Play and Development:
Evolutionary, Sociocultural,
and Functional Perspectives

The Jean Piaget Symposium Series
Available from LEA

Play and Development: Evolutionary, Sociocultural, and Functional Perspectives

Artin Göncü

University of Illinois at Chicago

and
Suzanne Gaskins

Northeastern Illinois University

LEA

LAWRENCE ERLBAUM ASSOCIATES, PUBLISHERS
2007   Mahwah, New Jersey   London

Lawrence Erlbaum Associates, Inc., Publishers
10 Industrial Avenue
Mahwah, New Jersey 07430
www.erlbaum.com

Cover design by Tomai Maridou

CIP information for this book can be obtained by contacting the Library of Congress

ISBN 0-8058-5261-1 (cloth : alk. paper)

Books published by Lawrence Erlbaum Associates are printed on acid-free paper, and their bindings are chosen for strength and durability.

Printed in the United States of America
10 9 8 7 6 5 4 3 2 1

Contents

Preface

One of the many activities that allows psychological research to progress is reflecting on the recent accomplishments and future questions in a given area of study. This book is one such effort. It developed as an extension of the 33rd annual meeting of the Jean Piaget Society (JPS), titled "Play and Development." Much like the previous statements on the status of play research (e.g., Bruner, Jolly, & Sylva, 1976; Power, 2000), we examine the status of play research and the uncontested assumptions on which play studies are based. However, our principal goal is to examine one pervasive assumption about play, namely, that it is a universal activity in humans with unique significant developmental outcomes. In the process of examining this assumption, we also reflect on the definitions of play and its measures with the purpose of identifying recent conceptual and empirical advances.

Partly due to the complexity of play and partly due to our tendency to take it for granted as an activity that is essential for human functioning, students of play assume that play occurs with a certain degree of universality. Theorists in many disciplines such as anthropology, folklore, and psychology consistently talk about play as a necessary activity for the interpretation of and experimentation with experience (Göncü & Perone, 2005). Following these claims and relying on our own daily Western experiences of engaging in play of many kinds (ranging from participating in an improv performance to cracking jokes with one another), we tacitly believe that play is ever paramount in every community for both adult and child. In fact, this belief is so strong that when we do not see sufficient kinds and amounts of play in children, we feel the obligation to provide intervention programs to help the "needy."

As play researchers with interests in the degree to which play is culture specific and universal, we wanted to address the universality assumption from every relevant perspective. Bringing together three communities of scholars whose work had direct or indirect bearing on this assumption appeared reasonable to us. One community examines play from an ethological perspective searching for continuities and discontinuities across different species. A second community focuses on the play of human children and adults with the aim of understanding the degree to which play is a socially and culturally constructed activity. Finally, the third community tries to understand how play can assert powerful influence on the lives of children in certain contexts even if play does not lead to similar developmental outcomes in all contexts of childhood.

Our effort to examine play in a holistic fashion has proved to be productive. The research reported here conducted from ethological perspectives indicates that not only is pretend play a human characteristic, but there is still an open debate about how human pretense differs from animal pretense because researchers have not been consistent in their definitions of and criteria for pretend play across species. Equally provocatively, rough-and-tumble play, which is often seen as the activity of animals, not only occurs in humans, but also may play a significant developmental role for them.

The work reported here that examines the universality assumption from a social and cultural perspective, although it reveals that play is at least to some extent a universal activity of childhood, also forcefully illustrates that children's play should be examined in relation to the value and meaning systems of children's communities to make sense of cultural variations that are found in research. Parallel to the research reported in this volume in the ethological framework, research reported in this volume in the cultural tradition illustrates that Western play researchers have been biased in their conceptualization and definition of play, especially in pretend play, calling for more emic examinations to provide accurate pictures of children's play in diverse cultures.

The research reported here that examines children's play from an applied point of view with interest in the developmental outcomes of play focuses sharply on pretend play as a form of self-expression. This line of research shows that pretend play serves to construct worlds of fantasy and narrative, as it also enables us to deal with stressful situations of life. The applied work offers support for claims about the significant developmental functions of pretend play in the Western world as it leaves open the question of whether pretend play serves similar functions universally.

Any integrative work that brings into dialogue perspectives that do not always speak to each other requires exceptional commitment to collaboration from all participants. The contributors to this volume, all veteran researchers of children and animal play, have been wonderful collaborators. This book is a continuation of the mutual conversation that began in June 2003, when we all met in Chicago for the JPS meetings and had the opportunity to listen to each other's presentations and to discuss them over the course of several days. As the editors of the volume, we have profited more than anyone, as we were able to continue those discussions through the process of developing the chapters for this book. We are grateful to the contributors of this book for keeping a collegial spirit during the entire process of writing, responding thoughtfully to our editorial comments, and respecting the deadlines we set. We also thank the Board of the Jean Piaget Society for their enthusiastic support by devoting one of their annual meetings to the topic "Play and Development," which allowed this rich discussion to happen in the first place.

REFERENCES

Bruner, J. S. , Jolly, A., & Sylva, K. (Eds.). (1976). *Play, its role in development and evolution*. New York: Basic Books.

Göncü, A., & Perone, A. (2005). Pretend play as a life-span activity. *Topoi*. 24: 137: 147.

Power, T. G. (2000). *Play and exploration in children and animals*. Mahwah, NJ: Lawrence Erlbaum Associates, Inc.

List of Contributors

Dr. Marc H. Bornstein
Child and Family Research
National Institute of
Child Health and Human Development
Building 31 -- Room B2B15
9000 Rockville Pike
Bethesda MD 20892-2030 USA
Tel: 301-496-6832
Fax: 301-496-2766
Marc_H_Bornstein@nih.gov

Dr. Cindy Dell Clark
Human Development and Family Studies
Penn State Delaware County
25 Yearsley Mill Road
Media PA 19063-5596 USA
Tel: 610-892-1265
cdc9@psu.edu

Dr. Suzanne Gaskins
Department of Psychology
Northeastern Illinois University
5500 N. St. Louis Ave.
Chicago, IL 60625 USA
Tel: 773-442-4903

Fax: 773-442-5850
s-gaskins@neiu.edu

Dr. Artin Göncü (also Jyoti Jain and Ute Tuermer)
College of Education M/C 147
University of Illinois at Chicago
1040 W. Harrison St.,
Chicago, IL 60607 USA
Tel: 312-996-5259
goncu@uic.edu

Dr. Wendy Haight
School of Social Work
University of Illinois at Urbana-Champaing
608 South Matthews,
Urbana, IL 61801 USA
Tel: 217-244-5212
wlhaight@uiuc.edu

Dr. Paul Harris
HGSE, 503A Larsen Hall,
Appian Way,
Cambridge, MA 02138 USA
Paul_Harris@gse.harvard.edu
Tel: 617-965-8231
Fax: 617-496-3963

Dr. David F. Lancy
Department of SSW&A
Utah State University
0730 Old Main Hill
Logan, UT 84322-0730 USA
Tel: 435-797-1230
dlancy@cc.usu.edu

Dr. Angeline Lillard
Department of Psychology
University of Virginia
PO Box 400400
102 Gilmer Hall

Charlottesville VA 22904-4400 USA
Tel: 434-982-4750
lillard@virginia.edu

Dr. Robert W. Mitchell
Department of Psychology
127 Cammack Building
Eastern Kentucky University
Richmond, KY 40475 USA
Tel: 859-622-3122
Fax: 859-622-5871

Dr. Ageliki Nicolopoulou
Lehigh University
Department of Psychology
17 Memorial Drive East
Bethlehem, PA 18015-3068 USA
Tel: 610-758-3618
agn3@lehigh.edu

Dr. Anthony Pellegrini
Department of Educational Psychology
University of Minnesota
214 Burton Hall
178 Pillsbury Drive, S.E
Minneapolis, MN 55455 USA
Tel: 612.625.4353
Fax: 612.624.8241
pelle013@umn.edu

Dr. Peter K Smith
Department of Psychology
Goldsmiths College
New Cross
London SE14 6NW USA
England
Tel: +44-20-7919-7898
Fax: +44-20-7919-7873
pss01pks@gold.ac.uk

Dr. Marjorie Taylor (and Anne M. Mannering)
1227 Department of Psychology
University of Oregon
Eugene OR 97403-1227 USA
Tel: 541-346-4933
mtaylor@uoregon.edu

I

INTRODUCTION

1

An Integrative Perspective on Play and Development

Artin Göncü
University of Illinois at Chicago

Suzanne Gaskins
Northeastern Illinois University

The work reported in this volume developed as an extension of the 33rd annual meeting of the Jean Piaget Society. The principal goal of the volume (as it was of the meeting) is to examine the uncontested assumption that play is a unique and universal activity in humans with significant developmental outcomes. Three separate lines of research converged as being relevant for unpacking the meaning of this assumption and examining its consequences for the future of play research. One line of research examines the unique universality assumption from an ethological perspective by seeking to establish continuities and discontinuities in play within and across different species. A second line of research questions the universality assumption in view of ever-growing knowledge of the extent to which play is socially and culturally constructed and supported. Finally, a third line of work seeks to examine the universality assumption by considering the specifics of varied applications of play in children's lives in order to illuminate the paths that play follows in different contexts of childhood.

Historically, play has proven to be a difficult topic to define and study. One of the important reasons for this difficulty is that play is not a monolithic behavior with a single source. If we continue to consider play as a spontaneous universal human behavior, as researchers have done in the past, play will remain a perplexing set of related behaviors that do not combine easily into a single phenomenon. If we can come to recognize play as a complexly determined behavior, however, we can work to integrate its multiple perspectives: We will come to understand that some of its characteristics are not fundamentally uniquely human, that play comes to be expressed in uniquely human or culturally specific forms over developmental time, and that the demands of specific contexts influence the ways that children use play. We first discuss how each of the three perspectives represented in this book sheds significant light on the assumption of human universality. Then we describe how all three perspectives collectively offer important new insights regarding play—its motivational origins, its nonliteral character, and its social features—and how these in turn influence the developmental outcomes that come from play. Finally, we argue for an integration of methodologies represented by the varied perspectives included in this book.

PLAY AS A UNIVERSAL AND CONTEXTUAL ACTIVITY

Parallel to its goal of examining play from ethological, cultural, and applied perspectives, the volume is organized into three parts. The first part is devoted to ethological perspectives and contains chapters by Smith (chap. 2), Mitchell (chap. 3), and Pellegrini (chap. 4). The next part is devoted to the social and cultural dimensions of play and contains chapters by Bornstein (chap. 5), Lillard (chap. 6), Göncü, Jain, and Tuermer (chap. 7), and Gaskins, Haight, and Lancy (chap. 8). The last part of the volume articulates contextually applied perspectives on pretend play and imagination in chapters by Harris (chap. 9), Taylor and Mannering (chap. 10), Nicolopoulou (chap. 11), and Clark (chap. 12).

The authors of the part on the ethology of play bring to our attention the significance of examining human and animal play in relation to one another, to determine fairly and accurately which features of play are shared across species and which are specific to a particular species. However, they also entertain informed hypotheses about the functions and developmental outcomes of human play. Smith (chap. 2, this volume) opens this part with a historical overview of theory and research providing the reader with background on the conceptualization of play from an evolutionary perspective. He discusses object play, rough-and-tumble play, and sociodramatic play, summarizing similarities and differences across different species in these kinds of play and discussing the differential benefits obtained by these three kinds of play by different species. In the next chapter, Mitchell (chap. 3, this volume) contributes to the study of pretend play by offering a comprehensive definition of pretense to be used in future research on all species. Through examining previous work on human and animal pretense, he demonstrates that scholars have been human-centric; that is, they have been generous in interpreting human infant behaviors as pretense while being stringent in interpreting animals' behaviors as pretense. In the last chapter of this part, Pellegrini (chap. 4, this volume) argues that rough-and-tumble play should be a focus of our work in developmental psychology, just as pretend play has been. After offering a definition and a theoretical orientation for the study of rough-and-tumble play, Pellegrini discusses the biological roots of rough-and-tumble play and its developmental course and functions, arguing that there is an important shift in the social function of rough-and-tumble play with the onset of adolescence.

The work of Smith, Mitchell, and Pellegrini collectively illustrates that understanding the similarities and differences in the emergence and developmental functions of play across different species holds important consequences for our understanding of human play and its potential role in development. Pretend play, which is often argued to be species specific for humans, if looked at carefully, appears to have striking similarities at its inception with behaviors of other species. If this similarity is granted, a new question arises from Mitchell's (chap. 3) research, of how pretense comes to develop its distinctly human characteristics over time in infancy and early childhood. On the other hand, rough-and-tumble play, which is often conceived of as being less significant in human development because of its close ties to behavior of other species, appears to play significant but different roles in social organization during middle childhood and adolescence. A second new question arises from Pelligrini's (chap. 4) research, then, of how biological characteristics of play, shared with other species, come to be integrated into culturally structured social organization, even as the principles of that play change over developmental time.

The review of ethological play research presented by Smith (chap. 2) suggests that these are only two of a wide array of important questions about the nature of human play that arise from considering an ethological perspective, all of which suggest that children's play may well be less human specific and more related to other species' play than many would like to think. At the same time, these authors argue that whatever inherited tendencies toward play humans may have, the expression of those tendencies is always shaped by children's experiences, especially as they are organized at a cultural level. The ethological perspective, even as it suggests that there is a significant biological component to human play (some of which is shared across species), also recognizes that play must be studied in the specific context of children's experiences.

The authors in the next part examine more directly the impact on play of the social and cultural worlds of children. Based on research conducted in Western and non-Western, urban and rural, middle- and low-income communities, these authors collectively state that play is, at least to some degree, a universal activity of childhood. However, the chapters in this section significantly qualify this claim by also documenting that important variations occur in children's play as a function of the economic, social, and cultural structure of children's communities. The chapters in this part provide extensive descriptions of how the structure of children's daily interactions contributes to the development of play. Taken as a whole, the research in this section suggests that play develops within a context of cultural traditions and adult values and ethnotheories about development that influence its type, frequency, partners, setting, and organization. In some cases, the variation may be large enough to influence play's role as a catalyst for development as it has been conceived of by Western play researchers.

Bornstein (chap. 5, this volume) opens this part with a discussion of how individual, interactional, and cultural features influence children's play. Bornstein acknowledges that the propensity to play is biological in origin but argues that its development and expression are influenced by caregiver–child interaction and the cultural priorities during infancy. In turn, Lillard (chap. 6, this volume) provides a detailed discussion of pretend play in middle-class European-American mother–child dyads and offers extensive data examining the construction of their pretend frames in interaction, providing evidence for the subtle and complex nature of how moment-to-moment interaction can build structured and enduring stances about pretend. The last two chapters focus on the influence of specific cultural priorities on children's play. Göncü, Jain, and Tuermer (chap. 7, this volume) discuss how the play of children in low-income African-American, European-American, and Turkish children is similar to and different from the middle-class Western children that have been the subject of research in developmental psychology. At the same time, these authors also address the variations in children's play across these three low-income communities. Gaskins, Haight, and Lancy (chap. 8, this volume) describe how children's play is differentially valued in the United States, China, Liberia, and Yucatan, Mexico, and thereby differentially supported in these cultures.

The play of middle-class European-Americans has served as the unexamined basis for the dominant theoretical model of play as spontaneous, individual expression of universal human behavior and a catalyst for development. With careful demonstrations like that provided by Lillard (chap. 6), we begin to realize that play is, at least in part, a socialized behavior that grows out of specific patterns found in daily interactions between children and caregivers. The other three chapters in this part argue further that the patterns of those daily interactions are structured by factors that are larger than the specific dyad—in particular, culture and social class. These chapters provide powerful illustrations that cultural and class variations in children's play need not be interpreted from the perspective of privilege or deficit as once believed. Rather, the differences are best understood in relation to canons of children's social and cultural context. For a theoretical understanding of play to be adequate, it must recognize the sociocultural influences on play—and the resulting differences in children's play behaviors—as fundamental and omnipresent. This not only allows us to bring a greater degree of accuracy to our understanding of play in general, but allows us to recognize that the specific characteristics of middle-class European-American play are a unique response to specific cultural pressures and leads us to examine how they function as such.

The authors in the final part discuss the emergence and functions of play in applied settings, primarily within European American culture. The particular characteristic that is taken up in this section is imagination; that is, pretense that goes beyond the child's experiences. The chapters explore how imagination develops and how it is used in a variety of contexts. This kind of play is clearly most highly developed and most strongly supported in European-American cultures. This part looks in depth at the amazing potential of a particular form of play to provide a medium for individual expression in everyday contexts while at the same time supporting cultural goals for development. Taken together, the chapters richly illustrate the power of such play to reflect on, expand on, and constitute valued experiences in Western children's lives.

Harris (chap. 9, this volume) illustrates the wide-ranging and adaptive capacity of children for imagining beyond experience. He demonstrates that young children are capable of entertaining imaginary premises that are independent of their empirical experience, of reasoning on the basis of hypothetical situations, and of making sense of unobservable evidence through the use of their imagination. Taylor and Mannering (chap. 10, this volume) provide a special case of the use of imagination in pretend play, imaginary companions. The authors describe the characteristics of children who have imaginary companions, the characteristics of imaginary companions themselves, and parental and cultural characteristics related to imaginary companions. They argue that having imaginary companions is an adaptive activity with positive correlates that transforms itself into various forms of creativity in adulthood. Based on her work in preschools and Headstart centers in the United States, Nicolopoulou (chap. 11, this volume) examines the independent development of two lines of expression of imagination—pretend play and storytelling. She argues that early pretend play involves the development of roles and characters whereas early storytelling emphasizes the development of events and plot. As these two activities develop, they also merge, and young children develop more sophisticated narratives with integrated plot and character development. Finally, Clark (chap. 12, this volume) argues that children on their own can use play for therapeutic purposes, much like adults use play as a therapeutic device in working with children. Clark shows that children suffering from asthma and diabetes can take an active role in directing themselves and the adults around them in imaginative pretense activities that help them cope with the fear, pain, and other emotionally challenging experiences that result from their illnesses.

The examples in this part show that imagination and pretend play can serve as important mediums for self-expression and can have important developmental consequences. They are testimony for the potential power in children's use of one particular kind of play. The authors here have variously suggested that the use of the imagination influences our understanding of science and religion, our ability to construct and populate personal social worlds of fantasy, our competence for producing complex narrative, and our ability to emotionally cope with overwhelmingly difficult situations.

However, our understanding of that power should be influenced by the arguments of the two preceding sections of this volume. Pretend play appears to be a human universal that is built on a more basic capacity, shared with other species, to take an "as-if" stance, yet it is also a socialized behavior that is supported differentially across cultures and social classes. None of the imaginative stances reported in this part could be found in other species, but exactly how are they different from those that are? Which of the imaginative stances reported in this part would be found in all human children and to what extent would they serve to foster the range of activities previously listed? Although this volume cannot provide definitive answers to those questions, our hope is that it will provide a motivation to ask them (and others like them) more consistently and to direct future research toward finding the answers.

CONCEPTUALIZING PLAY AS A BIOLOGICAL, CULTURAL, AND APPLIED ACTIVITY

This volume illustrates that children's play and its developmental functions conceived of as an activity of the sole individual child, as formulated by Piaget (1945), Erikson (1963), Freud (1950), Vygotsky (1978), and others can actually be best understood by considering the extra-individual contributions to play that act as an integrated structuring force on children's individual expression. This book illustrates that play does not, as once assumed, exist more or less equally for all the children of the world as an intrinsically motivated, social, and symbolic activity. Rather, these features of play are filtered through biological, sociocultural, and specific ecological contexts of childhoods during development. We take up each issue in turn.

The work reported in this volume suggests that children's motivations to play, and in particular, to play in certain ways, are complexly determined and that all three perspectives offer important insights into the structure of a child's motivation to play. First of all, biology can be an important determining factor of motivation, affecting groups of children differentially. Pellegrini (chap. 4) argues, for example, that boys have more desire to engage in rough-and-tumble play than girls, and older boys have a different motivation for such play than younger ones. Second, Göncü et al. (chap. 7) and Gaskins et al. (chap. 8) argue that children's engagement in play, as with other activities such as schoolwork, chores, and economic activity, is guided and constrained by the cultural context. How much children play, what kinds of play in which they choose to engage, and what they gain from any specific play activity are all culturally variable and dependent in part on what other activities are available to the children. Third, specific contexts of experience can also be highly significant in influencing the type of play in which a child engages. Clark's (chap. 12) work clearly illustrates that children with asthma and diabetes come to rely on pretend play for coping with their problems in ways that are distinctive from healthy children. If we consider play to be simply an intrinsically motivated behavior, we miss the complex network of constraints and encouragements that come from specific contexts. These influences, which reflect a child's biology, culture, and experiences, contribute to the motivation to play. If we ignore such influences, we can only partially understand why children play in particular ways. By incorporating a broader view of sources of motivation, we have a more difficult practical task of identifying all the contributions, but to the extent that we succeed—even partially—we come closer to understanding the actual influences on the child's motivation.

We also can begin to understand a developmental trajectory of play motivation, as well. Some biological influences may be constant throughout development (like the gender difference in rough-and-tumble play) but others may not (like the shift in that play from affiliation to competition in adolescence). Cultural differences are likely to become more pronounced as the child gets older. Effects on motivation from specific contexts will vary based on the child's personal experiences, but, like cultural effects, they are likely to become more pronounced over time, if the context stays consistent. In general, the complexity of sorting out motivation based on individual experience from motivation based on socially shared experience should become greater over developmental time. By the time a boy of 4 or 5 is invoking a lively superhero to help him deal with a painful procedure, his motivation to do so is made up of a mixture of general cultural support of fantasy pretense, a contextual need for dealing with pain, individual encouragement and coparticipation of a caregiver, and, perhaps, a contribution from biology for more physically aggressive play.

Regarding the representational nature of play, this volume is unique in offering a comprehensive review of the concepts of pretend, nonliterality, and symbolic expression. To begin with, as discussed by Smith (chap. 2), Mitchell (chap. 3), and Lillard (chap. 6), there has been a considerable restlessness in the field about the meaning of these terms, their applications in research, and their significance. These three authors examine these notions from different perspectives but taken together they provide a clear proposal for a framework for differentiating one notion from another. One important point that emerges from this work is that pretend may not always incorporate symbolic representation (see Mitchell, chap. 3), differentiating much of animal play from human play.

Göncü et al. (chap. 7) suggest that pretend may take widely different forms depending on children's broad cultural traditions. For example, middle-class Western children may pretend by assuming social roles, whereas low-income Western children pretend by using their words to represent nonliteral meanings as evidenced in their teasing. Their analysis suggests that it is important to consider not only the behavior but the function of the behavior. In particular, the symbolic function could be met in various cultures through pretend play, teasing, myths, or other mediums that use symbolic meanings. Whether these different mediums would have differential impact on development is not known. Gaskins et al. (chap. 8) make a different developmental argument—that cultural constraints on play, in this case, multiaged playgroups, can have an impact on the developmental potential of certain behaviors. If symbolic play reaches its peak of expression at different ages, its potential developmental impact is altered.

The chapters in this volume give numerous examples of how social interaction in play is influenced by all three perspectives. Gender-specific play partners in middle childhood, as described by Pelligrini (chap. 4), is a strong example of a biological influence on social play. Many chapters in this volume address cultural differences in social interaction in play. There are contexts in which young children's social play is encouraged, supported, and even shared by caregivers. Emergence of play during infancy in the context of Western caregiver–child interaction is described extensively by Bornstein (chap. 5), Lillard (chap. 6), and Gaskins et al. (chap. 8). Furthermore, the play of preschool-age children gets additional cultural support in their Western schooling, as described by Nicolopoulou (chap. 11) and Göncü et al. (chap. 7). Additional evidence of how play is supported and coconstructed by caregivers in the Western world is found in the work of Taylor and Mannering (chap. 10) and Clark (chap. 12). In contrast to this pattern, Kpelle (cf. Gaskins et al., chap. 8) and coconstructed by caregivers (cf. Göncü et al., chap. 7), due to their workload or sense of appropriateness, value play only as distinct children's activity and do not engage in play themselves, and the Yucatec Maya (cf. Gaskins et al., chap. 8) do not even encourage play in children. In cultures where play is less central and less frequent, other contexts for social interaction become more important. This is in contrast to the children studied by Taylor and Mannering (chap. 10), where social interaction can be completely incorporated into pretense in the form of imaginary companions. The obvious conclusion is that play is one medium, not the medium, for social interaction in childhood. The question then becomes what is distinctive about the medium of play compared to other mediums for social interaction.

These biological, sociocultural, and contextual differences in children's motivations for playing, in the expression of symbolic representation, and in social interaction in play suggest that there is a significant amount of variation in children's experiences in play. If play's developmental impact is derived through experience, then such differences in experience imply that there are also important differences in the developmental consequences of play. Interestingly enough, those differences can come from either belonging to different groups that have different experiences (e.g., boys vs. girls or low-income African-American vs. low-income Turkish) or from failing as an individual to meet the group normative behavior (e.g., boys who do not like rough-and-tumble play or a child who is too sick to play). In the first instance, we would have group developmental differences; in the second, individual ones. These differences could be based on biological, cultural, or contextually applied circumstances, but they all argue against the idea of play as a universal developmental force.

That said, there are a number of theories, accompanied by rich descriptions, in this volume of how play contributes to children's development in Western cultures. The work of Clark (chap. 12), Nicolopoulou (chap. 11), and Göncü et al. (chap. 7) provide illustrations that play is an activity of interpretation, as assumed by the forefathers of play theory such as Erikson (1963), Freud (1950), Piaget (1945), and Vygotksy (1978). These theorists argued that when children pretend, they appropriate affect-laden experiences either in solitary or in intersubjective play, promoting the development of self and providing emotional ballast. Furthermore, Smith (chap. 2), Harris (chap. 9), Lillard (chap. 6), and Taylor and Mannering (chap. 10) all provide conceptual background and considerable empirical support for a relation between pretending and entertaining hypotheses about others' thinking (i.e., theory of mind). Lillard (chap. 6) provides descriptions of how pretending with caregivers additionally enables young children to differentiate play communication from nonplay communication, noting children's developing abilities to make sense of extralinguistic messages. Taylor and Mannering (chap. 10) also propose that pretending is correlated with other measures of fantasy, levels of energy, and concentration. Last, but not least, a hypothesis is advanced by Pellegrini (chap. 4) regarding the developmental function of rough-and-tumble play: It is used in middle childhood to establish cooperation and affiliation, whereas it is used during adolescence to establish aggressive dominance in heterosexual relationships.

These chapters in this volume, and many other works, have argued that the play produced by middle-class European-American children has a significant impact on development. What is less clear is what developmental impact other patterns of play might have. The argument that there is significant cultural variation in children's play is made throughout the first two parts of this book. This point is taken up in all three chapters in the part on ethological perspectives. Smith (chap. 2), Mitchell (chap. 3), and Pellegrini (chap. 4) all explicitly state that biology cannot be taken as destiny because expression of our inherited abilities is shaped by the tools of culture, guiding the reader to consider the consequences of play in relation to children's culture. In the second main part of the volume, this argument is made even more specifically and in more detail. Should we conclude that children whose play looks significantly different from Western children's play do not develop a sense of self, emotional ballast, a theory of mind, metalinguistic distinctions, energy and concentration, cooperation, or dominance—or any number of other developmental outcomes that have been connected to play? Or should we conclude that play is not the only way to achieve each of these developmental outcomes? The first conclusion leads us to endorse a model of development that predicts radically different outcomes based on children's play experiences; the second leads us to endorse a model of play with radically reduced inherent importance. We suspect that the truth falls somewhere in between but is closer to the second than the first. That is, play in Western culture may indeed have important developmental impact because it is a highly frequent, highly complex, and highly valued activity of young children. In other cultures, or for specific groups of children, in which play is not so frequent, complex, or valued, its developmental importance is significantly reduced, and other everyday activities serve to provide the experiences that children need to grow cognitively, socially, and emotionally. At the same time, we do not want to rule out that there may indeed be culturally specific developmental outcomes that reflect the demands and the opportunities in specific cultures. In terms of play, one example discussed by Gaskins et al. (chap.8) is that in cultures where there is less stress placed on children, play may be less necessary to provide emotional ballast, and therefore children's pretend play in those cultures would reflect fewer individually specific themes of emotional importance. Neither of these interpretations diminishes the power of play that is represented by the chapters in the final part in this book. It does, however, identify them as culturally specific cases, not as universal experiences.

PROPOSAL FOR AN INTERDISCIPLINARY
METHODOLOGY

In addition to proposing a more integrated interdisciplinary approach to the theory of children's play and development, this volume invites researchers to broaden their perspectives in determining the methodologies that are appropriate for the examination of play. The richness of play lends itself to the adoption of a wide range of methodologies that has not yet been adopted as a canon of the field. Guided by a concern to provide "objective" results that can be generalized, research has been constrained mostly to experimental research and quantitative analyses. Unfortunately, play as an activity resists reduction to an easily codable and quantifiable behavior. Thus, those certain features of play that have been accepted as passing the scientific criteria adopted by journal policies have been most closely examined. Creative experimental work has made significant contributions to our understanding of play. This point is well illustrated in this volume by Harris's (chap. 9) work on the development of imagination, and Lillard's (chap. 6) work on mother–child dyadic metacommunication about pretense.

More often, however, as both Smith (chap. 2) and Mitchell (chap. 3) note, neither animal nor human play can be studied productively using experimental methods. There is a compelling argument here that the field of play research and its publication outlets should make wider provisions for observational studies. One type of observational method, often used in animal studies, involves coding of the species' behaviors as they occur in their natural habitat according to a set of criteria developed a priori, illustrated in this volume by Bornstein's (chap. 5) research on human infants and their caregivers. Coding from observations can also be done from videotapes of everyday behavior using a coding system that is developed gradually through multiple viewings of the tapes, as done by Göncü et al. (chap. 7). Although observational studies have had their place in the field, due to their cost (in terms of both time and money), they have been rare. Support needs to be given for more observational research that addresses animal and human play in its natural contexts.

Research with humans, unlike that with animals, can also take advantage of our species' ability to reflect on our own behavior and to communicate about it verbally. Some researchers rely on these abilities by using questionnaires as a way of collecting information about play behavior. When done thoughtfully, such a methodology can provide important information about rare or private play behavior that the children (or caregivers) are consciously aware of and willing to share (e.g., Göncü et al., chap. 7; Taylor & Mannering, chap. 10). But many play phenomena are not planned or readily reported, so, like experiments, this is not an ideal methodology for the field at large. Rather, it should be reserved for topics for which it is well suited.

The type of methodology we most need for understanding the rich tapestry of children's play is the ethnographic method. It is both relatively uncommon and labor intensive, relying on both open-ended naturalistic observation and extensive communication with participants about their thoughts, feelings, and interpretations of behaviors. Such an ethnographic method can be seen in language socialization research (e.g., Brice-Heath, 1983; Miller, 1982, Ochs, 1988). With respect to children's play, rare examples include Lancy (1996) and Goldman (1998). In this volume, this method is illustrated in the chapters by Göncü et al. (chap. 7), Gaskins et al. (chap. 8), Nicolopoulou (chap. 11), and Clark (chap. 12). We believe that the meaning of play activities and their role in development, especially when looking at play in communities other than middle-class European-American ones, can be understood best when we look at the activities from an emic perspective; that is, the perspective of the participants.

The most important methodological need is that there is an acceptance of a broad range of quantitative and qualitative methods so that researchers are free to choose the methodology best suited to their research question. Without this open-mindedness, we are limited as researchers to investigate only those research questions that can be answered by accepted methodologies. If we are to embark on a more interdisciplinary approach to play as called for in this volume, the need for more flexibility and creativity in methods is even more critical. Neither an ethological or a cultural perspective on play can be fully supported by a limited methodological toolbox.

CONCLUSION

In summary, this volume has embraced a number of theoretical and methodological perspectives in the service of providing a broader and more integrated understanding of children's play and its relation to development. We think that any comprehensive understanding of children's play will consider the ethological contributions to play, including how human play relates to nonhuman play; the various evolutionary functions of play behaviors; and how biological differences in development influence play behavior. Along with ethological approaches to play, and equally necessary, we think that sociocultural approaches bring an important respect for the environmental context in which play occurs, with a focus on the cultural structuring of children's everyday activities. Whereas cultural groups can influence the various specific forms that play can take, perhaps—and even more important—groups can differ on the extent to which they emphasize play's role in experience and, consequently, its role in development. Western culture appears to maximize play's role in children's lives and places particular emphasis on pretense and imagination in play. How imaginative play is applied in various contexts provides a strong demonstration of the diverse roles play can have in children's experience and how play can have important developmental consequences. Whatever theoretical perspective one takes, whether it is ethological, cultural, or applied, it is important that we continue to recognize that children themselves are the ones who, in play, integrate these various levels of influence into a seamless stream of creative play behavior, leading to individual expression and variation.

Play has traditionally held a position of prominence in most developmental theories. Primarily, this prominence has been due to claims in developmental psychology, as well as education, anthropology, and sociology, that play makes significant contributions to development in a variety of domains, including affect, cognition, interpersonal relations, and language. Secondarily, scholars have been fascinated by the changes in play in ontological time; that is, the influence of development on play. It is only from an integrative perspective like the one presented in this volume that we can hope to begin to understand the complex relation between play and development in childhood. Through articulating these various arguments throughout the following chapters, we hope that this volume will establish a new agenda for future play research—an agenda that recognizes play as a complex activity that is simultaneously biological and learned, both shared with other species and culturally variable, and created and articulated by individual children playing in their everyday worlds.

REFERENCES

Brice-Heath, S. (1983). *Ways with words: Language, life, and work in communities and classrooms*. New York: Cambridge University Press.

Erikson, E. (1963). *Childhood and society*. New York: Norton.

Freud, S. (1950). *Beyond the pleasure principle*. New York: Liveright.

Goldman, L. (1998). *Child's play: Myth, mimesis, and make-believe*. New York: Berg.

Lancy, D. F. (1996). *Playing on the Mother Ground: Cultural routines for children's development*. New York: Guilford.

Miller, P. J. (1982). *Amy, Wendy, and Beth: Learning language in South Baltimore*. Austin: University of Texas Press.

Ochs, E. (1988). *Culture and language development*. Cambridge, UK: Cambridge University Press.

Piaget, J. (1945). *Play, dreams, and imitation in childhood*. New York: Norton.

Vygotsky, L. S. (1978). *Mind in society*. Cambridge, MA: Harvard University Press.

II

BIOLOGICAL/ETHOLOGICAL PERSPECTIVES OF PLAY AND DEVELOPMENT

2

Evolutionary Foundations and Functions of Play: An Overview

Peter K. Smith
Goldsmiths College, University of London

In this chapter I give an overview of how evolutionary theory has impacted the study of children's play. There have been distinct ups and downs in this influence since evolutionary theory originated, and I start with a historical account of this. I also mention the play ethos that influenced much research in the 20th century. I delineate what I regard as four important characteristics of an evolutionary approach, useful at the present time. I then discuss the relevance of such an approach to the main forms of play—physical activity and rough-and-tumble play, object play, and pretend and sociodramatic play. I take the opportunity to cross-refer to the following chapters by Mitchell (chap. 3, this volume), and Pellegrini (chap. 4, this volume), where appropriate. I end with a brief discussion of genetic and cultural evolution and of future directions in this field.

EVOLUTIONARY PERSPECTIVES ON PLAY: AN OVERVIEW

With the advent of evolutionary theory in the latter half of the 19th century, and its extension from animal to human behavior (Darwin, 1859, 1871), it was natural that play behavior should be a topic for evolutionary speculation in regard to its nature, origin, and function. Darwin did not write extensively on play (Gruber, 1974), but Spencer (1878/1898), in his book *The Principles of Psychology*, suggested that the higher animals are better able to deal with the immediate necessities of life, and that their more highly developed nervous systems, rather than remaining inactive for long periods, stimulate play: "Thus it happens that in the more-evolved creatures, there often recurs an energy somewhat in excess of immediate needs.... Hence play of all kinds—hence this tendency to superfluous and useless exercise of faculties that have been quiescent" (pp. 629–630). He proposed that play is "an artificial exercise of powers which, in default of their natural exercise, become so ready to discharge that they relieve themselves by simulated actions in place of real actions" (p. 630), and that play is carried out "for the sake of the immediate gratifications involved, without reference to ulterior benefits" (p. 632)—an approach commonly labeled the *surplus energy theory*.

The writings of Groos (1898, 1901) provide an integrative view of play that ascribed greater functional significance to it. Play provided exercise and elaboration of skills needed for survival: "The utility of play is incalculable. This utility consists in the practice and exercise it affords for some of the more important duties of life" (1898, p. 76). Indeed Groos thought that a main reason for childhood was so that play could occur: "Perhaps the very existence of youth is largely for the sake of play" (1898, p. 76). In his books *The Play of Animals* (1898) and *The Play of Man* (1901) he criticized Spencer's theory, arguing that a "superabundant nervous force is always ... a favorable one for play, but it is not its motive cause, nor, as I believe, a necessary condition of its existence" (1898, p. 24).

Hall (1908), in his book *Adolescence* and elsewhere, thought that play was a means for children to work through primitive atavisms, reflecting our evolutionary past; "we rehearse the activities of our ancestors" (p. 202), and "play is not doing things to be useful later, but it is rehearsing racial history" (p. 207). The function of play was thus cathartic in nature, and allowed the playing out of those instincts that characterized earlier human history. Hall attacked Groos's practice theory as "very partial, superficial, and perverse" (p. 202) because it simply saw play as practice for contemporary activities.

Although these views and quotations reflect the level of scientific knowledge at the time, and might appear dated, they raise important issues that still concern us. Does play have real functions selected for in evolution, or is it just a by-product of selection for other processes? Would any functions selected for in evolutionary history still apply in contemporary environments? Does play function for future skills, or for present circumstances?

After this promising beginning, evolutionary perspectives on play were neglected from the 1920s to the 1970s. Evolutionary theory continued to develop, of course, with the full integration of genetic theory into the modern synthesis or neo-darwinian revolution (Huxley, 1942). However, in the social sciences generally, including psychology, the first decades of the 20th century saw a reaction against deterministic biological views, with (what now seem to us as) deterministic cultural views. This was marked by the work of cultural determinists in anthropology (including Mead's work on childhood in "primitive" societies), and by Watson's behaviorist program in psychology.

As far as more practical applications of play research were concerned, although Hall's writings inspired a wave of interest in early childhood behavior, linked with the setting up of many child development or child welfare institutes in North America in the 1920s, the observational methods employed there were used simply to describe typical age and sex differences and ways of managing children's behavior and lacked any evolutionary perspective (Smith & Connolly, 1972).

Furthermore, the 1920s seem to have seen the start of a play ethos that took a very simplistic view of the (biological) importance of play, and in fact may have distorted play research for many decades, especially in the 1970s and 1980s (Smith, 1988). The play ethos is an uncritical and extreme assertion of the functional importance of play, well embodied in this quote by Isaacs (1929), professor of educational psychology at the Institute of Education in London, and a pivotal figure in the education of nursery school teachers: "Play is indeed the child's work, and the means whereby he grows and develops. Active play can be looked upon as a sign of mental health; and its absence, either of some inborn defect, or of mental illness" (p. 9). Such statements are often found in child development texts and teacher handbooks, and the cumulative effect is well stated in a U.K. government report from the 1970s: "The realisation that play is essential for normal development has slowly but surely permeated our cultural heritage" (Department of the Environment, 1973, p. 1).

Meanwhile, from around the 1920s to the 1970s, anthropological work largely (with some exceptions) avoided a biological or evolutionary perspective, and indeed little was written on children's play—a lack pointed out by Schwartzman (1978) and Lancy (1980) when they came to review what literature there was in the 1970s. In psychology, not only was evolutionary thinking neglected, but even observational methods fell out of favor in the 1940s and the experimental paradigm predominated through to the 1970s and 1980s (Plotkin, 2004).

The primary psychological theorists on play in this period were Vygotsky and Piaget. In their writings (Piaget, 1951; Vygotsky, 1933/ 1966) they discussed the nature of play, the immediate psychological mechanisms for playing, and the relations among play, thought, and language. Their views differed as to whether play is primarily assimilating new experiences to existing schema (Piaget) or showing creativity through being liberated from immediate situation constraints (Vygotsky). This research, and indeed most psychological research on play through to the 1970s at least, concentrated on object and pretend play; these were more specifically human forms of play, and were perceived as educationally relevant.

A resurgence in evolutionary perspectives on play can be dated from the 1970s and 1980s. There appear to be two strands to this. One was a return of observational methods to respectability, in the guise of human ethology. Following their decline in the 1940s (Arrington, 1943), observational methods used in natural surroundings were not in favor with psychologists, who espoused a supposedly scientific model of experimentation. I encountered this prejudice myself in the late 1960s when I was working on my doctoral thesis (Smith, 1970). This was based on natural observations of play behavior of 2- to 4-year-olds in day nurseries. This was seen as radical, and some colleagues criticized me for not having hypotheses to test.

Animal ethologists had of course been using observations in natural surroundings for decades, with a generally well-balanced program of research that employed natural observations when needed to describe behavior in a new species and understand the full range of natural behavior, with experimentation when wanted, to test hypotheses genuinely rooted in the natural ecology and behavior patterns of the species (Tinbergen, 1951). Blurton Jones, a doctoral student of Tinbergen's, pioneered this approach as applied to human (mostly child) behavior, and his edited book *Ethological Studies of Child Behaviour* (Blurton Jones, 1972) provided a benchmark. Some of the chapters in this book were mainly observational, whereas others were more explicitly guided by evolutionary thinking—although thinking still of the presociobiology era.

The other strand from the 1970s is the new evolutionary thinking embodied at the time in Wilson's (1978) book *Sociobiology: The New Synthesis*, integrating the recent ideas about kin selection, reciprocal altruism, parent–offspring conflict, and similar insights into a comprehensive overview of animal and human behavior. The term *sociobiology*, and the program, met a lot of initial resistance and hostility; and of course, as with any program, there was some loose writing and loose theorizing. However, the core ideas have gradually become accepted as not only central to understanding animal behavior, but also as at least of some relevance to understanding human behavior. The debate now is a more reasoned one about the extent of influence, and the terminology has changed to one of evolutionary psychology and notably of evolutionary developmental psychology (Bjorklund & Pellegrini, 2002), with an explicit realization of the interplay of genetic predispositions and environmental influences in development.

Of course, the sociobiological revolution reinvigorated animal as well as human ethology. Fagen's (1981) book *Animal Play Behavior* was a masterful synthesis of animal and human play, and this, together with Smith's (1982) review plus commentaries in *Behavior and Brain Sciences*, and his edited book *Play in Animals and Humans* (Smith, 1984), rekindled an interest in the evolutionary perspective on play. Fagen (1981) considered different classes of effects of animal play, which might be candidates for functional hypotheses. The one he considered as the most supported was training of physical capabilities and cognitive and social skills (for later use, although Fagen did not place much emphasis on the immediate or delayed benefits distinction in this context). Smith argued that most forms of play were selected for practice functions, when a lot of direct practice might be difficult or dangerous (e.g., in fighting). These broadly functional perspectives were productively challenged by Martin and Caro (1985), who argued that the costs (time, energy, danger) of play were not very great, and that play had a low priority when times were difficult. They correspondingly argued that any benefits of play should be relatively modest.

After what appears to have been a lull from the mid-1980s to the mid-1990s, research on play from an evolutionary perspective picked up again with an edited collection by Bekoff and Byers (1998), *Animal Play: Evolutionary, Comparative and Ecological Approaches*, and by Power's (2000) overview *Play and Exploration in Children and Animals*. Power saw the strongest case for an evolutionary function for play with rough-and-tumble play, but concluded generally that research on developmental functions of play needs more conclusive results, and more studies of social as well as cognitive effects of play, before firm functional statements can be made. Bjorklund and Pellegrini (2002), however, reasserted a functional significance for play. Documenting time and energy budgets and other costs of play (e.g., injury), they believed that physical, object, and pretend play would not be so prevalent if they had not been selected for in our evolutionary history. Pellegrini and Smith (2005), in the edited book *The Nature of Play: Great Apes and Humans*, focused on the evolutionary comparisons with humans to our nearest genetic relatives, the great apes; however, they also drew attention to the great cultural variability in human play. Developments in life history theory as applied to human evolution and childhood (Bock, 2002; Kaplan, Lancaster, Hill, & Hurtado, 2000) have provided a further impetus to new thinking in this area.

ASPECTS OF THE EVOLUTIONARY APPROACH

What is distinctive about an evolutionary approach to play? It is easy to draw facile comparisons between kittens playing and young children rough-and-tumbling. Does it go further than that? I think the perspective is important, in at least four ways.

First, it makes it clear that play embraces a variety of behaviors that likely have different functions. The following main types of play are well recognized: physical activity play (rhythmic stereotypies, exercise play, rough-and-tumble play), object play, and pretend play (including sociodramatic play as a particularly complex form). Of these, physical activity play and object play are seen widely in other species of mammals. Pretend and sociodramatic play are only seen in humans, apart from some possibly very elementary forms of pretense in great apes (Mitchell, chap. 3, this volume). A related concept in developmental psychology is that of games. Games with rules describe more organized forms of play in which there is some clear and publicly expressed goal (e.g., winning the game in a manner accepted by other players); games with rules are not reviewed further in this chapter. For a discussion of games from an evolutionary perspective, see Parker (1984).

Second, it focuses questions naturally on what the functions of different kinds of play might be. If some forms of play behavior are common in a species (including humans), then there is at least a time cost (the time could have been spent doing other things—eating, watching, exploring, resting, etc.), and almost certainly an energy cost compared to resting, and possibly a risk-of-injury cost, especially for exercise and rough-and-tumble play. From an evolutionary perspective, these costs should be counterbalanced by some benefits. These benefits should ultimately be for reproductive success; but more proximately, this might be via increased strength, agility, cognitive skills, social skills, dominance or rank in the social group, or other proxies that might now (immediate benefits) or later (delayed benefits) enhance reproductive fitness (ultimately, offspring surviving into future generations).

Of course, such benefits could be expected to vary by species and by type of play. Benefits might change developmentally. Benefits might be very important, or relatively slight. It might be the case that play was a vital mechanism to achieve such benefits; or, play might be just one of several routes to achieving this (Smith, 2005).

Several well-known methods are available to examine functional hypotheses. The form of the play behavior should be such as to make it a plausible candidate for the functions suggested (e.g., Symons [1978] argued that the forms of rough-and-tumble play make it a plausible candidate for training in fighting skills). Age changes in the nature, frequency, and intensity of play should be consistent with postulated benefits. Sex differences provide another very important source of evidence. Sex differences link in to broader features of species difference in sexual organization, and principles of sexual selection, explored by Pellegrini (chap. 4, this volume). Individual differences in play frequencies could be predicted to lead to later developmental outcomes linked to the benefits of play. Finally, deprivation or enrichment of play experiences should result in measurable outcomes. Deprivation or enrichment can be due to natural circumstances; for example, in some monkey troops, food shortages can lead to less play as youngsters spend more time foraging (Baldwin & Baldwin, 1976). However, they can also be experimentally manipulated, and play deprivation studies have been carried out experimentally, for example, with rodents (Hole & Einon, 1984). With human children, variation in the amount of play occurs naturally in some socioeconomic groups (Smilansky, 1968), and play deprivation has been carried out at least quasi-experimentally for exercise play in schools (Pellegrini, 1995b). Play enhancement studies have been carried out rather frequently with pretend and sociodramatic play (Smilansky, 1968; Smith, 1988).

A third aspect of the evolutionary perspective is perhaps less obvious, but is nonetheless important. This is an awareness of different perspectives on play. If play has benefits, then benefits for whom? A basic impetus for this question comes from Trivers's (1974) writings on parent–offspring conflict. Trivers made it clear that there were conflicts of (reproductive) interest between parents and offspring, and also between siblings, as they are not genetically identical (leaving aside the occasional case of identical twins). Just as nonrelatives are in reproductive competition, so are relatives, even if this is partially moderated by relatedness. Parents are in a position to strongly influence or manipulate children's behavior (and children can influence parents, too, via crying, demands for suckling, etc.); thus, we have to consider whether a child's play behavior, or lack of it, is representing benefits for the child or the parent.

More broadly, this awareness of the importance of different perspectives meshes with more recent thinking in sociology and anthropology, and with a more systemic view of human behavior that acknowledges the profound impact of culture and cultural variation on human behavior (Cole, 1998; Göncü, 1999; Rogoff, 2003; Lancy, 1996). Theories of genetic evolution, so brilliantly elaborated over the last century, are still grappling with the complexities of culture and with developing useful biocultural theories (Klein, 1989). Besides thinking of benefits in individual terms (child, parent, etc.) we clearly also need to consider influence and manipulation at the level of cultural ethos and societal pressure. The effects of the play ethos belief system have already been mentioned, but even more evident in contemporary society are the effects of toy manufacturing and advertising as a corporate investment process that has its own impetus and that will surely impact children's play behaviors (Kline, 1995).

Fourth, but related to all the preceding, evolutionary theory encourages us to look at a behavioral phenomenon such as play in a life-history perspective. Human life history differs appreciably from that of other mammals, including other primates (Bogin, 1999; Kaplan et al., 2000). There is a longer period of helpless infancy and a long period of childhood from around 3 to 7 years, during which the child is weaned but still dependent on adults for food and protection. There is then what has been described as a separate juvenile period from around 7 years to adolescence, in which individuals are no longer dependent on parental care, but are not yet sexually mature. This is followed by a longer adolescent period before full adult stature and strength is reached (Bogin, 1999; Pereira, 1993). For comparison, growth is complete at around age 11 for chimpanzees and gorillas, but only at around age 20 for humans.

Lancaster and Lancaster (1987) argued that the long period of immaturity in humans was adaptive for an environment in which extensive parental investment could pay off in terms of skill acquisition by offspring, given that immediate productive activity by children might be difficult due to hazards (e.g., hunting) or difficulty of extracting resources (e.g., foraging). Skill acquisition here could include both physical growth-related capabilities (strength, general coordination), as well as cognitive and social learning; in general it has to do with acquiring useful competencies for later life (but not necessarily very much later, bearing in mind that in preindustrial societies both subsistence responsibilities and reproductive opportunities would have started much earlier than is common in modern Western societies).

The parental (and also grandparental) investment envisaged by Lancaster and Lancaster (1987) and others (e.g., Hawkes, O'Connell, Blurton Jones, Alvarez, & Charnov, 1998; Kaplan et al., 2000) might take the form of allowing or encouraging play activities, a view consonant with Smith's (1982) hypothesis that play was broadly selected for when practice would be dangerous or ineffective. This view of play as especially important as a characteristic of human childhood does not necessarily go so far as Groos's (1901) view that childhood largely existed so that play could occur, but it does see play as part of a package of adaptations involving prolonged immaturity, opportunities for learning (in a broad sense), and parental investment in such learning (Lovejoy, 1981).

In the next sections of this chapter I review physical activity and rough-and-tumble play, object play, and pretend and sociodramatic play from an evolutionary perspective, bearing in mind the characteristics of an evolutionary approach, delineated earlier. This naturally includes a discussion of what the functional significance of such forms of play might be in the light of relevant evidence.

PHYSICAL ACTIVITY AND
ROUGH-AND-TUMBLE PLAY

Pellegrini and Smith (1998) argued that physical activity play (involving large muscle activity) has three main types following overlapping but sequential time courses. The first is early physical activity play in infancy, such as rhythmic stereotypies (Thelen, 1979). Years 3 to 6 are character-ized by exercise play (running, climbing, and other large body or muscle activity), which increases in frequency from toddlers to preschool and peaks at early primary school (childhood) ages, then declines in frequency. Finally, rough-and-tumble play (play fighting and play chasing) increases from toddlers through preschool and primary school ages, to peak at late primary or middle school ages (juvenile period) and then decline.

There are two main functional hypotheses regarding exercise play. One is that it supports neural maturation and synaptic differentiation at impor-tant critical periods in development (Byers & Walker, 1995). Pellegrini and Smith (1998) argued that this applies to rhythmic stereotypies in infancy, such as body rocking and foot kicking. Relatedly, exercise play in childhood is hypothesized to enhance physical training of muscles, for strength and endurance, and skill and economy of movement. This is consistent with the design features of exercise play, and with the results of deprivation studies that show that children engage in longer and more intense bouts of exercise play after being confined in smaller spaces or prevented from vigorous exercise (i.e., in classroom settings). Such rebound effects appear more important in the childhood and juvenile periods, when children are more likely to get restless after long sedentary periods, than with adults (Pellegrini, 1995b), although proper cross-sectional studies would put this generalization on a better footing.

A second hypothesis relating to an adaptive function for exercise play is the cognitive immaturity hypothesis (Bjorklund & Green, 1992). This argues that exercise play encourages younger children to take breaks from being overloaded on cognitive tasks and that nonfocused play activities, such as those found at school break times, provide a release from more focused school work. This is also consistent with the deprivation studies, and with results that suggest that exercise play in break time results in improved attention to school tasks (Pellegrini, 1995b). However, school tasks did not characterize ancestral human environments, so it is possible that this is not a function originally selected for, but rather an incidental benefit of exercise play.

Although rough-and-tumble play was neglected for a long time by psychologists, there is now a reasonable body of literature on this form of play, common in children (and indeed in many mammals). Functional hypotheses for rough-and-tumble play need to take account of the form of the behavior (design features), age trends (with a peak frequency in middle childhood), sex differences, and individual differences (Pellegrini, 2002; Smith, 1989).

Play fighting in the primates takes forms similar to human rough-and-tumble play—chasing, grappling—though with other elements such as mock biting usually absent in humans. It often looks like real fighting, and Symons (1978) argued on the basis of these design features that for rhesus monkeys, play fighting served as relatively safe practice for real fighting skills. It is relatively safe due to design features such as self-handicapping, choice of friends as play partners, and choice of safer spaces and surfaces for play fighting. Smith (1982) argued a similar case for human play fighting. The argument is consistent with age trends (inverted U, with real fighting becoming more important by adolescence), and sex differences (both play fighting and real fighting more frequent for males). However there has been an absence of confirmatory evidence from individual differences (are children who play fight less often, less good fighters), or from enrichment or deprivation studies.

Pellegrini (chap. 4, this volume) reviews the nature of rough-and-tumble play, and discusses its likely functions, especially in relation to sex differences and sexual selection theory. He argues for social affiliation benefits of play fighting in preadolescence, although my personal view is that this would be an incidental benefit, and that an affiliation function would not fully explain the design features or sex differences in play fighting.

Fagen's (1981) insight into the possibilities of cheating or manipulation in play fighting (see Smith, 1989), and Pellegrini's own empirical research with human children (Pellegrini, 1995a, 2002), has led to the hypothesis of a developmental shift in the function of rough-and-tumble play. Pellegrini (chap. 4, this volume) proposes a developmental change in function, from being primarily cooperative and affiliative in middle childhood, to being mainly concerned with dominance in adolescence, for boys (and possibly with "push-and-poke" courtship exchanges, for girls).

Symons (1978) explicitly attacked the idea that monkey play fighting could function to assert or maintain dominance, precisely because of the self-handicapping and reversals that often occur. A dominant youngster may allow himself or herself to be "rolled over" into the inferior position by a younger or weaker partner. However, it is a common observation in mammals including primates that play fighting becomes rougher with age; in human children, partner choice becomes influenced by strength ranking, by 11 years (not before; Humphreys & Smith, 1987). Pellegrini (1995a) found partner choice related to dominance status in adolescent boys; and in early adolescence, it appears that some boys may take advantage of the play fighting convention to encourage another into a rough-and-tumble play bout, and then inflict some actual hurt or display dominance, justifying this as "just being playing" (Neill, 1976). Pellegrini (chap. 4, this volume; Pellegrini & Long, 2003) found direct correlational evidence that boys who engage in play fighting at age 12 have higher dominance status, which in turn relates to a measure of dating popularity. Thus, Symons's (1978) argument against a dominance function might not hold for adolescent boys, who might be using play fighting, sometimes shading into real fighting, perhaps deliberately "cheating" with the conventions, to show off their physical strength and prowess at a developmental period when this could be important for reproductive competition and success. Pellegrini (2002) pointed out that gauging strength can still occur despite self-handicapping, and that self-handicapping and similar features are less prominent in adolescence when cheating becomes more common.

Pellegrini (2002) related the sex difference in rough-and-tumble play to sexual selection theory. In a polygamous or culturally imposed monogamous mating system (as humans can be argued to be), there is increased competition among males for access to "choosy" females, and thus males must invest more in dominance-related activities, especially as they approach reproductive maturity. Of course, not many 12- to 14-year-old boys will become fathers in the near future. However, our reference point here might more appropriately be ancestral human populations, hunter-gatherer or foraging peoples, who characterized 90% or more of the duration of human evolution. Fry (2005) documented how, in many foraging societies, adolescence is a period of male physical contests; these are quite ritualized—the intent is not to kill the other or even to harm them severely—but also quite serious in their intent and outcome. For example, Gusinde (1931, pp. 1623–1625 quoted in Fry, 2005, pp. 76–77) wrote of the Ona Eskimo people:

> The example of the adults often spurs them on, for, when an opportunity presents itself, they also valiantly fall to and never tire in their rivalry to down an opponent.... They choose soft earth, preferably dry mossy ground, where women and children and watching men form a large circle, in the inner space of which the wrestlers step.... Although the two opponents seize each other resolutely and gradually increase their efforts to the utmost, the wrestling never degenerates into ill-feeling, even though the stronger one finally knocks the weaker one to the ground with such force that he can sometimes get up only with difficulty. Many a man may be badly hurt, to be sure, but in the long run he may not escape further fights, but must venture on to increasingly stronger opponents in order not to get the reputation of a weak coward. For a very long time afterwards such a performance stimulates constant discussions, comparisons, and various opinions.

Fry (2005, p. 78) argued that the rougher kinds of rough-and-tumble play we see in present-day adolescents in Western societies may be analogous to these ritualized contests in foraging peoples, and that they may

> provide practice at participating in restrained, rule-based competitive struggles later in life? If so, we may have a convergence, in adolescence, of practice and dominance functions of R&T.

However there are important cultural differences in the extent of rough-and-tumble play, which may provide some challenge to this functional approach. In some societies, both play fighting and real fighting are infrequent. This is true for example of the Semai of Malaysia (Fry, 2005), of the La Paz Zapotec community in Mexico (Fry, 1990), and among the Parakana Indians of the Brazilian Amazon (Gosso, Otta, Salum e Morais,

Ribeiro, & Bussab, 2005). It is not clear how closely this relates to Pellegrini's (chap. 4, this volume) ecological and sexual selection model. Pellegrini would presumably predict that we would find less rough-and-tumble play, and certainly less of a sex difference in rough-and-tumble play, in ecologically imposed monogamous societies (his examples being Lapps and some Eskimo groups). There is actually little evidence to test this hypothesis at present, but Fry (2005, and see previous quote) certainly presents evidence of frequent male rough-and-tumble play and male dominance conflicts in Eskimo communities.

Gosso et al. (2005, p. 233) actually challenged the functionality of rough-and-tumble play in humans. They wrote:

> Parakanã children, both boys and girls, do know what fighting means, but both play fighting and actual fighting are very rare indeed.... It is our view that play fighting, so important in so many mammals, may have lost nearly all of its relevance for humans. Its abundance in other mammals relates to adult male's need to fight for status, females, territory and food.... Polygynic species exhibit more adult fighting, sexual dimorphism, and juvenile play fighting.... In our view, at some early point of human evolution, those benefits resulting from superior fighting abilities must have declined. Vertical hierarchy gave way to horizontal cooperation among males (and females). Access to females ceased to be the direct or indirect result of fights. A unique food-sharing pattern, devoid of priorities and disputes, made obsolete the advantages of superior fighting abilities.

However, even if there is little internal fighting in some hunter-gatherer or foraging communities, and excessive interpersonal aggression is not tolerated (Boehm, 1999), rates of aggression appear to be very variable in such groups, and fights with neighboring groups can occur (Boehm, 1999; Fry, 2005). So far as the practice function of rough-and-tumble play is concerned, I would argue that this remains as a facultative adaptation. In so far as fighting and aggression are valued or not valued, children's rough-and-tumble play may be encouraged or discouraged. So far as the dominance function in adolescence is concerned, as Fry (2005) documented, male skill in contests seems to predict prestige and standing in the community, and therefore probably reproductive success for males.

OBJECT PLAY

In traditional societies, play with objects is typically with surrounding materials, often involving pretend subsistence activities. For example Konner (1972) described! Kung children playing with sticks and pebbles, pretending to hunt animals and herd cattle. Gosso et al. (2005) described South American Indian children making pretend houses with mud and making baskets out of palm leaves. In modern societies, play with objects typically involves toys purpose-made for children's play, often based on mass media prototypes. There is no pronounced sex difference in the frequency of object play between boys and girls; any sex differences reported seem to vary with respect to age, and type of object play. Object play in boys is typically more vigorous (Gosso et al., 2005; Pellegrini & Gustafson, 2005).

Pellegrini and Bjorklund (2004) argued that object play develops skills useful in subsistence activities—such as hunting for boys and gathering for girls. This is consistent with arguments from design, as seen earlier. There are two main positive sources of evidence for this view—observations in traditional societies and experimental studies in modern societies.

The best evidence of the first kind comes from Bock's (1995, 2002, 2005) work with five ethnic groups living in traditional communities in the Okavango Delta, Botswana. His most detailed analyses relevant to this debate are observations on play pounding of grain, which is common in young girls. Their parents might tolerate or even encourage this play, or they might require girls to take part in subsistence activities, such as actually pounding and sifting grain. Pounding grain requires some combination of strength and skill, and it takes a few years for children to acquire proficiency approaching that of adults.

Bock's observations show that the frequency of play pounding in girls follows a characteristic inverted-U curve, peaking at around ages 5 to 6 years and falling off steeply at around ages 8 to 9 years. It is at 8 to 9 years old that girls' skill and productivity in actually pounding grain makes them useful in this respect, enabling their mothers to reallocate their own time to mongongo nut processing, which is a more demanding skilled process. Bock's analysis certainly supports the hypothesis that the play pounding helps develop skills in real pounding, and that these are put to use as soon as it is productive to do so, in the sense that a reasonable level of skill has been reached and that further play brings diminishing returns.

The evidence from this and from other less quantified analyses of object play in traditional societies (Gaskins, 1999, 2000; Gosso et al., 2005; Morelli, Rogoff, & Angelillo, 2003) suggests that parents tolerate children playing, even though they could be doing other productive tasks (e.g., food gathering or processing), and that they might even encourage children to play when the benefits of skill acquisition with future payoff outweigh the benefits of immediate productivity. However, there is a developmental trade-off between the child doing actual productive work (albeit at low efficiency), or engaging in play that is not productive in immediate terms but can improve skills for later use. As Bock pointed out, there will be some conflict of interest between parents and children on time allocation to play or engage in other activities, as parents are likely to value the actual work of the children rather higher than the child himself or herself (who might benefit from spending more time playing).

Data such as these remain essentially correlational. There have been a number of experimental studies on object play. These were inspired by Bruner (1972), who, taking an evolutionary perspective, emphasized the flexible nature of object play, and hypothesized its role especially for creative problem solving—finding solutions in new situations. Several experimental studies (Dansky & Silverman, 1973, 1975; Smith & Dutton, 1979; Sylva, Bruner, & Genova, 1976) appeared to support this hypothesis. These were carried out with children, usually of nursery-school age. Some children were given some play experience with objects; others were given an instructional session, or an alternative materials condition (e.g., drawing), or put in a no-treatment control group. After the sessions were over, the children were given an assessment of creativity (e.g., thinking of unusual uses for the objects they played with), or problem solving (e.g., using the objects to make a long tool to retrieve a marble).

Although the results of these studies were positive, in the sense that the children in the play condition did best at the creativity assessments, Smith and Simon (1984) argued that these studies were methodologically unsound. They were susceptible to experimenter effects; when the same experimenter administers the conditions and tests the children immediately after, unconscious bias could come in (especially if the researchers have strong positive expectations regarding the results; see earlier discussion of the play ethos). When experimenter effects were controlled for, there was little evidence that the play experience helped more than the others (Smith & Whitney, 1987). Indeed, there is not much evidence that any of the sessions had much impact; most lasted only about 10 minutes, and Smith and Simon (1984) concluded that either the benefits of object play in real life occur over a longer time period, or they are not substantial enough to measure by this sort of experimental procedure. The time period argument is probably important, in the light of the anthropological observations; in the play pounding observations by Bock, girls spent 2 to 4 years play pounding before switching to real pounding activities.

Pellegrini and Gustafson (2005) reported research that improves on these short-term experimental studies. Unlike the previous studies, criticized for lack of ecological validity because of their short duration (Smith & Simon, 1984), they used observational data of constructive play and tool use in 3- to 5-year-old children, gathered over an entire school year. They assessed children on problem-solving tasks at the end, and controlled statistically for spatial intelligence. Observed exploration, construction, and tool use during play over the last year were negatively related to measures of time, number of hints needed, and number of swipes at the lure, in a lure retrieval task (i.e., performance was improved). Their results do support the hypothesis that children spending time in construction play may be getting important practice and learning opportunities for problem solving. However such benefits might require more time than the earlier generation of experimental studies had initially suggested.

PRETEND AND SOCIODRAMATIC PLAY

There are clear similarities in the forms of rough-and-tumble play seen in mammalian species, especially nonhuman primates, and humans. In the case of pretend play, matters are very different. At least by the criteria we use for assessing pretend play in human children, it is entirely lacking in most animal species, although there may be exceptions, especially with the great apes (Gómez & Martín-Andrade, 2005). We generally surmise that pretend play forms part of a package of symbolic abilities, including self-awareness, theory of mind, and language, which characterizes humans and of which we see only simple precursors even in the cognitively most advanced nonhuman species. In this section I discuss the definition of pretense and levels of representation in pretense (and other) play, before moving on to consider the possible role of pretend play in theory of mind development.

Lillard (1994) defined pretense as involving six defining features: a *pretender*, a *reality*, and a *mental representation* that is *projected onto reality*, with *awareness* and *intention* on the part of that pretender. This can be regarded as a tough definition, which would rule out most or all nonhuman pretense. Mitchell (chap. 3, this volume) provides an illuminating discussion of the meaning of pretense and its applicability to nonhuman species. He provides a definition of pretense as follows: "Pretending is intentionally allowing an idea, at least part of which an agent knows to be inaccurate about or unrelated to current reality (i.e., fictional), to guide and constrain the agent's behaviors (including mental states)." Mitchell points out the considerable overlap between pretense, and deception. Incidentally, these are definitions of pretense, not of pretend play. The definition of play, is of course, another minefield, but we could take pretend play to be pretense that has the usual attributes associated with play—it is fun, done for its own sake, emphasizing means rather than ends (so, it is not important to convince someone of the reality of your actions, a criterion indicative of deception rather than pretense).

A tough definition of pretense, like that of Lillard (1994), implies conscious intention, an awareness of both the pretend reality and the actual reality. They imply some metarepresentational ability. Yet, much pretend play in younger infants (say, 15 months to 2 years) need not and probably does not satisfy such requirements (Jarrold, Carruthers, Smith & Boucher, 1994; Lillard, 1993), and this is likely true of the nonhuman examples also. Generally, nonhuman pretend, and that of young infants, too, are simple imitative actions done in a nonfunctional context (e.g., feeding or cuddling a "baby"). We do not know to what extent the pretender is aware of intentionally simulating reality. Really, we only become certain of this when slightly older children use language to explicit assign roles ("You be daddy") or negotiate or explain pretense ("It's not for real, we're only pretending").

Mitchell's (chap. 3, this volume) definition of pretense does not require the same level of conscious awareness as Lillard's definition; Mitchell considers that "the pretender could enjoy creating part of something, but not the whole thing, and enjoy that, and it would be pretend. In some sense that involves awareness of the pretend and actual realities, but not at a very deep level at all—the pretender could simply recognize incompleteness without concerning itself with realities of one sort or another" (personal communication, May 10, 2005). This allows Mitchell to consider human and nonhuman pretense on more equal terms, and he suggests some simpler precursors to full-blown pretense. Schematic play is "enactment of schemas based on relatively canalized processes for perceptual-motor integration that is not based on associative learning or imitation of another's actions." His example of play fighting can illustrate schematic play, and possibly the pet badger play fighting with a bush (which Mitchell argues is not schematic play; but following his line of reasoning, this might depend on how much prior experience of actual play fighting activity the badger had).

In a previous discussion of the ontogeny and phylogeny of theory of mind (Smith, 1996), I made use of Karmiloff-Smith's (1992) levels of representation; this may also be useful here in discussing the ontogeny and phylogeny of pretense and pretend play. Karmiloff-Smith posited a representational redescription model with several levels. Level I was implicit; the representation is available for use (whether inborn or through imitative or associative learning), but is not available to link with other representations in a flexible way. Level E1 means having representations explicit at the level of cross-system availability of procedural components; "component parts [of a procedure] ... become accessible to potential intra-domain links" (p. 20). Level E2 means representations are explicit at the level of conscious access or awareness, and Level E3 means available at the level of verbal report. In fact, these two last levels are not so clearly separated in Karmiloff-Smith's account as are the others, and I refer to it as E2/3.

For example, play fighting in mammals can be considered as at Level I. It is an easily learned repertoire of actions associated with certain cues and contexts. Developmental changes in the roughness of play fighting are in principle explicable in terms of maturational and hormonal changes in the individual, and their response to differing stimuli from their play fighting partners. However the picture is different when play fighting is used for other ends, such as by a rhesus monkey mother to distract her infant from suckling (Breuggeman, 1978). This surely requires some E1 ability. So, too, would cheating in play fighting. Cheating in play fighting that is done with awareness and conscious intent would of course be E2/3 level, but we have no clear evidence of this except from human children who are at or near adolescence, where the evidence comes from observation (Neill, 1976) but also from verbal self-report (Boulton, 1992; Smith, Smees, & Pellegrini, 2004).

Returning to pretend play, Karmiloff-Smith's (1992) Level I seems to correspond well to Mitchell's schematic play level. Mitchell continues by discussing the idea of presymbolic play or functional symbolic play. He suggests that these involve imitation, plus some ability in visual-kinesthetic matching. Procedures visually observed in others (feeding a baby) may be imitated though one's own body actions. This seems to correspond to Karmiloff-Smith's Level E1, where there is availability of procedures across domains, but as yet without conscious awareness or verbal report—therefore, not yet fully symbolic pretend play. Only her Level E2/E3 would correspond to this.

Karmiloff-Smith (1992) argued that chimpanzees (and a fortiori, other nonhuman species) did not get beyond Level I, or if there is any further level representation, "the higher-level codes into which representations are translated during redescription are very impoverished" (p. 192). My own view (see also Smith, 1996) is that this is rather harsh on chimpanzees and other great apes (see also Gómez & Martín-Andrade, 2005) and possibly other species such as dolphins (Mitchell, chap. 3, this volume); and especially when we consider enculturated apes, who possibly show more joint attention, show more deferred imitation, and provide most of the examples of possible pretend play. However, I see no compelling reason to put chimpanzees or any other nonhuman species at the E2/3 level, or as showing fully symbolic pretend play. As I argued before in relation to theory of mind (and the same argument holds for pretense), I think we would need apes to be able to talk to us, to convince us they were pretending (as aware, intentional beings). I also think that they would have needed language as social support to have evolved abilities to have this level of awareness (the greater representational level found in enculturated apes is a partial pointer to the importance of this).

Verbal self-report is also important in knowing whether play with objects involves pretense. Smilansky (1968) distinguished construction play from symbolic or pretend play, and this distinction has been widely used (e.g., Rubin, Watson, & Jambor, 1978). A 3- or 4-year-old child assembling bricks or Lego blocks might be classed as engaged in construction play. However, if you say to that child "Tell me what you are doing," he or she might reply "Making a spaceship" or "Making a cage to put monsters in" (Takhvar & Smith, 1990). The verbal report allows us to infer an awareness of intent to pursue an idea that is known in part to veer from current reality—that is, symbolic pretend play.

PRETEND PLAY AND THEORY OF MIND

Mitchell (chap. 3, this volume) considers various aspects of pretend play—actions directed to self or others, use of substitute or imaginary objects (including whether miming is done by one's own body part or an imaginary substitute); and the traditional constructs of integration, decentration, and decontextualization. Interestingly, he regards integration as being the most indicative of developmental change in pretend as children get older. He ends by suggesting that "pretending about others was adaptive because of the utility of imaginative planning or apprenticing (learning by matching one's own actions to another's)." This is not too dissimilar to my own earlier (Smith, 1982) argument that pretend makes play more complex and challenging than it would otherwise be, and Alexander's (1989) argument that social-intellectual play (or pretense) allows practice in "an expanding ability and tendency to elaborate and internalize social-intellectual-physical scenarios," using these to "anticipate and manipulate cause–effect relations in social cooperation and competition" (p. 480).

There is by now quite a long history of theorizing and of empirical investigation concerning the possible developmental benefits or adaptive value of pretend play (see Smith, 2004, 2005, for fuller discussions). The evidence, whether from correlational studies or from experimental (usually, enrichment) studies, remains equivocal. There is certainly evidence that pretend play experience and ability correlates with other developmental changes (e.g., increased cognitive, language, and social skills), but this means little unless general intelligence or age-related ability is factored out. Similarly, experimental play tutoring studies usually show gains in such skills along with the augmented play skills, but these studies usually lacked control for equivalent nonpretend play experiences, and when such controls were included, few if any differential effects of play tutoring were found (Smith, 1988). My own view is that this is consistent with pretend play being a useful facilitative experience, but not having a major or essential adaptive role in development.

This also applies to the evidence relating pretend play to theory of mind. This has been a vigorous research area recently. There is a good case to be made for relating these two abilities both ontogenetically (symbolic pretend play and theory of mind both emerge at around 3 years) and phylogenetically (rudimentary signs of both in great apes, otherwise seem limited to humans); and the design features of pretend play—its largely social nature, the negotiation of roles, and the need to understand others to keep an extended sociodramatic play sequence going—are consistent with it helping to acquire theory of mind skills. However there is very little relevant experimental evidence (Dockett, 1998; Smith, 2005), although there are a number of correlational studies.

Mitchell's (chap. 3, this volume) discussion usefully draws attention to the different components of pretend play. These might relate differently to outcomes. For example, if integration is a good indicator of developmental change in pretend play, this might relate more strongly to other outcomes than, say, decontextualization or decentration. Table 2.1 shows a summary of correlations obtained in nine studies, between theory of mind abilities (e.g., false belief tasks, deception tasks) and various pretend play measures. In all cases except one (as indicated) these correlations are partialed for age, or a general age-related measure (e.g., picture vocabulary score, mean length of utterance). In fact the picture is a very patchy

TABLE 2.1
Correlations Between One or More Measures of Pretend Play and
Theory of Mind in 3- to 5-Year-Old Children in Nine Different Studies

Measure	Study
Amount of fantasy/pretend play, or general fantasy/pretense measure	
.16	Astington & Jenkins (1995)
ns, .26	Youngblade & Dunn (1995)
.16* (ns at 3 years, .27* at 4 years)	Taylor & Carlson (1997)
.09	Nielsen & Dissanayake (2000)
Diversity of themes, etc.	
ns, ns	Youngblade & Dunn (1995)
.27	Lillard (1999)
Imaginative play predisposition	
.07	Taylor & Carlson (1997)
.06, .46**	Schwebel, Rosen, & Singer (1999), first study
Favorite play activity	
.11	Taylor & Carlson (1997)
Solitary pretend play	
.12, .27	Schwebel et al. (1999), first study
.17, −.22, .07	Schwebel et al. (1999), second study
Joint pretend play	
.14, .36*	Schwebel et al. (1999), first study
.18, .03, .36**	Schwebel et al. (1999), second study
Joint proposals	
.49**	Astington & Jenkins (1995)
Role assignment, explicit	
ns, ns	Youngblade & Dunn (1995)
.37**	Astington & Jenkins (1995)
.35*	Nielsen & Dissanayake (2000)
Role enactment, role play	
.31*, ns	Youngblade & Dunn (1995)
.24	Nielsen & Dissanayake (2000)
Imaginary companion	
.20*, .08	Taylor & Carlson (1997)
Impersonation	
21**, .17*	Taylor & Carlson (1997)
.15	Lillard (1999)
Pretend actions, object substitution, transformations	
.26**, .13	Taylor & Carlson (1997)
.01	Lillard (1999)
.17, .03, .29*	Schwebel et al. (1999), first study
.35*	Nielsen & Dissanayake (2000)

(Continued)

TABLE 2.1   *(Continued)*

Body part as object pantomime	
ns	Suddendorf, Fletcher-Flinn, & Johnston, (1999)
.09	Nielsen & Dissanayake (2000)
Imaginary object pantomime	
.25**	Suddendorf et al. (1999)
.35*	Nielsen & Dissanayake (2000)
Identify pretense	
.26, .16, .08	Rosen, Schwebel, & Singer (1997), no controls
Brain pretend questions	
.14	Lillard (1999)
Attribution of animacy	
.23	Nielsen & Dissanayake (2000)
Moe task	
ns	Lillard (1999)

$*p < .05. **p < .01.$

one. It does seem that just the amount of pretense or pretend play is not a major correlate with theory of mind. Verbal indicators such as making joint proposals or explicit role assignment have higher correlations, but not consistently in the latter case.

The Importance of Cross-Cultural Evidence

Another reason for some skepticism about pretend play having a major adaptive role is the low profile it has in a number of traditional societies. Gaskins (1999, 2000) observed 1- to 5-year-old children in a Mayan village community in the Yucatan, Mexico. Pretend play was rare in these children. It was not encouraged by adults, and early work demands were placed on the children. In general, although in agricultural communities pretend play is seen, it is rather simple in nature, mainly imitative of adult routines such as feeding a baby, herding cattle, and so on, which are readily observed. It is possible that some pretend subsistence activities, such as play pounding among Botswanan girls (Bock, 2002, 2005), has adaptive value in training for the adult equivalent skills. However, in many domains, children seem to learn by observation and by actually doing tasks or activities—often much earlier than in Western industrialized societies, in which the child is much more separated from adult work routines, and for whom toys and educative play are encouraged (Morelli et al., 2003). In other words, children become well-functioning adults in that society without necessarily doing much pretend play, and, the skills they need to be well-functioning adults can be acquired in many ways.

Sociodramatic play, more than other kinds of play, appears sensitive to adult involvement and encouragement, and may reflect effects of increased parental investment (Haight & Miller, 1993; MacDonald, 1993). This investment can be seen in a positive light as fostering the skills that sociodramatic play provides (whether as a main evolutionary function, which is debatable, or as incidental benefits, which are rather well documented). On the other hand, parents' interests are not identical with children's interests, and parents might be attempting to switch children from exercise and rough-and-tumble play (which they might find noisy and irritating) to more "educational" forms of play; this might or might not be in the child's own interests. Parents themselves can be manipulated by media, commercial, and manufacturing interests to purchase and consume toys, backed up by a prevalent play ethos (Smith, 1994; Sutton-Smith, 1986).

SUMMARY

After a century of considerable vicissitudes, an evolutionary perspective on human play (as with other areas of human behavior) has become established. It has valuable perspectives to offer. It places human play in a broad, phylogenetic framework, allowing us to see it in relation to the play of other species. It helps us ask searching questions about the functions of play—questions not yet fully answered, but about which we now know much more than a generation or so ago. It helps us be aware of how function might vary according to the type of play being considered, the point in the human life span that we are considering, and the perspective that we are taking—for example, child, parent, or social group. Not least, it is compatible with a view of human play and human activity as situated in a cultural context. An evolutionary approach embraces both universals and cultural variations in play. It would differ from a cultural determinist view, however, in seeing human play predispositions as being influenced by our genetic inheritance, in interaction with cultural environments that themselves might vary to greater or lesser extents from the kinds of environments in which we evolved. A fuller rapprochement between evolutionary developmental psychology and cultural-ecological models of development is a promising task for the next decade.

ACKNOWLEDGMENTS

I thank the School of Social Sciences and Humanities, University of Ballarat, Australia, for support during the completion of this chapter, and the editors for their constructive comments.

REFERENCES

Alexander, R. D. (1989). Evolution of the human psyche. In P. Mellars & C. Stringer (Eds.), *The human revolution* (pp. 455–513). Edinburgh, UK: Edinburgh University Press.

Arrington, R. E. (1943). Time sampling in studies of social behaviour: A critical review of techniques and results with research suggestions. *Psychological Bulletin, 40*, 81–124.

Astington, J. W., & Jenkins, J. M. (1995). Theory of mind development and social understanding. *Cognition and Emotion, 9*, 151–165.

Baldwin, J. D., & Baldwin, J. I. (1976). Effects of food ecology on social play: A laboratory simulation. *Zeitschrift für Tierpsychologie, 40*, 1–14.

Bekoff, M., & Byers, J. (Eds.). (1998). *Animal play: Evolutionary, comparative and ecological approaches*. New York: Cambridge University Press.

Bjorklund, D., & Green, B. (1992). The adaptive nature of cognitive immaturity. *American Psychologist, 47*, 46–54.

Bjorklund, D. F., & Pellegrini, A. D. (2002). *The origins of human nature: Evolutionary developmental psychology*. Washington, DC: APA Press.

Blurton Jones, N. (Ed.). (1972). *Ethological studies of child behaviour*. Cambridge, UK: Cambridge University Press.

Bock, J. (1995). *The determinants of variation in children's activities in a southern African community*. Unpublished doctoral dissertation, Department of Anthropology, University of New Mexico, Albuquerque.

Bock, J. (2002). Learning, life history, and productivity: Children's lives in the Okavango Delta, Botswana. *Human Nature, 13*, 161–197.

Bock, J. (2005). Farming, foraging, and children's play in the Okavango Delta, Botswana. In A. D. Pellegrini & P. K. Smith (Eds.), *The nature of play: Great apes and humans* (pp. 254–281). New York: Guilford.

Boehm, C. (1999). *Hierarchy in the forest: The evolution of egalitarian behavior*. Cambridge, MA: Harvard University Press.

Bogin, B. (1999). Evolutionary perspective on human growth. *Annual Review of Anthropology, 28*, 109–153.

Boulton, M. J. (1992). Rough physical play in adolescents: Does it serve a dominance function? *Early Education and Development, 3*, 312–333.

Breuggeman, J. A. (1978). The function of adult play in free-ranging Macaca mulatta. In E. O. Smith (Ed.), *Social play in primates* (pp. 169–191). New York: Academic.

Bruner, J. S. (1972). The nature and uses of immaturity. *American Psychologist, 27*, 687–708.

Byers, J. A., & Walker, C. (1995). Refining the motor training hypothesis for the evolution of play. *American Naturalist, 146,* 25–40.

Cole, M. (1998). Culture in development. In M. Woodhead, D. Faulkner, & K. Littleton (Eds.), *Cultural worlds of early childhood* (pp. 11–33). London: Routledge.

Dansky, J., & Silverman, I. (1973). Effects of play on associative fluency of preschool-age children. *Developmental Psychology, 9,* 38–43.

Dansky, J., & Silverman, I. (1975). Play: A general facilitator of associative fluency. *Developmental Psychology, 11,* 104.

Darwin, C. (1859). *The origin of species.* London: Murray.

Darwin, C. (1871). *The descent of man and selection in relation to sex.* Appleton: New York.

Department of the Environment. (1973). Children at play. In *Design bulletin* (p. 27). London: HMSO.

Dockett, S. (1998). Constructing understandings through play in the early years. *International Journal of Early Years Education, 6,* 105–116.

Fagen, R. (1981). *Animal play behavior.* New York: Oxford University Press.

Fry, D. P. (1990). Play aggression among Zapotec children: Implications for the practice hypothesis. *Aggressive Behavior, 16,* 321–340.

Fry, D. P. (2005). Rough-and-tumble social play in children and adolescents. In A. D. Pellegrini & P. K. Smith (Eds.), *The nature of play: Great apes and humans* (pp. 54–85). New York: Guilford.

Gaskins, S. (1999). Children's lives in a Mayan village: A case of culturally constructed roles and activities. In A. Göncü (Ed.), *Children's engagement in the world: Sociocultural perspectives* (pp. 25–61). New York: Cambridge University Press.

Gaskins, S. (2000). Children's daily activities in a Mayan village: A culturally grounded description. *Journal of Cross-Cultural Research, 34,* 375–389.

Gómez, J.-C., & Martín-Andrade, B. (2005). Fantasy play in apes. In A. D. Pellegrini & P. K. Smith (Eds.), *The nature of play: Great apes and humans* (pp. 139–172). New York: Guilford.

Göncü, A. (Ed.). (1999). *Children's engagement in the world: Sociocultural perspectives.* New York: Cambridge University Press.

Gosso, Y., Otta, E., Salum e Morais, M. de L., Ribeiro, F. J. L., & Bussab, V. S. R. (2005). Play in hunter-gatherer society. In A. D. Pellegrini & P. K. Smith (Eds.), *The nature of play: Great apes and humans* (pp. 213–253). New York: Guilford.

Groos, K. (1898). *The play of animals* (E. L. Baldwin, Trans.). New York: Appleton.

Groos, K. (1901). *The play of man.* New York: Appleton.

Gruber, H. E. (1974). *Darwin on man: A psychological study of scientific creativity.* London: Wildwood House.

Haight, W. L., & Miller, P. J. (1993). *Pretending at home: Early development in a sociocultural context.* Albany: State University of New York Press.

Hall, G. S. (1908). *Adolescence.* New York: Appleton.

Hawkes, K., O'Connell, J. F., Blurton Jones, N. G., Alvarez, H., & Charnov, E. L. (1998). Grandmothering, menopause, and the evolution of human life histories. *Proceedings of the National Academy of Sciences, USA, 95,* 1336–1339.

Hole, G. J., & Einon, D. F. (1984). Play in rodents. In P. K. Smith (Ed.), *Play in animals and humans* (pp. 95–117). Oxford, UK: Basil Blackwell.

Humphreys, A. P., & Smith, P. K. (1987). Rough-and-tumble play, friendship, and dominance in school children: Evidence for continuity and change with age. *Child Development, 58,* 201–212.

Huxley, J. S. (1942). *Evolution: The modern synthesis.* London: Allen & Unwin.

Isaacs, S. (1929). *The nursery years.* London: Routledge & Kegan Paul.

Jarrold, C., Carruthers, P., Smith, P. K., & Boucher, J. (1994). Pretend play: Is it metarepresentational? *Mind and Language, 9,* 445–468.

Kaplan, H. S., Lancaster, J. B., Hill, K., & Hurtado, A. M. (2000). A theory of human life history evolution: Diet, intelligence, and longevity. *Evolutionary Anthropology, 9,* 156–183.

Karmiloff-Smith, A. (1992). *Beyond modularity.* Cambridge, MA: MIT Press.

Klein, R. G. (1989). *The human career: Human biological and cultural origins.* Chicago: University of Chicago Press.

Kline, S. (1995). The promotion and marketing of toys: Time to rethink the paradox? In A. D. Pellegrini (Ed.), *The future of play theory* (pp. 165–185). Albany: State University of New York Press.

Konner, M. (1972). Aspects of the developmental ethology of a foraging people. In N. Blurton Jones (Ed.), *Ethological studies of child behaviour* (pp. 285–304). Cambridge, UK: Cambridge University Press.

Lancaster, J. B., & Lancaster, C. S. (1987). The watershed: Change in parental-investment and family-formation strategies in the course of human evolution. In J. B. Lancaster, J. Altmann, A. S. Rossi, & L. R. Sherrod (Eds.), *Parenting across the lifespan: Biosocial dimensions* (pp. 187–205). New York: Aldine.

Lancy, D. F. (1980). Play in species adaptation. *Annual Review of Anthropology, 9,* 471–495.

Lancy, D. F. (1996). *Playing on the mother-ground.* New York: Guilford.

Lillard, A. S. (1993). Pretend play skills and the child's theory of mind. *Child Development, 64,* 348–371.

Lillard, A. S. (1994). Making sense of pretense. In C. Lewis & P. Mitchell (Eds.), *Children's early understanding of mind* (pp. 211–234). Hove, UK: Lawrence Erlbaum Associates.

Lillard, A. S. (1999). Pretending, understanding pretense, and understanding minds. In S. Reifel (Ed.), *Play and culture studies: Vol. 3. Theory in context and out* (pp. 233–254). Norwood, NJ: Ablex.

Lovejoy, C. O. (1981) The origin of man. *Science, 211,* 341–350.

MacDonald, K. (1993). Parent–child play: An evolutionary perspective. In K. MacDonald (Ed.), *Parent–child play* (pp. 113–143). New York: SUNY Press.

Martin, P., & Caro, T. (1985). On the function of play and its role in behavioral development. In J. Rosenblatt, C. Beer, M. Bushnel, & P. Slater (Eds.), *Advances in the study of behaviour* (Vol. 15, pp. 59–103). Orlando, FL: Academic.

Morelli, G. A., Rogoff, B., & Angelillo, C. (2003). Cultural variation in young children's access to work or involvement in specialized child-focused activities. *International Journal of Behavioral Development, 27,* 264–274.

Neill, S. R. S. (1976). Aggressive and non-aggressive fighting in twelve-to-thirteen year old pre-adolescent boys. *Journal of Child Psychology and Psychiatry, 17,* 213–220.

Nielsen, M., & Dissanayake, C. (2000). An investigation of pretend play, mental state terms and false belief understanding: In search of a metarepresentational link. *British Journal of Developmental Psychology, 18*, 609–624.

Parker, S. T. (1984). Playing for keeps: An evolutionary perspective on human games. In P. K. Smith (Ed.), *Play in animals and humans* (pp. 271–293). Oxford, UK: Blackwell.

Pellegrini, A. D. (1995a). A longitudinal study of boys' rough-and-tumble play and dominance during early adolescence. *Journal of Applied Developmental Psychology, 16*, 77–93.

Pellegrini, A. D. (1995b). *School recess and playground behavior.* Albany: State University of New York Press.

Pellegrini, A. D. (2002). Rough-and-tumble play from childhood through adolescence: Development and possible functions. In P. K. Smith & C. Hart (Eds.), *Blackwell handbook of social development* (pp. 438–453). Oxford, UK: Blackwell.

Pellegrini, A. D., & Bjorklund, D. F. (2004). The ontogeny and phylogeny of children's object and fantasy play. *Human Nature, 15*, 23–43.

Pellegrini, A. D., & Gustafson, K. (2005). Boys' and girls' uses of objects for exploration, play, and tools in early childhood. In A. D. Pellegrini & P. K. Smith (Eds.), *The nature of play: Great apes and humans* (pp. 113–135). New York: Guilford.

Pellegrini, A. D., & Long, J. D. (2003). A sexual selection theory longitudinal analysis of sexual segregation and integration in early adolescence. *Journal of Experimental Child Psychology, 85*, 257–278.

Pellegrini, A. D., & Smith, P. K. (1998). Physical activity play: The nature and function of a neglected aspect of play. *Child Development, 69*, 577–598.

Pellegrini, A. D., & Smith, P. K. (Eds.). (2005). *The nature of play: Great apes and humans.* New York: Guilford.

Pereira, M. E. (1993). Evolution of the juvenile period in mammals. In M. E. Pereira & L. A. Fairbanks (Eds.), *Juvenile primates* (pp. 17–27). Oxford, UK: Oxford University Press.

Piaget, J. (1951). *Play, dreams, and imitation in childhood.* London: Heinemann.

Plotkin, H. (2004). *Evolutionary thought in psychology: A brief history.* Malden, MA: Blackwell.

Power, T. G. (2000). *Play and exploration in children and animals.* Mahwah, NJ: Lawrence Erlbaum Associates.

Rogoff, B. (2003). *The cultural nature of human development.* New York: Oxford University Press.

Rosen, C. S., Schwebel, D. C., & Singer, J. L. (1997). Preschoolers' attributions of mental states in pretense. *Child Development, 68*, 1133–1142.

Rubin, K. H., Watson, K. S., & Jambor, T. W. (1978). Free-play behaviors in preschool and kindergarten children. *Child Development, 49*, 534–536.

Schwartzman, H. (1978). *Transformations: The anthropology of children's play.* New York: Plenum.

Schwebel, D. C., Rosen, C. S., & Singer, J. L. (1999). Preschoolers' pretend play and theory of mind: The role of jointly constructed pretense. *British Journal of Developmental Psychology, 17*, 333–348.

Smilansky, S. (1968). *The effects of sociodramatic play on disadvantaged preschool children*. New York: Wiley.

Smith, P. K. (1970). *Social and play behaviour of preschool children*. Unpublished doctoral dissertation, University of Sheffield, Sheffield, UK.

Smith, P. K. (1982). Does play matter? Functional and evolutionary aspects of animal and human play. *Behavioral and Brain Sciences, 5*, 139–184.

Smith, P. K. (Ed.). (1984). *Play in animals and humans*. Oxford, UK: Basil Blackwell.

Smith, P. K. (1988). Children's play and its role in early development: A reevaluation of the "play ethos." In A. D. Pellegrini (Ed.), *Psychological bases of early education* (pp. 207–226). Chichester, UK: Wiley.

Smith, P. K. (1989). The role of rough-and-tumble play in the development of social competence: Theoretical perspectives and empirical evidence. In B. Schneider, G. Attili, J. Nadel & R. P. Weissberg (Eds.), *Social competence in developmental perspective* (pp. 239–255). Dordrecht, The Netherlands: Kluwer.

Smith, P. K. (1994). Play training: An overview. In J. Hellendoorn, R. van der Kooij, & B. Sutton-Smith (Eds.), *Play and intervention* (pp. 185–194). New York: State University of New York Press.

Smith, P. K. (1996). Language and the evolution of mindreading. In P. Carruthers & P. K. Smith (Eds.), *Theories of theories of mind* (pp. 344–354). Cambridge, UK: Cambridge University Press.

Smith, P. K. (2004). Play: Types and functions in human development. In B. J. Ellis & D. F. Bjorklund (Eds.), *Origins of the social mind: Evolutionary psychology and child development* (pp. 271–291). New York: Guilford.

Smith, P. K. (2005). Social and pretend play in children. In A. D. Pellegrini & P. K. Smith (Eds.), *The nature of play: Great apes and humans* (pp. 173–209). New York: Guilford.

Smith, P. K., & Connolly, K. J. (1972). Patterns of play and social interaction in preschool children. In N. Blurton Jones (Ed.), *Ethological studies of child behaviour* (pp. 62–95). Cambridge, UK: Cambridge University Press.

Smith, P. K., & Dutton, S. (1979). Play and training in direct and innovative problem solving. *Child Development, 50*, 830–836.

Smith, P. K., & Simon, T. (1984). Object play, problem-solving and creativity in children. In P. K. Smith (Ed.), *Play in animals and humans* (pp. 199–216). Oxford, UK: Basil Blackwell.

Smith, P. K., Smees, R., & Pellegrini, A. D. (2004). Play fighting and real fighting: Using video playback methodology with young children. *Aggressive Behavior, 30*, 164–173.

Smith, P. K., & Whitney, S. (1987). Play and associative fluency: Experimenter effects may be responsible for previous findings. *Developmental Psychology, 23*, 49–53.

Spencer, H. (1898). *The principles of psychology*. New York: Appleton. (Original work published 1878)

Suddendorf, T., Fletcher-Flinn, C., & Johnston, L. (1999). Pantomime and theory of mind. *Journal of Genetic Psychology, 160*, 31–45.

Sutton-Smith, B. (1986). *Toys as culture*. New York: Gardner.

Sylva, K., Bruner, J. S., & Genova, P. (1976). The role of play in the problem-solving behaviour of children 3–5 years old. In J. S. Bruner, A. Jolly, & K. Sylva (Eds.), *Play: Its role in development and evolution* (pp. 244–261). New York: Basic Books.

Symons, D. (1978). *Play and aggression: A study of rhesus monkeys.* New York: Columbia University Press.

Takhvar, M., & Smith, P. K. (1990). A review and critique of Smilansky's classification scheme and the "nested hierarchy" of play categories. *Journal of Research in Childhood Education, 4*, 112–122.

Taylor, M., & Carlson, S. M. (1997). The relation between individual differences in fantasy and theory of mind. *Child Development, 68*, 436–455.

Thelen, E. (1979). Rhythmical stereotypies in normal human infants. *Animal Behaviour, 27*, 699–715.

Tinbergen, N. (1951). *The study of instinct.* Oxford, UK: Clarendon.

Trivers, R. L. (1974). Parent–offspring conflict. *American Zoologist, 14*, 249–264.

Vygotsky, L. S. (1966). Play and its role in the mental development of the child. *Voprosy Psikhologii, 12*, 62–76. (Original work published 1933)

Wilson, E. O. (1978). *Sociobiology: The new synthesis.* Belknap, MA: Harvard University Press.

Youngblade, L. M., & Dunn, J. (1995). Individual differences in young children's pretend play with mother and sibling: Links to relationships and understanding of other people's feelings and beliefs. *Child Development, 66*, 1472–1492.

3

Pretense in Animals: The Continuing Relevance of Children's Pretense

Robert W. Mitchell
Department of Psychology
Eastern Kentucky University

Do animals pretend? This deceptively simple question with its modern ring was critically examined more than 100 years ago by Groos (1898, 1901). Before and since, diverse reasons have been offered for or against the proposition (Mitchell, 2002b). Darwin (1871/1896) and his supporters easily accepted the idea that animals are pretending when play-fighting, playing with objects, teasing, and deceiving. For them, such activities showed imagination, even though (unlike children's pretenses) animal pretenses seemed limited in scope. Groos offered an alternative interpretation of apparent pretense in play: These activities are simply the pleasurable acting out of instincts prior to their usefulness in adult life; they simulate adult behaviors, but without awareness of the simulation, functioning as practice. Yet Darwin's interpretation was, Groos believed, potentially accurate: When animal players had experienced the real activity that was practiced in play, they might (as human children do) become aware of the similarities and differences between their play behavior and the behavior it simulates, and thus come to act out a role while playing. The two views of play, as either unintentional (often instinctual) simulation, usually for practice (see Smith, chap. 2, this volume), or intentional simulation (pretense), perhaps also for practice, remain active interpretations of animal play (Mitchell, 1990, 2002b). However, pretense is broader than play.

Pretending is a term often used without too much reflection. In normal usage, *pretense* and its congener *make-believe* apply to a broad array of activities and experiences, including those of con artists, theatrical actors and their audience, adults looking at works of art or reading a novel, and infants offering a drink from an empty bottle. However, for scientists, pretending often has restricted meanings. For some, pretending must be symbolic, or employ an imaginary object, or be verbally characterized by the pretender. Some of these restrictions may disallow animal pretending by definition, but they also contradict normative uses of the term. Concerns about restricting the term derive in part from the plausible idea that pretense is a symbolic activity linked to language (Piaget, 1945/1962). However, such restriction tends to ignore the perplexing questions of how symbolic activities develop (Fein & Moorin, 1985) and evolve (Parker & McKinney, 1999).

Consider this example of pretense:

> [L.] takes great delight in a sort of slight-of-hand trick that she has devised by herself, thus: she hides (by covering it up with her leg) a glass ball when it is rolled to her, then says invariably Gone! ..., and then suddenly produces it with leg and hand, and acts as if much pleased by her little magic. (Dearborn, 1910, p. 156)

Or this more elaborate one:

> [T.] would beg me for [my keys] until finally I gave them to her, and she would immediately hide them, under an arm or between her legs, or in the grass beneath her. Then she would go through an elaborate routine of showing me that she didn't have them at all by calling attention to every place on her body where they might be except the one where they were. She might, for instance, hide them under her left armpit, then carefully lift her right arm to show me that they weren't under that one, point to the inside of her elbow, open both of her hands to show me that they weren't there, spread her legs and show me the soles of her feet. Sometimes she threw them away in the grass and then if after a long and futile hunt I told her that she must get them for me, she would trot to them immediately and bring them back. (Hoyt, 1941, p. 149)

L. and T. are pretending that an object has disappeared or cannot be found. Imagine that both are apes (sign-using ones, if need be). Does it still seem as if both are pretending? Besides chauvinism, I cannot conceive why anyone would doubt it. Yet many scientists would deny that these actions are pretense if enacted by apes but not if by children. Some argue that calling animals' activities pretend is an anthropomorphic "conceptual leap" (Taylor & Carlson, in Mitchell, 2002b, p. 168), but this erroneously implies that the term pretense is earmarked as relevant solely to people—the *Oxford English Dictionary* indicates no such implication.

Knowledge of human pretense is clearly relevant to understanding animal pretense: What we think about human abilities, especially young children's, influences any ideas we apply to animals' abilities. In what follows, I provide a definition of pretense, apply the definition to human activity, elaborate the development of human pretense, and then apply all this to animals' activities.

DEFINING PRETENSE

The disparities among definitions of pretense make for confusion unconducive to scientific study; most phenomena need a clear and coherent definition to be studied. I begin with this one: "Pretense or make-believe is a mental activity involving imagination that is intentionally projected onto something" (Mitchell, 2002b, p. 4; see also Lillard, in Mitchell, 2002b). More elaborately, pretense is "the use of … props in imaginative activities" (Walton, 1990, p. 67), where props are "objects of imaginings" (p. 25). The props, or what imagination is projected onto, can include the imaginer himself or herself, his or her behavior (including mental states), as well as things outside the imaginer. As such, detecting another's pretense requires psychological inference from behavior.

Imagination is a key term, yet it is difficult to encompass (Walton, 1990). In Darwin's (1871/1896) *Descent of Man* and the subsequent literature on children's early pretenses, imagination indicates that children and animals are acting as if something is the case, when it is literally and obviously not the case. Children's actions are pretenses because they evince such imagination: They dramatize an idea (or schema), conform to an idea that is inaccurate or "untrue," or imitate actions of another that fit an idea. The pretending child "is possessed by an idea, and is working this out into visible action" (Sully, 1896, p. 37) or, in more modern terms, "seems to explore what it means to do something without having to do it" (Fein & Moorin, 1985, p. 67). This dissociation between the idea and reality indicates imagination. Yet imagination per se is not peculiar to pretense (Walton, 1990). What makes the imagination in pretense so important to its definition is that the goal of pretense (which constrains the behaviors engaged in) is to enact imagination. Thus, pretending is intentionally allowing an idea, at least part of which an agent knows to be inaccurate about or unrelated to current reality (i.e., fictional), to guide and constrain the agent's behaviors (including mental states).

This definition, in my view, simultaneously captures the usual ideas about pretending and leaves open many scientists' unnecessary and inappropriate requirements for pretense:

- The standard view of pretense—that it is, or originates from, a (usually but not necessarily playful and therefore "unreal") simulation of a real activity—fits the definition.
- Using this definition, pretenses can be realistic (i.e., simulative), indeed very realistic, but they need not be, and they need not be based on real experiences.
- Pretenders may pretend about real objects using these objects, realistic toys, substitutes for the real objects, or nothing at all.
- Pretenses may or may not be indicated to be pretense by the pretender, and may not be detectable as pretense by outsider observers while they are happening.
- Pretenses may or may not be playful, and pretense per se does not indicate play; indeed, intentional deceptions can be pretenses.
- Pretenses may or may not be symbolic.
- Finally, the definition provides a level playing field within which to compare human and animal pretense and incorporates both simple and complex phenomena, thereby allowing for the possibility of development in pretense. (See Mitchell, 2002b, for discussion of all of these points.)

Before I present evidence of pretense by animals that fits my definition, I need to show that my definition fits human pretenses accurately and specifically.

HUMAN PRETENSES AND THEIR DEVELOPMENT

Intentional simulation is a standard marker of pretending by young children, who borrow the structure of their early pretenses from reality. Simulations are things (e.g., actions) designed to resemble something else. Simulation in action satisfies my definition if the actors know that at least part of the idea they are acting out is incommensurate with reality. A girl who normally threw a ball would not be pretending if she threw an apple, as she is not intending to simulate the act of throwing (cf. Gómez & Martín-Andrade, in Mitchell, 2002b), but the child would be pretending if she "threw" an imaginary ball or threw an apple while imagining it to be a ball. (This latter pretense may be indiscernible as pretense to outsiders, to whom it may appear as merely throwing an apple.) That children act intentionally, and that children intentionally simulate, are rarely contentious points for researchers of children.

The tricky part of the definition is discerning the pretender's knowledge that part of the idea is inaccurate (does not fit current reality) or is unrelated to (not based on) current reality. That this aspect is essential to pretense is hardly novel (Bretherton, 1984; Fein & Moorin, 1985; McCune & Agayoff, in Mitchell, 2002b). There are diverse reasons for attributing knowledge of their activity's "unreality" to pretenders; the most common is the activity's being an incomplete simulation. The fact that children's earliest pretenses are usually simulations of something real they have experienced, but for a different purpose, suggests that the children know that they are simulating. For example, a 3.5-month-old boy who repeatedly cried violently when his father moved out of sight but chuckled when he reappeared (Valentine, 1942/1950, p. 87) must have had some sense of the unreality of his cry—his real violent cries did not, one assumes, end abruptly with chuckling. Another more well-studied pretense is acting as if offering liquid to someone—initially themselves, later others, and later still dolls as well (Fein & Moorin, 1985). Pretense occurs when a drinking action is performed with no liquid in the bottle or cup, or when the child himself or herself acts only as if taking liquid from the bottle (whether full or empty), or when the child performs the action toward an inanimate, such as a doll. These infants are pretending, rather than just performing an appropriate action with a bottle or cup, because they know that no one is really drinking; they are acting out the idea of drinking that they know does not cohere with reality, an idea that derives from repeated drinking activities. The idea of drinking (well known to the infant) is enacted but unfulfilled. Such resemblance of form without similar function helps us to detect pretense when the pretender knows from experience about the real function of the action. Intentional deceptions are also pretenses—"pretenses presented for real" (Sinclair, 1996, p. 166)—that rely on resemblance of form that deceivers know has a dissimilar function (Mitchell, 1994; Reddy, 1991). Indeed, the word *pretense* originates from ideas of feigning and providing a false appearance.

But what about when a child does not know the real function of an action he or she appears to be pretending to do? In this case, even with simulation as a guide, detecting "whether the child is merely performing the appropriate action with an object or pretending ... as well" can be difficult (Bretherton, 1984, p. 16). One-year-olds "pretend-telephoning" do not understand telephoning, and 19-month-olds "pretending" to read a newspaper do not know what reading or a newspaper are (Bretherton, 1984). These actions are pretense if they indicate a "projection of another person's behavior onto the self" (p. 10)—a dissociation between the idea enacted and reality. Some researchers appear to assume this dissociation, calling all deferred imitation of others pretense (Bates, Benigni, Bretherton, Camaioni, & Volterra, 1979). Still, a child might be re-creating what another did without any knowledge of unreality, in which case he or she is imitating but not pretending. Note the difficulty—just because a child's knowledge of unreality is necessary to detect pretense does not guarantee that this knowledge is easily discernible (Piaget, 1945/1962). Knowledge of unreality can come from any aspect of the pretense; it is not necessary that children understand all aspects of the real thing on which their imitation is based. Children can "think babies, like dolls, are filled with sawdust" (Hall, 1914, p. 183). Children can pretend to be Einstein without understanding relativity.

Because detection of pretense so often depends on recognition of simulation, "an observer must know how the culture in which the child is reared goes about eating, sleeping, transporting, loving, or fighting in order to perform the proper matching operation" (Fein & Moorin, 1985, p. 63; Gaskins & Göncü, 1992). (Which imaginings are fun to enact may, of course, have instinctual prompting.) In addition, one must know how the individual pretender and his or her companions go about doing these things, and with which objects (Musatti & Mayer, 1987; Piaget, 1945/ 1962). Because repeated activities are likely to become ritualized, separated from their original purposes, and simulated in pretense, one's knowledge of pervasive regularities in the child's social world is helpful for pretense detection. For those immersed in a child's culture, "the simulation is often apparent," yet "there may be simulations too subtle to detect" (Fein & Moorin, 1985, p. 63).

To support his interpretation that pretense involves representation and symbolism, Piaget (1945/1962) required that the action approximate the child's normal action without the normal objects. He argued that pretense first appears with the "union" of the "application of ... schema to inadequate objects and evocation for pleasure" (p. 97), the latter evinced by laughing or smiling. The "inadequate objects" are substitute or imaginary objects that represent or are symbolic of real objects. Such symbolism or representation in action helps us to discern young children's pretending, as their knowledge of unreality is clear, and also helps to distinguish pretenses from simple reenactments of past behavior, but it is unclear to me that symbolism is essential for pretending. Precise replications of normal activities with normal objects can be pretense. Stage actors pretend in many cases by really doing what they pretend to be doing (Walton, 1990). A child can pretend to sleep by going to her bed and precisely re-creating her normal sleeping activities, and even use it as a form of teasing—which Valentine's (1942/1950) son did at 21 months. In addition, the earliest pretenses are probably not representational: "It may be useful to classify [an infant's playful] feeding behavior at 12 months as pretense, but to interpret the behavior as presymbolic ... sucking or drinking can be playful and simulative, if the infant wishes it to be, but the sense in which the behavior might be viewed as symbolic or representational requires further specification" (Fein & Moorin, 1985, p. 74). Such presymbolic pretense occurs in functional pretend play, which employs realistic objects used conventionally. By contrast, and in concert with Piaget's idea of pretense, symbolic pretend play is "substituting one object for another, attributing an imaginary property to something or someone [including oneself], and referring to an absent object as if it was present" (Lewis, Boucher, Lupton, & Watson, 2000, p. 119), each of which indicates decontextualization.

Psychologists view symbolic pretense as more developed than functional pretense because the imaginings in symbolic pretense are not prescribed by the objects used (which need not even be present). Yet functional pretense may be more common than symbolic pretense among adults, who enjoy functional pretense when experiencing art (Walton, 1990): Particular imaginings are prescribed by the art itself, as when portraits of people afford easy imagining about people (rather than about atoms or elephants). Our perceptual systems are organized to give us some imaginative experiences simply because of resemblance between real objects and their simulations (Mitchell, 1994). For children, real objects and their facsimiles (e.g., toys, dolls) can be thought to similarly prescribe imaginings, and thus induce pretense. Indeed, children's symbolic pretense results almost always when realistic objects are unavailable for functional pretense (Musatti & Mayer, 1987).

Children can know that what they are doing is not what it appears to be, without thinking through all the implications. For example, 2.5- to 6-year-old children engage in pretend play by pretending to be an animal (Elder & Pederson, 1978; Myers, in Mitchell, 2002b; Pederson, Rook-Green, & Elder, 1981). Yet it is only by 4 years of age that children appear to know that an intention to simulate something x is required for their own pretending to be x, and it is after 6 years of age that they seem to understand the same about others. When told that their own actions or another's looked like those of an animal that neither had intended to look like, and were asked if they or the other were pretending to be that animal, 4.5- to 6.5-year-old children tended to say that they were not pretending, but that the other person was (Lillard, in Mitchell, 2002b; Mitchell & Neal, 2005).

The difference in children's thinking about their own and another's pretense seems based on a greater willingness to believe that the other person's actions, but not their own, actually looked like actions of the animal suggested (even though neither intended their actions to look like those of the animal). On several tasks we (Mitchell & Neal, 2005) asked the child, or a confederate (while the child observed), to perform actions, and asked the performer if he or she were intending to look like a particular animal. On denial by the performer, we told him or her that his or her actions looked like those of that animal, and then asked the child two questions, in counterbalanced order: if he or she (or the other person) looked like that animal, and if he or she (or the other person) was pretending to be that animal. Children usually (75% of the time) gave the same answer to both questions (usually "no" if the questions were about their own actions, and "yes" if about the confederate's). What is interesting is that, if a child said "yes" to the question about either his or her own or the confederate's actions looking like those of an animal, the child usually also agreed that the person was pretending, even though the person had not intended to resemble the animal, even if the person was the child himself or herself. These children must have been experts at symbolic pretending, yet they did not recognize that someone must intend to look (act) like the animal to be pretending to be it. They apparently thought that just looking like something x is enough to be pretending to be x, and not looking like x is enough not to be pretending to be x. So pretending symbolically cannot require that you always think of yourself as intending to create a similarity, even though you intend to simulate when pretending. Rather, all you need to do (in the case of imitative pretense) is recognize the similarity (and nonidentity) between the real and the simulation. Pretenses are actions (including mental states) intentionally controlled by (or conforming to) an idea the actor knows does not cohere with current reality. Awareness of this intention is not required to pretend, even to pretend symbolically. Neither is simulation: When asked how they could pretend to be a (nonexistent) animal they had never heard of (e.g., a "crillbo"), some children produced actions as if they were such an animal (Mitchell, 2000).

During ontogeny, the ideas embodied in pretenses become more elaborate and their dissociation from or lack of relation to reality becomes more acceptable to the pretender. Researchers have articulated, following ideas set out by Piaget (1945/1962), a development from early play to later pretense that proceeds along three trajectories: integration of schemes, decontextualization, and decentration (see, e.g., Bretherton, 1984). Of these, only the latter two indicate knowledge of fictionality or unreality.

Increasing integration of schemes is evident in more elaborate sequences of actions relevant to an idea such as a script or a scene. Infants using the same action toward self, others, and dolls show single-scheme integration, and those using diverse actions with the same entities show multischeme integration, as when the child has a doll drive a car to a store, get groceries, and drive home. More sequentially appropriate actions indicate greater integration. Multischeme integration is particularly prevalent in role play, dramatic play, and complicated deceptions; in all, children begin with the ability to replicate their own or another's actions, and increase the number of appropriately sequential actions as they come to imitate or inhabit roles more precisely or elaborately. However, increasing integration occurs in the development of any activity or skill.

Decontextualization is present in the use of imaginary objects supported by other objects, in the use of substitute objects, and in the creation of gestures indicating completely imaginary objects. Objects themselves or replicas of these (toys) are presumed to provide the context for their conventional use, and thus "contextualize" pretense. Object use is decontextualized only if imaginary objects (e.g., liquid) are present with use of a conventional object (e.g., a cup) that supports the imaginary object, or if the objects are used in nonconventional ways (i.e., are substitute objects). It is unclear whether any decontextualized pretense is symbolic (Fenson, Kagan, Kearsley, & Zelazo, 1976), or only pretenses with greater decontextualization (using substitute objects and gestures about imaginary objects; Lewis et al., 2000). Young players prefer more contextualized pretense. They can show object-supported imaginary object use at 9 months of age, but exhibit it more frequently between 13 and 22 months (Fenson et al., 1976; Ungerer, Zelazo, Kearsley, & O'Leary, 1981). Children under 3 years only infrequently use substitute objects or gestures for imaginary objects in free play when realistic objects are present (Corrigan, 1987; Fenson, in Bretherton, 1984; Lyytinen, 1991), perhaps because more realistic objects induce greater engagement in pretense (Walton, 1990). In fact, when children imitate actions of same-age play companions, "unavailability of a given object to be used for displaying a given activity seems to be the driving force behind the production of acts of object substitution" (Musatti & Mayer, 1987, p. 234).

Decentration represents a development away from acting on the self to acting on (increasingly fictional, decontextualized) others. In centered pretense, the child acts on himself or herself; decentration increases as the child's pretenses develop to acting on objects (including "animate" objects, such as live entities and dolls, as well as "passive" objects, such as cups), to animating dolls to do things, and later to having imaginary companions (Fenson, in Bretherton, 1984; Taylor & Carlson, in Mitchell, 2002b). Decentration and decontextualization are combined in studies examining children's doll play with objects (Corrigan, 1987); using dolls as agents making gestures indicating entirely imaginary objects, normal for 2.5-year-olds, would show the most developed level for both (Lowe, 1975). Another aspect of decentration is children's move from reenacting their own behavior to reenacting another's behavior (Bretherton, 1984; Piaget, 1945/1962). With language, Piaget noted, pretenses based on one's own and others' actions in role play games seem to develop simultaneously, but the actions themselves are often not obviously simulative without linguistic markers (see also Lyytinen, 1991).

The substitute objects that indicate decontextualization vary in the similarity of their form and function to the objects they replace. By 3 years of age most children can perform most varieties, but none are common: Fewer than half of the children tested at 14 to 34 months showed any substitute object use (Jackowitz & Watson, 1980; Ungerer et al., 1981). The properties of the objects used as substitutes may influence the pretense. Obvious affordances of objects tend to suggest similar affordances in pretense, and interfere with different uses in pretense (Crum, Thornburg, Benninga, & Bridge, 1983; El'konin, 1969; Pederson et al., 1981; Ungerer et al., 1981). Even by their third year, children only infrequently substitute objects that are dissimilar in form and function to the objects they represent (Crum et al., 1983; Elder & Pederson, 1978). To increase children's decontextualized responses, researchers cited earlier in this paragraph provided modeling of actions and instructions to pretend or imitate to stimulate children to use substitute objects or gestures for imaginary objects. Modeling and verbal prompting are believed to provide scaffolding for pretend actions, but even under more naturalistic conditions, young children only infrequently use dissimilar substitute objects (Musatti & Mayer, 1987).

Gestures indicating an imaginary object include using a body part as an object (e.g., holding a fist to your ear in pretend telephoning) as well as acting as if using an imaginary object (e.g., as if actually holding a phone). Gestures of either kind indicating imaginary objects were exhibited infrequently by 25- to 36-month-old children (Crum et al., 1983; Elder & Pederson, 1978). Although imaginary object use is spontaneously generated more frequently by older than younger children, who more frequently use a body part as the object, in fact even younger (3-year-old) children show the more mature form sometimes and 4-year-old children show either form, depending on instructions or situation (Acredolo & Goodwyn, 1985; Boyatzis & Watson, 1993; Kaplan, 1977; Lyons, 1986; Overton & Jackson, 1973). Surprisingly, researchers who test children for their "spontaneous" gestures (Nielsen & Dissanayake, 2000; Taylor, Cartwright, & Carlson, 1993) provide instructions or situations that induce children to use the supposedly less developed form of body part as object.

Object-related actions engaged in frequently even by very young children can be reenacted without objects. Through repetition, the actions become ritualized—easily repeated in sequence (Piaget, 1945/1962). For example, one 12-month-old boy enjoyed giving and receiving imaginary gifts, laughing after pretending to put imaginary things in his father's hand (Valentine, 1942/1950), and 15-month-old children can pretend to receive and eat an imaginary cake following adult modeling and prompting (see Baudonnière et al., in Mitchell, 2002b). Once ritualized, "All that is needed for the ludic ritual to become a symbol is that the child, instead of merely following the cycle of his habitual movements, should be aware of the make believe, *i.e.*, that he should 'pretend' to sleep" or eat or whatever (Piaget, 1945/1962, pp. 93–94; see also Musatti & Mayer, 1987). However, this awareness of make-believe need be neither extensive nor explicit:

> As understood by the child, nonliteralness [i.e., pretense] may originate in part from experiences in which the child establishes sufficient control over well-mastered behavior to detach it from consummatory outcomes; sucking (or mouthing) on a full nipple without drawing liquid seems a dramatic illustration of such control. (Fein & Moorin, 1985, p. 73)

Pretense seems to originate in a child's recognizing that his or her current actions are similar to other actions he or she has performed (Groos, 1901). It is unclear whether children start with the intention to simulate (as Piaget [1945/1962] suggested) or first simply notice, in replicating some action they have repeated previously, that the new action resembles (and differs from) the old (see Davis, 1989).

Decontextualization, decentration, and scheme integration are particularly evident in the development of particular pretenses, with the consequence that, as the child's array of activities increases during ontogeny, these categories can be applied more globally to pretense development in general. Once children begin to pretend, how decontextualized, decentered, or integrated a pretense is seems to depend less on the children's age than on their experience with the actions employed, and the context in which the actions are situated, including the objects and potential play partners available and the instructions given.

Although simulation is useful as a first approximation for detecting pretense, as we age pretending can be increasingly divorced from realistic origins; simulation is not essential because language can create a wholly imaginary idea (Fenson, in Bretherton, 1984). Language users can pretend to do things neither they nor anyone else in their experience has done and become absorbed or engaged in this created "reality," but there need be no reality on which the pretense is based (Walton, 1990). For example, one 31-month-old girl "pretended her knitting needles were knives and cut imaginary slices of meat from her sister's knee and handed them round to each of us" (Valentine, 1942/1950, p. 160), and a 4-year-old pretended to have an invisible companion who lives in the white light of a lamp (Taylor & Carlson, in Mitchell, 2002b). Numerous depictions in novels, paintings, movies, and theater are there for us to imagine—but they need not directly map to anything real, although some aspects are likely to (people exist, move, feel sadness at a loved one's death; Walton, 1990). Pretense that is not simulative, or in which the real activity simulated is not obvious, may be difficult if not impossible to discern without language (Lowe, 1975, pp. 35–36). Without language, *detection* of pretense (but not pretense itself) may require simulative action.

ANIMAL PRETENSE AND
THE EVOLUTION OF PRETENSE

To determine if animals pretend, we must apply the same methods used to decide if humans pretend, otherwise comparison is confounded. Yet the same methods are almost never applied.

- Children's and animals' pretenses are observed in disparate contexts. Most studies of children's pretense are inherently developmental. Initially researchers looked at the same individuals as they grew, and articulated the developmental variations in their simulations. More recently, researchers also studied children of various ages on the same tasks to determine developmental milestones. For animals, many instances of pretense in the wild are not observed in a developmental context; rather, they are detected because of apparent simulation or strangeness. Almost no one is looking for development of pretense in animals; animals' ages are rarely provided.

- Speech and toys are predominantly used in studies of children's pretense, whereas these are absent in the experiences of most animals. Other than pets, only apes in linguistic experiments experience language and toys regularly. Without dolls or toys, decentration and decontextualization are less apparent.

- Many studies of children use modeling and prompting to get their most developed pretenses, but these are unintentional or rare with animals. Oddly, evidence that animals were prompted serves to discount what they do as pretense.

- Furthermore, observation of simulation requires elaborate knowledge of the animals being evaluated that cannot be taken for granted from the start, as it usually is with children who are from the same culture as the researcher. What is one to make, for example, of the zoo chimpanzees who often used a hose to make a semicircle around themselves and placed objects between themselves and the hose, and attacked any chimpanzees who came nearby (Mignault, 1985)? Clearly more than the few hours the animals were observed over a 4-year period is needed to understand what, if anything, chimpanzees might be simulating. One can expect the best evidence of pretense in animals, even if it is infrequent, in longitudinal studies.

Any answer to the question of pretense in animals requires a definition of pretense, and the definition I provided directs us to concerns about animals' knowledge about their own actions. Often at issue in interpreting animals' activities as pretense is whether animals know that some part of their activities is "unreal" (Groos, 1898; Piaget, 1945/1962). One might believe that any apparent simulation in play indicates recognition of simulation, but often animals have never experienced the real actions that their play actions look like, and thus cannot be pretending about them (Mitchell, 1991). For example, the play-fighting of dogs and chimpanzees suggests pretending to fight (Valentine, 1942/1950), but they engage in play-fighting before they engage in fighting. Such playful, instinctually

motivated actions that resemble other actions are *schematic play*, enactment of schemas based on relatively canalized processes for perceptual-
motor integration that is not based on associative learning or imitation of
another's actions (Mitchell, 1990). In schematic play, the simulation is in
the eye of the observer, not the player. For example, maternal behaviors
enacted toward objects by wild apes (or by children toward dolls) might
be instinctually motivated and not pretending, because they enact similar behaviors even when they have no experience of babies (Gómez &
Martín-Andrade, in Mitchell, 2002b). However, once animals have
experience of infants, they may recognize differences between an infant
and another object as they act maternally toward it, and thus pretend.
What begins as schematic play could, following experience of the real
activity, become pretending. An example is mature rhesus monkeys that
engage in play-fighting from an early age; they sometimes pretend to
play-fight to indicate a real threat to another when an actual threat might
bring retaliation (Breuggeman, 1978). So do human children (Smith,
1997).

   To decide if an animal is pretending, we use the same definition as that
used with infants and children. Consider a pet badger who several times
"invited a bush to play" when its normal play partners (a human and a
dog, with whom it had played repeatedly) were unavailable: "He displayed his bravado behavior toward a bush, then touched the twigs and
pulled them," acting as he did toward a normal play partner (Eibl-
Eibesfeldt, 1950/1978, p. 145; see similar activity by a chimpanzee in
Hayaki, 1985). Is the badger pretending? Although the skeptical reader is
likely to believe that the badger's behavior indicates schematic play, in
fact its behavior fits the definition of pretense: Unless we are to believe
that it is remarkably stupid, its action is intentionally controlled by an
idea that it knows does not cohere with current reality. Given that the
badger acts as if the bush is a potential player, yet must know (being an
intelligent mammal) that the bush is not, it pretends that the bush is a
player. The badger, like children, developed pretense after "establish[ing]
sufficient control over well-mastered behavior [in this case, social play] to
detach it from consummatory outcomes" (Fein & Moorin, 1985, p. 73)—
that is, through ritualization. Similarly ritualized activities that turned
into pretense with imaginary objects are bonobos' pretend eating
(Savage-Rumbaugh & McDonald, 1988), the human-reared chimpanzee
Viki's play with an imaginary pull-toy after extensive play pulling toys
(Hayes, 1951), and the sign-using orangutan Chantek's pretending that
an invisible cat was present through signing "cat" or acting fearful or both

(Miles, 1986). Animals such as monkeys and apes engage in play in which they close or cover their eyes and attempt to move about without seeing (Gómez & Martín-Andrade, in Mitchell, 2002b; Russon, Vasey, & Gauthier, in Mitchell, 2002b). I suspect that these animals are acting as if they cannot open or uncover their eyes—a relatively simple pretense based on repetition and control of their own actions of closing or covering their eyes. Whether or not some repeated actions become pretense, however, is uncertain. For example, are dogs and bonobos that appear disinterested in a play object, but then quickly regain their interest when their human partner attempts to obtain it, pretending to be disinterested (Savage-Rumbaugh & McDonald, 1988), or really disinterested (Mitchell, 2002b)?

In thinking about the play of intelligent mammals, Lorenz (1950/1971) argued that they might be pretending to experience feelings, rather than to act in a particular way. For example, the same pet badger described earlier (Eibl-Eibesfeldt, 1950/1978), when engaged in play-fleeing with his normal human partner, pretended to be afraid; he

> runs toward the caretaker, but stops short at 4 m distance with his hair raised.... The whole posture expresses a tendency to withdraw. ... the badger almost "waits" to be frightened. If one runs toward him, he does not wait as long as during the introductory fighting play but he runs away with a hissing sound, his hair standing on end and his tail drawn in. He stops again at some distance, "waits," and the play repeats itself often. (p. 146)

Badgers are very likely to experience fear quite early in life. If the badger were feeling real fear, it would run away (see Walton, 1990); it must know that its fear is unreal, so it is pretending to be afraid. Feelings are props about which animals know a great deal from experience, however much they are instinctually derived. In this light, consider the pet dog that playfully attacked and "growled at his play objects ... although one could never assume that he was angry, because he vigorously wagged his tail when doing so" (Eibl-Eibesfeldt, 1950/1978, pp. 147, 148). We need to know if this dog had experienced anger prior to this play to even consider the idea that it was pretending to be angry.

All examples of pretense by animals described so far are enactments of the animals' own activities, showing limited decontextualization and decentration. Pretenses based on others' actions are rare among nonhuman animals, found almost exclusively among great apes and dolphins. Simulation of one's own behavior or another's, substituting one object for another, acting as if something or someone has an imaginary property, and acting as if something absent were present, are some of the pretenses shown by these animals (see Mitchell, 2002b). Table 3.1 provides a tallying of different types of pretense by the most extensively studied great apes and dolphins (some of which occurred once or infrequently), using categories derived from children's pretenses. Pretenses by human-reared, relatively language-savvy great apes—gorilla Koko, orangutan Chantek, bonobo Kanzi, and chimpanzees Viki and Washoe—simulate their own and human actions (Fouts, with Mills, 1997; Gardner & Gardner, 1969; Hayes, 1951; Mitchell, 2002b; Miles, 1986; Miles, Mitchell, & Harper, 1996; Savage-Rumbaugh & McDonald, 1988). Functional pretend play, such as making toy animals bite and feeding them, is quite prevalent among these apes. The captive chimpanzees (all less than 7 years old, which is relatively young) had actions modeled for them by humans in some instances (Mignault, 1985); the wild chimpanzees were observed by Goodall (1986). Dolphins' pretenses simulated actions of humans and sea lions they interacted with in captivity (Tayler & Saayman, 1973). Examples of symbolic pretense include simple actions, such as acting as if looking at something interesting when nothing is there (Chantek, Viki), repeatedly signing a well-known sign incorrectly for fun (Chantek, Koko), pretending to fish for termites in an imaginary nest (wild chimpanzee), and pretending to eat from a bowl with the handle of a spoon (captive chimpanzee), as well as more decentered, decontextualized activities, such as having a doll sign (Koko), pulling an imaginary pull-toy (Viki), and acting as if cleaning their tank with fish and letting out bubbles of air in simulation of a human scuba diver who cleaned their tank with sponges (dolphins). A surprising symbolic pretense is a young dolphin's imitative action: After observing, through an underwater window, a person exhaling cigarette smoke, she left the window, obtained a mouthful of milk from her mother, returned to the window, and squirted the milk underwater in simulation of smoke. Washoe's bathing a doll is symbolic pretense because Washoe's script for bathing was derived only from being bathed herself (Gardner & Gardner, 1969); similar actions by other apes are not so clearly decentered (i.e., based on others' actions). Another symbolic pretense is invented signs, such as Chantek's for "eye-wash" (putting his sign for "drink"—extending his thumb from his fist—near his eye) that used a body part in place of an object, and for "balloon" (putting thumb and finger at lips, as he did when blowing up a balloon, and blowing, as if into a balloon) that acted as if holding an imaginary object.

Not surprisingly, apes and dolphins that have interacted extensively with humans, especially apes involved in language learning, provide the

TABLE 3.1
Example of Pretense Consonant With Those by Children Shown by Great Apes and Dolphins

	Gorilla Koko	Orangutan Chantek	Bonobo Kanzi	Viki	Chimpanzees Washoe	Captive	Wild	Captive Dolphins
Functional pretense								
Repetition of conventional behavior with realistic objects	x	x		x		x	x	
Doll repeating conventional behavior with realistic objects	x	x						
Symbolic pretense = attributing an imaginary property								
To one's actions								
When repeating one's own actions (deception)	x	x		x	x	x		x
When using body parts as object	x	x						
When imitating another's actions	x	x		x		x		x
To one's emotions	x	x						
To some thing (object substitution—decontextualization)								
Where thing is similar to real	x			x				x
Where thing is ambiguous, or dissimilar to real	x			x				x
Where nondoll is treated as animated							x	
To another (doll or live entity—decentration)								
By doing to doll or other what you do to yourself	x	x	x		x	x	x	
By imitating on the doll or other what others do to you					x			
By having doll or other do what you do	x	x						
By having doll or other do what another does	x		x^a		x			
To nothing (imaginary object—decontextualization)								
By acting as if absent object or entity is present								
With real object support	x	x	x	x	x	x	x	
Using gesture appropriate to imagined object		x	x	x	x			
Using signs	x	x						
Using signs along with other behavior		x						

^aThis action was performed by a sign-using bonobo other than Kanzi.

most extensive examples of pretense. Of course one might also anticipate that these are the most anthropomorphized of all the apes, both in method and interpretation, which might lead to skepticism. Indeed, when Patterson provided videotapes of the sign-using gorilla Koko's play actions that she offered as potential pretenses at the 2003 Piaget Society meeting, most of these actions involved toy manipulation that did not appear to be pretend (see Matevia, Patterson, & Hillix, in Mitchell, 2002b, for clearer instances of pretense with signing by Koko). Several scientists in the audience denied that any of the videotaped actions were pretense. However, three instances were functional pretense, all likely resulting from ritualization and verbal prompting. Koko (at just under 12 years old) had an alligator hand mitt bite toy animals and (unexpectedly) Patterson, and then made two toy animals kiss by moving their mouths together (supplying repeated exaggerated kissing noises on her own). Also, when asked "Where does the baby drink?" Koko (at 19 years old) methodically molded the baby orangutan doll's hand to sign "Drink" then "mouth" on the doll's own face. Some pretenses by Koko and other apes might be overinterpreted, but not all are (see Mitchell, 2002b).

At present, pretenses about others appear almost nonexistent in animals other than great apes and dolphins. Consider the following pretense by a rhesus monkey:

> A 2-year-old female, 7N, moved after her mother, [AC], while [AC] carried 7N's infant brother in the ventral position. 7N clasped a piece of coconut shell with one hand to her ventrum. When AC stopped, she lay on her side and rested one hand on her infant's back. Just a few feet away, 7N adopted the exact posture of AC, while still holding the coconut shell to her ventrum. (Breuggeman, 1973, p. 196)

This is the only clear example of imitative pretense with object substitution by a monkey, occurring when the desired real object (a baby) was unavailable. Imitating another's actions, with or without objects, is exceedingly rare among monkeys (Mitchell, 2002a; Zeller, in Mitchell, 2002b). Most potentially pretend actions by monkeys seem to be simpler repetitions of the monkey's own actions, or limited repetition of others' actions toward objects—behaviors that Piaget (1945/1962) would classify as secondary or tertiary circular reactions, rudiments for pretense (Parker & McKinney, 1999)—but some deceptive pretenses employ imaginary components the monkeys know to be inaccurate about current reality.

We know little about the development of pretense in animals. Ritualization seems a likely process leading to some pretenses of apes showing decontextualization and decentration, but the ritualization is not extensive. Animals show little integration of schemes (scripts) in their pretenses, including their deceptions; even those by great apes are mostly straightforward repetitions of their own actions and action combinations (Mitchell, 1999, 2002b). If animals pretend about events, they do not offer elaborate presentations. By contrast, orangutans' attempts to really do what humans do can show detailed integration of schemes (Russon & Galdikas, 1993).

If pretense requires knowledge of unreality, how do animals and humans discern unreality? As suggested previously (see Davis, 1989; Groos, 1901), awareness of unreality likely derives initially from knowledge of simulation—knowledge that something like x is, simultaneously, not x. If so, how is simulation recognized or created? The answer is that simulation, and ultimately pretense, depends on intra- or intersensory matching (or both), of which ritualization is one form (Guillaume, 1926/1971; Mitchell, 1991, 1994; Piaget, 1945/1962). For example, pretending with objects requires visual–visual matching, and pretending to be another by sounding like them requires auditory–auditory matching. (People in many cultures make simulation based on visual–visual matching salient for children by using real and miniature objects as toys.)

Pretending about others requires a little more. The reason that humans, great apes, and dolphins can pretend about others is that, in addition to having the intrasensory matching common to mammals and birds, they have kinesthetic–visual matching (Mitchell, 1994, 1997). Thus, they can recognize the spatial or bodily similarity between their visual experience of another and their own kinesthetic experience, and create a match. The most elaborate pretenders among animals are also the most prolific imitators; animals that rarely imitate others' actions also rarely pretend to be others or do what others do. Well-developed skill at kinesthetic–visual matching (along with intrasensory matching skills) seems likely to be the basis for a suite of activities, including generalized bodily imitation, pretending to be another, mirror self-recognition, elaborate planning, and pantomime (Guillaume, 1926/1971; Mitchell, 1994, 2002a, 2002b).

If the intersensory matching of kinesthetic–visual matching is the basis for pretending about others, it suggests a means by which this pretense could develop evolutionarily. Mammals and birds can match within sensory systems, such that at least within a given sense modality similar experiences and images are recognized as such (a by-product of perception), and some of these animals (but particularly primates) use these matching abilities to re-create their own activities with variations, to influence others as well as to enact their own behaviors in pretense (Mitchell, 1994). The question is how intersensory matching could occur. According to Guillaume (1926/1971), intersensory matching is essentially entrained. Initially children try to re-create the effects other people have on objects, and only gradually come to re-create other people's actions. By repeated attempts at re-creation, the child learns to match his or her own kinesthetic feelings to the visual actions of another, and also becomes aware of what he or she looks like to others, as in a mirror. How humans, apes, and dolphins are organized such that this entrainment through ritualization is possible is under debate (see Nadel & Butterworth, 1999), but it appears that even monkeys have a basis for such entrainment in neurons that are responsive to the similarity between the monkey's own and another's actions directed toward an object (the so-called mirror neurons; Gallese, Fadiga, Fogassi, Rizzolatti, 1996). If the rare pretense of a monkey can be accepted as evidence of a rudiment of kinesthetic–visual matching, it suggests that intersensory matching skills may randomly appear in populations that are mostly without it. This could occur through variations in neural connections, which may depend on particular experiences (Stein, Wallace, & Stanford, 1999). The possessor of kinesthetic–visual matching might also naturally reproduce for its progeny the kinds of experiences that led it to develop kinesthetic–visual matching in the first place. Once in place, matching between kinesthesis and vision would have beneficial consequences for its possessor, who not only could replicate potentially useful actions of others, but also imagine itself in visual images and use these to plan its kinesthetically produced actions and develop skills by repetitively pretending to be another (Piaget, 1945/1962). Indeed, pretending about others was adaptive because of the utility of imaginative planning or apprenticing (learning by matching one's own actions to another's) or both (Mitchell, 1994; Parker & Gibson, 1979; Parker & McKinney, 1999).

WHERE DO WE GO FROM HERE?

I have provided a definition of pretense that aptly characterizes standard instances of pretense in human children and adults, as well as instances in animals. Other definitions of pretense can be provided that cannot be applied to nonhuman animals, although I suspect that such definitions would also be inapplicable to many instances of human pretense. Definitions are always dependent on the purposes of the definer, but it is unclear what reasonable purpose a definer would have to exclude animal pretenses. What I have presented should raise doubts about the reasonableness of criteria that deny, by definition, the possibility of pretense in animals. This is not to say that animals' pretenses parallel all human pretenses; they do not. Humans, supported by extensive linguistic skills, show greater complexity and imagination in pretense than animals do. However, at present, at least for some members of ape and dolphin species, it is unclear whether some of the differences in pretense between animals and young children arise from methodology or biology.

This chapter should at least prompt us to look for opportunities to find new evidence for or against the existence of pretense in animals. My review offers some ideas about why pretenses might appear, how we can detect them, and the species most likely to show particular types. First, we must engage in longitudinal studies of individual animals. If we assume that the ontogenetically earliest pretenses are simulative, we must know what normal activities are available to be simulated. Second, pretenses about others are going to be present almost exclusively in species with members capable of kinesthetic–visual matching; that is, great apes and dolphins. Third, pretenses involving substitute objects tend to occur when a real object is unavailable to fulfill animals' desires, as when the badger initiated social play with a bush, the macaque used a coconut shell for a baby, dolphins used fish as sponges, and young children imitated what their same-aged play companions were doing. Finally, it is extensively repeated activities, and activities that are interesting to the animals, that they will exhibit in pretense. These last ideas suggest that we should engage in experiments within longitudinal studies: Once we discern objects particular animals repeatedly desire and find interesting to interact with, we can make the objects unavailable, but then provide objects of varying types (similar, dissimilar) and see what happens.

Interestingly, my review also suggests that we have work to do in understanding pretenses by human infants. Given that animals such as gorillas show behaviors suggestive of pretend mothering without ever experiencing real mothering by self or other, we need to see if human children base all of their pretenses on experience. It would appear that they do not, that some pretenses (e.g., pretend caretaking of a doll) occur without experience of babies. Just as the study of pretense in children has shed light on pretense in animals, perhaps the study of pretense in animals can now provide new interpretations of what we take for granted in children's pretense.

ACKNOWLEDGMENTS

I appreciate the patience and effort of the editors in helping me to develop this chapter.

REFERENCES

Acredolo, L. P., & Goodwyn, S. W. (1985). Symbolic gesturing in language development. *Human Development, 29,* 40–49.

Bates, E., Benigni, L., Bretherton, I., Camaioni, L., & Volterra, V. (1979). *The emergence of symbols.* New York: Academic.

Boyatzis, C. J., & Watson, M. W. (1993). Preschool children's symbolic representation of objects through gestures. *Child Development, 64,* 729–735.

Bretherton, I. (Ed.). (1984). *Symbolic play.* New York: Academic.

Breuggeman, J. A. (1973). Parental care in a group of free-ranging rhesus monkeys (*Macaca mulatta*). *Folia Primatologica, 20,* 178–210.

Breuggeman, J. A. (1978). The function of adult play in free-ranging *Macaca mulatta*. In E. O. Smith (Ed.), *Social play in primates* (pp. 169–191). New York: Academic.

Corrigan, R. (1987). A developmental sequence of actor–object pretend play in young children. *Merrill-Palmer Quarterly, 33,* 87–106.

Crum, R. A., Thornburg, K., Benninga, J., & Bridge, C. (1983). Preschool children's object substitutions during symbolic play. *Perceptual and Motor Skills, 56,* 947–955.

Darwin, C. (1896). *The descent of man.* New York: Appleton. (Original work published 1871)

Davis, W. (1989). Finding symbols in history. In H. Morphy (Ed.), *Animals into art* (pp. 179–189). London: Unwyn Hyman.

Dearborn, G. V. N. (1910). *Moto-sensory development: Observations on the first three years of a child.* Baltimore: Warwick & York.

Eibl-Eibesfeldt, I. (1978). On the ontogeny of behavior of a male badger (*Meles meles* L.) with particular reference to play behavior. In D. Müller-Schwarze (Ed.), *Evolution of play behavior* (pp. 142–148). Stroudsburg, PA: Dowden, Hutchinson & Ross. (Original work published 1950)

Elder, J. L., & Pederson, D. R. (1978). Preschool children's use of objects in symbolic play. *Child Development, 49,* 500–504.

El'konin, D. B. (1969). Some results of the study of the psychological development of preschool-age children. In M. Cole & I. Maltzman (Eds.), *A handbook of contemporary Soviet psychology* (pp. 163–208). New York: Basic Books.

Fein, G. G., & Moorin, E. R. (1985). Confusion, substitution, and mastery: Pretend play during the second year of life. In K. E. Nelson (Ed.), *Children's language* (Vol. 5, pp. 61–76). Hillsdale, NJ: Lawrence Erlbaum Associates.

Fenson, L., Kagan, J., Kearsley, R. B., & Zelazo, P. R. (1976). The developmental progression of manipulative play in the first two years. *Child Development, 47,* 232–236.

Fouts, R., with Mills, S. T. (1997). *Next of kin.* New York: Morrow.

Gallese, V., Fadiga, L., Fogassi, L., & Rizzolatti, G. (1996). Action recognition in the premotor cortex. *Brain, 119,* 593–609.

Gardner, R. A., & Gardner, B. T. (1969). Teaching sign language to a chimpanzee. *Science, 165*, 664–672.

Gaskins, S., & Göncü, A. (1992). Cultural variation in play: A challenge to Piaget and Vygotsky. *Quarterly Newsletter of the Laboratory of Comparative Human Cognition, 14*, 31–35.

Goodall, J. (1986). *The chimpanzees of Gombe*. Cambridge, MA: Harvard University Press.

Groos, K. (1898). *The play of animals*. New York: Appleton.

Groos, K. (1901). *The play of man*. New York: Appleton.

Guillaume, P. (1971). *Imitation in children*. Chicago: University of Chicago. (Original work published 1926)

Hall, G. S. (1914). *Aspects of child life and education*. Boston: Ginn.

Hayaki, H. (1985). Social play of juvenile and adolescent chimpanzees in the Mahale Mountain National Park, Tanzania. *Primates, 26*, 343–360.

Hayes, C. (1951). *The ape in our house*. New York: Harper.

Hoyt, A. M. (1941). *Toto and I: A gorilla in the family*. Philadelphia: Lippincott.

Jackowitz, E. R., & Watson, M. W. (1980). Development of object transformations in early pretend play. *Developmental Psychology, 16*, 543–549.

Kaplan, E. (1977). The development of praxis. In B. Wolman (Ed.), *International encyclopedia of neurology, psychiatry, psychoanalysis and psychology* (Vol. 9, pp. 26–29). New York: Aesculopius.

Lewis, V., Boucher, J., Lupton, L., & Watson, S. (2000). Relationships between symbolic play, functional play, verbal and non-verbal ability in young children. *International Journal of Language and Communicative Disorders, 35*, 117–127.

Lorenz, K. (1971). Part and parcel in animal and human societies. In K. Lorenz, *Studies in animal and human behavior* (Vol. 2, pp. 115–195). Cambridge, MA: Harvard University Press. (Original work published 1950)

Lowe, M. (1975). Trends in the development of representational play in infants from one to three years: An observational study. *Journal of Child Psychology and Psychiatry, 16*, 33–47.

Lyons, B. G. (1986). Zone of potential development for 4-year-olds attempting to simulate the use of absent objects. *Occupational Therapy Journal of Research, 6*, 33–46.

Lyytinen, P. (1991). Developmental trends in children's pretend play. *Child: Care, Health and Development, 17*, 9–25.

Mignault, C. (1985). Transition between sensorimotor and symbolic activities in nursery-reared chimpanzees (*Pan troglodytes*). *Journal of Human Evolution, 14*, 747–758.

Miles, H. L. (1986). How can I tell a lie? Apes, language, and the problem of deception. In R. W. Mitchell & N. S. Thompson (Eds.), *Deception* (pp. 245–266). Albany: State University of New York Press.

Miles, H. L., Mitchell, R. W., & Harper, S. (1996). Simon says: The development of imitation in an enculturated orangutan. In A. Russon, K. Bard, & S. T. Parker (Eds.), *Reaching into thought: The minds of the great apes* (pp. 278–299). New York: Cambridge University Press.

Mitchell, R. W. (1990). A theory of play. In M. Bekoff & D. Jamieson (Eds.), *Interpretation and explanation in the study of animal behavior: Vol. 1. Interpretation, intentionality, and communication* (pp. 197–227). Boulder, CO: Westview.

Mitchell, R. W. (1991). Bateson's concept of "metacommunication" in play. *New Ideas in Psychology, 9*, 73–87.

Mitchell, R. W. (1994). The evolution of primate cognition: Simulation, self-knowledge, and knowledge of other minds. In D. Quiatt & J. Itani (Eds.), *Hominid culture in primate perspective* (pp. 177–232). Boulder: University Press of Colorado.

Mitchell, R. W. (1997). Kinesthetic–visual matching and the self-concept as explanations of mirror-self-recognition. *Journal for the Theory of Social Behavior, 27,* 101–123.

Mitchell, R. W. (1999). Deception and concealment as strategic script violation in great apes and humans. In S. T. Parker, R. W. Mitchell, & H. L. Miles (Eds.), *The mentalities of gorillas and orangutans* (pp. 295–315). Cambridge, UK: Cambridge University Press.

Mitchell, R. W. (2000). A proposal for the development of a mental vocabulary, with special reference to pretense and false belief. In P. Mitchell & K. Riggs (Eds.), *Children's reasoning and the mind* (pp. 37–65). Hove, UK: Psychology Press.

Mitchell, R. W. (2002a). Imitation as a perceptual process. In K. Dautenhahn & C. L. Nehaniv (Eds.), *Imitation in animals and artifacts* (pp. 441–469). Cambridge, MA: MIT Press.

Mitchell, R. W. (Ed.). (2002b). *Pretending and imagination in animals and children.* Cambridge, UK: Cambridge University Press.

Mitchell, R. W., & Neal, M. (2005). Children's understanding of their own and others' mental states: Part A. Self-understanding precedes understanding of others in pretense. *British Journal of Developmental Psychology, 23,* 175–200.

Musatti, T., & Mayer, S. (1987). Object substitution: Its nature and function in early pretend play. *Human Development, 30,* 225–235.

Nadel, J., & Butterworth, G. (Eds.). (1999). *Imitation in infancy.* Cambridge, UK: Cambridge University Press.

Nielsen, M., & Dissanayake, C. (2000). An investigation of pretend play, mental state terms and false belief understanding: In search of a metarepresentational link. *British Journal of Developmental Psychology, 18,* 609–624.

Overton, W. F., & Jackson, J. P. (1973). The representation of imagined objects in action sequences: A developmental study. *Child Development, 44,* 309–314.

Parker, S. T., & Gibson, K. R. (1979). A developmental model for the evolution of language and intelligence in early hominids. *Behavioral and Brain Sciences, 2,* 367–408.

Parker, S. T., & McKinney, M. L. (1999). *Origins of intelligence.* Baltimore: Johns Hopkins University Press.

Pederson, D. R., Rook-Green, A., & Elder, J. L. (1981). The role of action in the development of pretend play in young children. *Developmental Psychology, 17,* 756–759.

Piaget, J. (1962). *Play, dreams and imitation in childhood.* New York: Norton. (Original work published 1945)

Reddy, V. (1991). Playing with others' expectations: Teasing and mucking about in the first year. In A. Whiten (Ed.), *Natural theories of mind* (pp. 143–158). Oxford, UK: Blackwell.

Russon, A. E., & Galdikas, B. M. F. (1993). Imitation in free-ranging rehabilitant orangutans (*Pongo pygmaeus*). *Journal of Comparative Psychology, 107,* 146–161.

Savage-Rumbaugh, E. S., & McDonald, K. (1988). Deception and social manipulation in symbol-using apes. In R. W. Byrne & A. Whiten (Eds.), *Machiavellian intelligence* (pp. 224–237). Oxford, UK: Oxford University Press.

Sinclair, A. (1996). Young children's practical deceptions and their understanding of false belief. *New Ideas in Psychology, 14*, 157–173.

Smith, P. K. (1997). Play fighting and real fighting: Perspectives on their relationship. In A. Schmitt, K. Atzwanger, K. Grammar, & K. Schäfer (Eds.), *New aspects of human ethology* (pp. 47–64). London: Plenum.

Stein, B. E., Wallace, M. T., & Stanford, T. R. (1999). Development of multisensory integration: Transforming sensory input into motor output. *Mental Retardation and Developmental Disabilities Research Reviews, 5*, 72–85.

Sully, J. (1896). *Studies of childhood.* London: Longmans, Green.

Tayler, C. K., & Saayman, G. S. (1973). Imitative behaviour by Indian Ocean bottlenose dolphins (*Tursiops aduncus*) in captivity. *Behaviour, 44*, 286–298.

Taylor, M., Cartwright, B. S., & Carlson, S. M. (1993). A developmental investigation of children's imaginary companions. *Developmental Psychology, 29*, 276–285.

Ungerer, J., Zelazo, P. R., Kearsley, R. B., & O'Leary, K. (1981). Developmental changes in the representation of objects in symbolic play from 18 to 34 months of age. *Child Development, 52*, 186–195.

Valentine, C. W. (1950). *The psychology of early childhood.* London: Methuen. (Original work published 1942)

Walton, K. L. (1990). *Mimesis as make-believe.* Cambridge, MA: Harvard University Press.

4

The Development and Function of Rough-and-Tumble Play in Childhood and Adolescence: A Sexual Selection Theory Perspective

Anthony D. Pellegrini
Department of Educational Psychology
University of Minnesota–Twin Cities Campus

The study of play, as evidenced by the chapters in this volume, is an important and active topic of research. It has occupied psychologists, biologists, and educators for much of the 20th century. Most of this research was, of course, motivated by Piaget's (1962) work. Following his lead, child and developmental psychologists have spent much of their time studying the pretend, or fantasy, play of children, often to the exclusion of other types of play. However, researchers in other fields such as ethology (e.g., Bateson, 1981) and behavioral biology (Fagen, 1981) have also been studying play, but instead of fantasy they usually parse play in terms of locomotor, object, and social play (Pellegrini & Smith, 2005).

In this chapter I integrate the ethological and developmental psychological play literatures. Indeed, such integration was called for explicitly by Piaget (1967): "There exists a parallelism, and a fairly close one, between biological doctrines of evolutionary variation and the particular theories of intelligence" (p. 11). To that end, I present a model for the development of rough-and-tumble play (R&T) utilizing both biological and developmental psychological principles. Specifically, I use sexual selection (Darwin, 1871) and parental investment theories (Trivers, 1972) as a way to explain the development and function of R&T during childhood and adolescence. I first define R&T. Next, I discuss basic tenets of sexual selection and parental investment theories and how these principles relate to gender differences in R&T. Third, I describe the context in which R&T develops by showing how sexually segregated peer groups in childhood is the venue in which boys use highly vigorous and competitive forms of play. Fourth, I outline the development and functions of play during childhood and adolescence. As part of this discussion, I present two views of function (immediate and deferred benefits). I present cost–benefit analyses to argue that R&T probably serves an immediate function during childhood as well as an immediate function during adolescence. Specifically, during childhood R&T probably is used by boys as a way in which to affiliate with other boys and to condition cardiovascular and muscular systems. During adolescence, R&T continues to relate to boys' cardiovascular and muscular conditioning but also relates to dominance and aggression and is later used as a strategy to initiate heterosexual contact.

WHAT IS R&T?

To my knowledge R&T was first used in the social and behavioral sciences by Harlow (1962) in his discussion of the social play of rhesus monkeys, where R&T resembled play-fighting. Similarly, R&T in preschool children often takes the form of play wrestling and fighting and is sometimes embedded superhero play.

Based on Harlow's work, and on the subsequent work with children by Blurton Jones (1972), R&T has been characterized by positive affect, or a play face, high-energy behaviors, exaggerated movements, and soft, open-handed hits or kicks. The play faces of the juvenile child and chimpanzee displayed in Fig. 4.1 clearly signal that the intent of these acts is playful, not aggressive. The exaggerated movements and gestures, as demonstrated by the child in Fig. 4.1, further helps signal the playful, not aggressive, intent to other players. In terms of structure, R&T is social and characterized by reciprocal role taking and self-handicapping. That is, in R&T players change roles, such that they alternate between being on top and on bottom and between being the aggressor and being the

FIG. 4.1. Play faces of chimpanzee and child.

victim. In cases where play involves unequal partners (e.g., a father and his son wrestling), the bigger and stronger typically self-handicaps. For example, a father may fall on the floor, allowing his son to be on top. In a chasing bout, the faster person slows or staggers, allowing the slower player to catch up. Self-handicapping probably maximizes players' motivation to sustain play by minimizing the boredom associated with limited role enactment.

Correspondingly, R&T is also considered playful by children. For example, in cases where children have been shown videotaped R&T and aggressive bouts, they clearly differentiated between the two and consider R&T playful (e.g., Costabile et al., 1991; Pellegrini, 1988; Smith, Hunter, Carvalho, & Costabile, 1992).

One of the interesting features of R&T is that, with development, its function seems to change. During the juvenile period it is, for most children, playful and related to peer affiliation and cooperative interaction, but during adolescence it seems to serve a dominance and aggressive purpose. This seems to be the case for both humans and nonhuman primates (Fagen, 1981). R&T also seems to be more important for males than females. As argued next, sexual selection theory (Darwin, 1871) accounts for this difference. Further sexual selection theory provides reasonable and testable explanations for the developmental contexts in which R&T develops.

Gender Differences in R&T: Sexual Selection Theory and Parental Investment Theory

There are reliable gender differences in children's R&T, favoring boys. Differences have been observed in industrialized societies as well as in pastoral and foraging societies (Bock, 2005; Fry, 2005; Gosso, Otta, Morais, Ribeiro, & Bussab, 2005; Pellegrini & Smith, 1998). That similar differences have also been observed in many monkey and great apes species (e.g., Lewis, 2005) suggests that the male bias in R&T has biological roots. These differences can be elegantly explained by Darwin's (1871) sexual selection theory.

Darwin (1871) recognized that males of many species, including humans, tend to be bigger, more physically active, and more physically aggressive than females. Darwin also suggested that the differences in body size and aggression were due to the fact that males are more competitive than females. Males, he observed, compete with one another for access to females. Males of many mammalian species also engage in R&T

more than females (Fagen, 1981), as part of this constellation of vigorous and competitive behavior. Darwin could not, however, determine why males were competitive and females choosy, and not vice versa.

This question was answered by Trivers, in the form of parental investment theory. Based on the earlier work of Bateman (1948), Trivers (1972) suggested that differences in parental investment are responsible for a number of sex differences in different species, including R&T and physical aggression. The basic consideration that sex is inexpensive for males (i.e., costs associated with copulation) and expensive for females (i.e., costs associated with copulation + gestation + protecting and provisioning the offspring). This leads to the general rule that high female parental investment leads to female choosiness in mates and concerns with maximizing investment in offspring. Females are therefore less likely than males to risk harm or danger through direct aggression or physically rough play because it would compromise their ability to provision and protect their offspring (Campbell, 1999, 2002). Behaviorally, this means that they are less competitive and more sedentary than males and use more indirect and safer strategies to access and protect resources.

Males, on the other hand, are much less choosy in mating and spend more time vigorously competing with each other for mates. To illustrate this point, Trivers (1985) gave examples of males from various species mating with members of other species and even with inanimate objects! This view is also supported by Buss's (1989) findings on human males' tendency toward promiscuity. The strategy of frequent mating and lack of paternal investment results in intrasexual competition, sexual dimorphism, and differences between the sexes in competitive behavior and physical aggression (Pellegrini, Long, & Mizerek, 2005). Boys' R&T may be the result of them being both more competitive and physically aggressive, relative to girls. During childhood boys may engage in R&T to learn the behaviors associated with male adult roles as competitors and fighters.

Contextual Moderation, Not Biological Determinism

Although I argue that evolutionary history has an impact on human development, I must further clarify the moderating role of context in understanding human development. This discussion is especially important given recent misunderstanding of our approach (e.g., Lickliter & Honeycutt, 2003). First, I do not take a deterministic view of phylogenetic history and genes on human behavior, even if continuity across common ancestry is found in dimensions of social behavior and organization.

My orientation, like that of many others, is that genes, environments, and behavior dynamically influence each other (Archer & Lloyd, 2002; Bateson & Martin, 1999; Bjorklund & Pellegrini, 2002; Gottlieb, 1998; Stamps, 2003; Suomi, 2002).

Specifically, the environment in which an individual develops, starting with conception, influences the ways in which genes and one's evolutionary history are expressed. Bateson and Martin (1999) suggested that individuals have a genetic endowment that can be realized through a wide variety of options but the specific developmental pathway taken by an individual is influenced by the perinatal environment (i.e., from conception through infancy) of the developing organism. Thus, a number of developmental pathways are possible, but which one is selected is determined by the environment in which the organism develops (Archer, 1992; Caro & Bateson, 1986).

For the purposes of this chapter, perhaps the most relevant aspect of the environment is nutrition as it affects mating patterns and sexual dimorphism in size, which, in turn, affects physically vigorous and competitive behavior, sexual segregation, and R&T. Specifically, the nutritional history of human mothers impacts the physical size of the offspring, and especially that of males (Bateson & Martin, 1999). Males' larger size, relative to females (i.e., sexual dimorphism), may be one of the factors responsible for sex differences in physical activity, competitiveness, and ultimately, R&T (Pellegrini, 2004; Pellegrini et al., 2005).

The interactive nature of genetic endowment and the environment in which one develops is illustrated by the fact that height (a dimension of sexual dimorphism) is highly heritable, yet the expression of this genotype is influenced by the fetus's perinatal environment; pregnant mothers experiencing nutritional stress will have relatively smaller offspring. Alexander, Hoogland, Howard, Noonan, and Sherman (1979) used the Human Relations Area File to examine the effect of nutrition, in the form of ecologically abundant and stressed societies, on mating systems and sexual dimorphism. They partitioned human societies as ecologically imposed monogamy (e.g., Lapps of Norway, Cooper and Labrador Eskimo), polygyny (e.g., Bedouin Arabs and Khmer), and culturally determined monogamy (most Western societies). They found that the ecological-imposed groups lived in less abundant ecologies and were significantly less dimorphic than the other two but there were no differences between the polygynous and culturally imposed monogamy groups. They argued that in ecologically imposed monogamous cultures efforts of both parents are needed to protect and provide for offspring, thus males competed less for mates, relative to polygynous societies. From this view, sexual dimorphism results from the confluence of ecological and mating systems. That is, differences in body size are antecedents to differences in physical activity and are associated with competitiveness, aggressiveness, and R&T such that males and females view themselves differently very early in development and then segregate (see Pellegrini et al., 2005, for a fuller discussion). Later, these differences are translated into different social roles and differences in R&T and agonistic behaviors associated with different energetic demands.

In short, the developmental option taken is related to the environment in which the individual develops. Given the vastly different environments into which individuals with the same genetic history are born, a single "genetic program" would not be equally effective across these different niches. Where resources are abundant, there will be a bias toward polygyny, and greater sexual dimorphism, with males being physically larger than females. These conditions, in turn, will result in males, relative to females, exhibiting more physically active and competitive behavior (including R&T) and physical aggression. In cases of severe environments, the sex differences should be moderated such that there would be less dimorphism and less difference in physical activity, competitive behavior, and R&T.

Sexually Segregated Groups as a Socialization Context

In this section I argue that the differences in male and female R&T are exacerbated in sexually segregated peer groups during childhood. Specifically and consistent with sexual selection theory, I posit that differences in the levels of physical activity in boys' and girls' groups is responsible for sex segregation (Pellegrini, 2004; Pellegrini et al., 2005). It is in these vigorous groups that boys' R&T develops as they refine the R&T-related behaviors they learned in father–son interactions and that relate to peer status in childhood.

I suggest that males' early bias toward physically vigorous and R&T serves an immediate benefit in terms of motor training. Motor training benefits, in turn, are associated with physical fitness and strength. Females avoid these active behaviors and interact with each other because they find vigorous behavior, especially in the presence of males, to be aversive and possibly dangerous. In segregated groups, males and females learn and practice, possibly through observational learning and reinforcement (Boyd & Richerson, 1985) the gender-appropriate social roles. Next I briefly document differences in energetics, social roles, and competition that may be responsible for sex differences in R&T.

Differences in Energetics and Social Roles.   Both males and females need vigorous physical exercise for physical conditioning and healthy muscular and skeletal growth and maintenance (Byers & Walker, 1995; Pellegrini & Smith, 1998) but physical exercise and competition may be more important for males, relative to females. Exercise is more important for juvenile males because it maximizes behavioral, brain, and muscular systems that are useful in competition, R&T, and aggression with other males (Pellegrini & Smith, 1998).

There is evidence for an early bias in males toward high-energetic behavior and this bias may be important for males choosing to interact with each other. According to three meta-analyses of sex differences in physical activity in humans, males are more active than females and these differences are observed from the prenatal period through the juvenile and adult periods (Campbell & Eaton, 1999; Eaton & Enns, 1986; Eaton, McKeen, & Campbell, 2001). These sex differences in activity increase during the early and middle childhood periods. That differences appear prenatally and are sustained through childhood suggests that differences in activity are only minimally affected by socialization.

The very early difference in activity preference helps to explain male infants' preference for high energy behaviors. For example, Kujawski and Bower (1993) demonstrated that infants used body movements to discriminate between boys and girls. Further, Campbell, Shirley, Heywood, and Crook (2000) conducted a longitudinal experiment with infants at 3, 9, and 18 months of age, using a visual preference paradigm, showing video clips of male typical activities (e.g., chasing, wrestling, climbing, jumping) and female typical activities (e.g., doll play, pat-a-cake, whispering, drawing). They found that male compared to female 9-month-olds preferred the male activities.

These differences, in turn, differentially bias males toward vigorous and competitive interaction with their peers. Indeed, during periods of segregation in childhood (3–11 years of age; Maccoby, 1998), we find sex differences in physical and competitive play (Pellegrini & Andrew, 2005, for a summary). For example, in one study, boys and girls in two age groups (6.8 years and 9.9 years) were studied and caloric expenditure was assessed using a behavioral checklist (Eaton et al., 1987), actometer readings, and heart rate monitors (Pellegrini, Horvat, & Huberty, 1998). Results showed that boys' behavior was more vigorous than that of girls.

These differences in physical activity are implicated in the different social roles enacted by males and females in segregated groups (Pellegrini, 2004; Pellegrini et al., 2005). Specifically, infants and very young children show preference for photos of same-sex peers and activity patterns (Shirley, 2000, cited in Archer & Lloyd, 2002). This orientation may lead to imitation of the behavior of same-sex models, which in turn, is reinforced by adults. The roles that young males and females enact, generally, reflect traditional male and female roles (Pitcher & Schultz, 1983). These roles are observed and reinforced initially with adults and then with peers.

Males are reinforced for expressing their physical activity in competitive and dominance-related roles, in the form of R&T and aggression, often by their fathers and later by their male peers. Fathers of young males spend significantly more time with sons, relative to their daughters (Parke & Suomi, 1981), thus providing same-sex models. During this time, fathers often engage in R&T and other forms of vigorous play with their sons (MacDonald & Parke, 1986).

The roles enacted in boys' groups are also more competitive than girls' groups. For example, in middle childhood, males' dominance and competitive roles are expressed in competitive and vigorous games and exhibited in male segregated groups (Pellegrini, Kato, Blatchford, & Baines, 2002). Males spend more time than females in vigorous games, such as chase and vigorous ball games, and their facility in these games increases with time. Further, males engage in more complex games, or games with a variety of rules to follow and roles to enact, such as basketball and soccer.

Facility with competitive games also is important in boys' status with their male peers. Specifically, peer popularity (i.e., the number of "like most" minus "like least" peer nominations) is predicted by the time they spend playing games and boys' teacher-rated facility in games. Game facility also correlated significantly with social leadership, as indicated by an attention structure, or the number of peers looking at the focal child, measure (Pellegrini et al., 2002). In short, leadership and competitive roles typify male groups and facility in these roles is related to their group status.

THE DEVELOPMENT AND FUNCTIONS OF R&T

In this section I document the development of R&T from childhood through adolescence by specifying the amount of time spent in R&T. Based on data from time, as well as caloric, budgets (both are measures of "cost"), I make inferences about the function (or benefits) of R&T. I use cost–benefit analyses to make inferences about function, following Krebs and McCleery (1984), but before I discuss the logic of this approach I first define what I mean by function.

What Is Meant by Function?

One view of function is a biological, or ultimate one, where function is defined in terms of reproductive (or inclusive) fitness. From this view, a behavior is functional to the extent that it relates to an individual's or his or her kin's number of reproducing offspring. In this chapter, however, I define function, as it often is in developmental psychology, in terms of beneficial consequences (Hinde, 1980). I also differentiate between deferred and immediate benefits.

A deferred benefit view of play is the commonly held view of play in developmental psychology such that benefits of play during childhood are reaped later in life. It reconciles the logical conundrum posed when one defines play in terms of it being "purposeless" and being more concerned with means than with ends, at the same time assigning functional importance to play: A deferred benefits argument for play solves the problem of how a behavior can be both purposeless and functional. Such a view would involve, for example, R&T in childhood predicting fighting skills during adulthood. Bateson (1981) labeled this the scaffolding view of play: Play is used in the building of a skill and once that skill is learned, play is disassembled.

R&T during the childhood period could also have immediate benefits, or benefits reaped during that period; for example, if it predicted cardio-vascular health during each period. Bateson (1981) referred to this view of function as the metamorphic role of play in development. From this view play has specific value to the niche of childhood. This view suggests that natural selection exerts pressure on all phases of development, including the juvenile period, not just adulthood (Burghardt, 2005; Stamps, 2003). Indeed, there may be a larger selective advantage for immediate, relative to deferred, benefits. Specifically, the earlier in life one reaps the benefits, the greater their cumulative effects (Caro, 1988).

Cost–Benefit Analyses and Function

Inferences about the extent to which a behavior is functional can be made by examining the ratio of costs to benefits associated with that behavior

(Martin & Caro, 1985). Specifically, a behavior will be beneficial if its benefits are greater than associated costs (documented in terms of caloric expenditure, survivorship, and time). The logic is that if behavior is costly across a closely related species, it was probably naturally selected. It has been further argued that if costs associated with juvenile play are moderate or high the benefits would probably be immediate, not deferred, given the relatively high risk of not surviving childhood. Reaping immediate benefits maximizes surviving the juvenile period and the benefits are also cumulative across the life span (Martin & Caro, 1985).

Caloric expenditure is an expense to the extent that calories used for play might be used for other activities. In times of nutritional shortage, for example, the play of children and other mammals decreases. The animal literature suggests that the caloric expense of play is modest, accounting for between 2.5% and 10% of the total energy budget (Fagen, 1981, for a general review; Martin, 1982, for an experimental study of cats). An estimate of caloric cost of primary schoolchildren's locomotor play is similar, at 2.5% (Pellegrini et al., 1998). Further, and as shown previously, the caloric cost of play for males is greater than for females.

Survivorship cost entails the dangers of injury and death associated with play. For example, bighorn sheep play on steep, risky slopes and a fall can be fatal (Byers, 1984). Similarly, many of the serious injuries in childhood occur in contexts that may have a playful dimension. Specifically, many deaths of children from 5 to 14 years of age are the result of accidents (Cataldo et al., 1986). Although most of these involve automobile accidents, a number may be play related. For example, children are frequently hit by cars while riding bicycles or drown while swimming and playing. Additionally, 700,000 children per year are injured by toys (Cataldo et al., 1986).

We simply do not have enough data on injuries and death during play, relative to other types of activity, to make inferences about this dimension of cost. However, the caloric data for children, although sparse, are consistent with the animal literature and suggest that the cost of play is "moderate" and probably serves an immediate function. In the next section I present data on another metric of cost, time spent in R&T, which is more familiar to developmental psychologists. Often developmentalists use time spent in a specific activity, such as play, as one way of documenting its developmental path. Based on these time estimates I make inferences about possible functions of play during childhood and adolescence. I suggest that both caloric and time costs are moderate and probably serve immediate function.

The Developmental Trajectory of R&T: Cost in Time and Benefits During Childhood and Adolescence

Time in play can be costly to the extent that time spent there to learn or practice a skill is time taken away from learning or practicing that same skill in another way, such as through direct instruction or imitation. Time budget information for all forms of play is limited, but those for fantasy play have been most thoroughly documented, although they too are limited. For the most part, descriptions are limited to those of children's play in their preschools or nursery schools; notable exceptions include the work of Haight and Miller (1993) and Bloch (1989). In this section I document time spent in R&T during childhood and adolescence and make corresponding inferences about its function in each period.

Time budgets of R&T are even less common than studies of other forms of play (see Pellegrini & Gustafson, 2005, for time budget analyses of object play). Most of what we know has been cobbled together from a variety of studies that included R&T and related forms of play, such as locomotor play and physical activity play; in studies of children in preschools, day care centers, and primary schools (most of these data come from observations on the playground at recess); and a few studies looking at children at home. The full details of and references to these studies can be found in Pellegrini and Smith (1998). In Fig. 4.2, I present a summary of the data taken from these studies.

The data clearly show that R&T follows an inverted-U curve, similar to other forms of play (see Fein, 1981). During the preschool period, R&T accounts for about 4% of all behavior, peaking during the primary school years at around 10%, and declining again in early adolescence to around 4%. These data, like the time and caloric costs documented in the animal literature, suggest that the time costs associated with R&T are modest.

There are also robust sex differences in time-related costs of R&T of children, cross-culturally (Bock, 2005; Fry, 2005; Gosso et al., 2005; Whiting & Edwards, 1973), as well as in many nonhuman animals (Lewis, 2005; Meaney, Stewart, & Beatty, 1985). Specific to the human case, Whiting and Edwards (1973) presented survey data (indicating alone that sex differences existed, not including the actual rate of behavior) for children 3 to 6 years and 7 to 11 years of age in six cultures, including the United States. For 3- to 6-year-olds, boys exhibited R&T more than girls in four of the six cultures and in five of the six cultures for the 7- to 11-year-olds. Their data showed that 3- to 6-year-old American girls engaged in R&T more than boys. DiPietro (1981) and Pellegrini

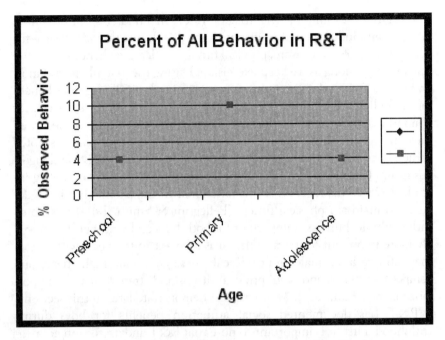

FIG. 4.2.   Percentage of all behavior in rough-and-tumble play.

(1989) found the opposite among American children. For example, Pellegrini observed elementary schoolchildren on their school playground during their recess period and found that for 5-year-old boys, R&T was four times greater than for girls, and for 7.5- and 9-year-olds it was three and two times greater, respectively. In terms of the total behavioral budget of outdoor behavior, boys' R&T accounted for 14% of all their behavior and girls' R&T was 7%.

In summary, it seems that R&T accounts for a modest portion of children's time and caloric budgets, yet it assumes a more important role for boys, relative to girls. Thus, we expect that R&T should have an immediate, not deferred, benefit in boys' development.

Benefits.   In this section I show how R&T serves different immediate benefits at different periods of development. I present evidence suggesting that R&T in childhood is related to peer affiliation whereas in early adolescence it initially relates to aggression and dominance and later is used as a strategy to establish heterosexual contact. Across development, R&T relates to physical conditioning.

I begin by examining the role of R&T in children's (mostly from Western and industrialized countries) immediate strength and physical fitness. As most of us are aware, physical fitness is a fleeting phenomenon. We stay fit only as long as we keep exercising. During the juvenile period most children are given the opportunity to engage in physically vigorous behavior, including R&T, during their school recess period, 5 days a week for 9 months of the year. Of course, they have many other opportunities when they are not in school, participating in organized sport or play. As noted earlier, boys, relative to girls, engage in more R&T, competitive and vigorous games (Pellegrini et al, 2002), and physically vigorous play (Pellegrini et al., 1998). This regimen seems functional to the extent that it is adequate to maintain physical fitness (Pellegrini & Smith, 1998). As noted earlier, physical fitness is important for both boys and girls, but it is probably more important for boys in that it is relevant to the peers with whom they affiliate in all-male groups. Recall these groups are high-energy and competitive places and boys' physical fitness and strength may be important for their status in these groups, as I demonstrate later in this section.

R&T has documented social affiliation benefits for boys during childhood. First, it is important to note that R&T and aggression are negatively and nonsignificantly related for primary school boys (Pellegrini, 1988). Further, looking at behaviors immediately following R&T, R&T does not lead to aggression and dispersal but does lead to continued affiliation, in the form of games with rules, at a greater than chance probability (Pellegrini, 1988); for example, chase can lead to tag games. This should not be surprising to the extent that it typically occurs between friends (Humphreys & Smith, 1987) and boys who engage in R&T tend to be popular and have a varied repertoire by which to solve social problems (Pellegrini, 1989). It may be the case that R&T affords opportunities to learn and practice a variety of social strategies for initiating and maintaining social interaction with peers. Those boys who have a varied repertoire in R&T also have a varied repertoire to solve social problems (Pellegrini, 1993).

The benefits of R&T in adolescence are different from its role in childhood. As in the animal literature (Fagen, 1981), R&T during adolescence seems to be used initially in the service of establishing dominance among males and related to aggression. More specifically, when males' peer groups are in the state of flux, such as when they change from primary to secondary schools, they use R&T and aggression with other males to establish dominance status in that group. After status is established, the frequency of both R&T and aggression should decrease. As

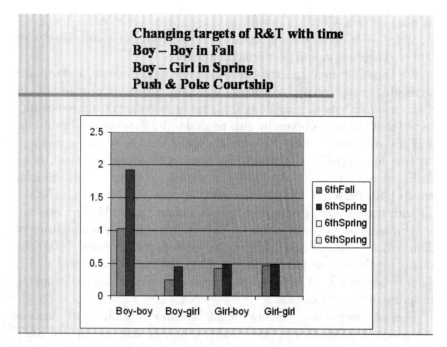

FIG. 4.3. Changing targets of rough-and-tumble play with time.

dominance is not an end onto itself, boys' dominance status is related to dating popularity with females.

The relation between R&T and aggression and dominance during adolescence was first pointed out by Neill (1976) in a factor analytical study of boys' behavior. Additionally, I (Pellegrini, 1995) found that observed R&T and aggression were significantly and positively interrelated in the sixth grade; in the second year of that study the correlation was positive but not significant. The sequential probability of R&T leading to aggression was significant in the sixth, but not in seventh grade. Observed R&T was, however, significantly and positively related to peer-rated dominance in both sixth and seventh grades. Further, sixth-grade R&T predicted seventh-grade dominance (Pellegrini, 1995).

In a more recent study of early adolescent males (Pellegrini, 2003), and consistent with the dominance hypothesis, boys' R&T was more frequently intrasexual than intersexual, as indicated in Fig. 4.3.

When peer groups are initially forming in middle school, boys engage in R&T with other boys, not with girls, to establish and maintain status in male groups. Consistent with this argument, observed frequency of R&T for adolescent boys was significantly and positively correlated with observed aggression and peer-rated dominance.

We also examined the extent to which R&T, dominance, and sexually segregated groups related to dating. We asked girls to nominate boys in their class to a hypothetical party (i.e., dating popularity) and results suggested that the boys chosen by girls tended to be dominant in both sixth and seventh grades. Our data clearly show that as male peer groups became less sexually segregated and boys' dominance increased, boys' dating popularity also increased (Pellegrini & Long, 2003). Similar results have been reported by Bukowski, Sippola, and Newcomb (2000).

With the passage of time, and after dominance is established, one can see the decrease in boy–boy R&T and corresponding to the stabilizing of dominance relationships (Pellegrini, 2003; Pellegrini & Long, 2003). At this point there is an increase in boy–girl R&T, as indicated in Fig. 4.2. That is, boy–girl R&T, although relatively infrequent, increased from fall to spring of the school year.

This occurrence can be interpreted in terms of adolescents' nascent heterosexual relationships. Specifically, it may be that intersexual R&T is a form of "push and poke" courtship (Maccoby, 1998; Schofield, 1981), whereby boys and girls are using playful and ambiguous behaviors, such as R&T, to initiate heterosexual interaction. These acts are sufficiently ambiguous that if the initiator is rebuffed he or she would not loose face among his or her peers. It could be put off as merely being playful. If, on the other hand, the behavior is reciprocated, successful heterosexual interaction was initiated. Thus, where male–male R&T is related to aggression and dominance, male–female R&T seems playful.

To more directly test this hypothesis I videotaped boys and girls engaging in R&T (Pellegrini, 2003) and showed the films to boys and girls who were participants in those events they were viewing and to their classmates who were not participating in the R&T bouts. The data showed participant–nonparticipant differences within each sex. That is, male participants saw the bouts as aggressive and contentious as they were experienced at R&T as adolescents. Male nonparticipants, because they did not engage in R&T at that point, saw the bouts as playful, as they were during childhood. Female participants, on the other hand, saw the bouts as playful, not aggressive because they were experiencing R&T in the context of playful push-and-poke courtship. Nonparticipating females, on the other hand, had little experience in these matters and saw R&T as aggressive.

For adolescents, then, R&T is initially used, along with aggression, to establish dominance. Once this is done, it is used as an early strategy for initiating heterosexual contact.

CONCLUSION

In this chapter I have documented the developmental trajectory of R&T and demonstrated that it, like other forms of play, follows an inverted-U development curve. Further, robust sex differences are observed, where boys engage in R&T more than girls. As part of this analysis, I suggest that R&T accounts for a modest portion of the time and energy budgets of male children and adolescents. This level of cost leads to a conclusion that the benefits, or function, of R&T are probably immediate.

Perhaps most interestingly, R&T may serve very different functions in childhood and adolescence. In childhood, R&T is generally not related to aggression and seems to serve a social affiliation function for boys. In adolescence, when aggression becomes more socially accepted, R&T is initially related to aggression and probably used to serve a social dominance function as boys enter secondary school. After dominance is established, boys seem to use R&T as a strategy to initiate heterosexual contact.

In terms of a broader theoretical picture, I used sexual selection theory to make inferences about the development and function of R&T. The theory predicts that R&T should be more important for males than females and that these differences are the result of differences in sexual dimorphism. That males are more competitive and physically bigger than females results in their being more energetic and physically aggressive. These differences, in turn, result in sexually segregated peer groups in which differences in R&T are associated with gender-appropriate social roles.

The evidence reviewed supports the claims derived from sexual selection theory. There are sex differences in the energetics and social roles enacted by children in segregated peer groups. Consistent with this theory, boys are more energetic, are more competitive, and engage in more R&T than girls. Ultimately, these differences reflect sex differences in the reproductive roles of males and females. Due to the greater variance in males' reproductive success, intrasexual competition for mates leads to their being more active and concerned with social dominance. Males segregate because their reproductive roles bias them to high energetics, relative to females. This is reflected in higher activity levels and their very early preference for more active props.

This conclusion is also supported by cross-sex comparisons in other species (Pellegrini, 2004; Pellegrini et al., 2005). These sex differences in activity may have implications for the development of neural and muscular systems, which are especially important in male roles both in R&T and as adults. Physically vigorous exercise, especially during the juvenile period, has been implicated in the development of brain and muscle systems used in skills associated with different forms of fighting. Specifically, the energetic characteristic of juvenile males' play seems to help develop the cerebellar synapse distributions and muscle fiber differentiation important in economical and skilled movements associated with R&T as well as fighting, predation, and hunting (Byers & Walker, 1995).

Based on this motor training, role enactment in male groups may provide the opportunity to practice and refine skills. During the juvenile and adolescent periods male groups provide the context to learn and practice their adult roles. Skills related to dominance, such as detecting weaknesses and coordinating skilled movements, may need extensive practice, perhaps through play with conspecifics, given their variety and complexity (Alexander, 1989). That dominance skills are especially important to males' functioning (Wrangham, 1999) points to the development of these activities taking place in a social context, most likely R&T and other forms of pretend. Indeed, human cross-cultural studies show that male juveniles are socialized into more competitive and aggressive roles, especially in polygynous societies where roles are not stratified (Low, 1989).

ACKNOWLEDGMENT

I acknowledge the comments of Artin Göncü and Suzanne Gaskins on an earlier draft.

REFERENCES

Alexander, R. D. (1989). Evolution of the human psyche. In P. Mellers & C. Stringer (Eds.), *The human revolution: Behavioral and biological perspectives on the origins of modern humans* (pp. 455–513). Princeton, NJ: Princeton University Press.

Alexander, R. D., Hoogland, J. L., Howard, R. D., Noonan, K. M., & Sherman, P. W. (1979). Sexual dimorphisms and breeding systems in pinnipeds, ungulates, primates, and humans. In N. A. Chagnon & W. Irons (Eds.), *Evolutionary biology and human social behavior* (pp. 402–435). North Scituate, MA: Duxbury.

Archer, J. (1992). *Ethology and human development.* Hemel Hempstead, UK: Harvester Wheatsheaf.

Archer, J., & Lloyd, B. (2002). *Sex and gender* (2nd ed.). London: Cambridge University Press.

Bateman, A. J. (1948). Intra-sexual selection in *Drosophilia*. *Heredity, 2,* 349–368.

Bateson, P. P. G. (1981). Discontinuities in development and changes in the organization of play in cats. In K. Immelmann, G. Barlow, L. Petrinovich, & M. Main (Eds.), *Behavioral development* (pp. 281–295). New York: Cambridge University Press.

Bateson, P. P. G., & Martin, P. (1999). *Design for a life: How behaviour develops.* London: Jonathan Cape.

Bjorklund, D. F., & Pellegrini, A. D. (2002). *Evolutionary developmental psychology.* Washington, DC: American Psychological Association.

Bloch, M. N. (1989). Young boys' and girls' play at home and in the community: A cultural ecological framework. In M. Bloch & A. Pellegrini (Eds.), *The ecological context of children's play* (pp. 120–154). Norwood, NJ: Ablex.

Blurton Jones, N. (1972). Categories of child–child interaction. In N. Blurton Jones (Ed.), *Ethological studies of child behaviour* (pp. 97–129). London: Cambridge University Press.

Bock, J. (2005). Farming, foraging, and children's play in the Okavango Delta, Botswana. In A. D. Pellegrini & P. K. Smith (Eds.), *The nature of play: Great apes and humans* (pp. 254–284). New York: Guilford.

Boyd, R., & Richerson, P. J. (1985). *Culture and the evolutionary process.* Chicago: University of Chicago Press.

Bukowski, W. M., Sippola, L. A., & Newcomb, A. F. (2000). Variations in patterns of attraction to same- and other-sex peers during early adolescence. *Developmental Psychology, 36,* 147–154.

Burghardt, G. (2005). *The genesis of animal play: Testing the limits.* Cambridge, MA: MIT Press.

Buss, D. M. (1989). Sex differences in human mate preferences: Evolutionary hypotheses tested in 37 cultures. *Behavioral and Brain Sciences, 12,* 1–49.

Byers, J. A. (1984). Play in ungulates. In P. K. Smith (Ed.), *Play in animals and humans* (pp. 43–65). Oxford, UK: Blackwell.

Byers, J. A., & Walker, C. (1995). Refining the motor training hypothesis for the evolution of play. *American Naturalist, 146,* 25–40.

Campbell, A. (1999). Staying alive: Evolution, culture, and women's intrasexual aggression. *Behavioral and Brain Sciences, 22,* 203–252.

Campbell, A. (2002). *A mind of her own: The evolutionary psychology of women.* Oxford, UK: Oxford University Press.

Campbell, A., Shirley, L., Heywood, C., & Crook, C. (2000). Infants' visual preference for sex-congruent babies, children, toys, and activities: A longitudinal study. *British Journal of Developmental Psychology, 18,* 479–498.

Campbell, D. W., & Eaton, W. O. (1999). Sex differences in the activity level of infants. *Infant and Child Development, 8,* 1–17.

Caro, T. (1988). Adaptive significance of play: Are we getting closer? *Trends in Ecology & Evolution, 3,* 50–54.

Caro, T. M., & Bateson, P. (1986). Ontogeny and organization of alternative tactics. *Animal Behaviour, 34,* 1483–1499.

Cataldo, M. F., Dershewitz, R., Wilson, M., Christophersen, E., Finney, J., Fawcett, S., et al. (1986). Childhood injury control. In N. A. Krasnegor, J. Arateh, & M. Cataldo (Eds.), *Child health behavior* (pp. 217–253). New York: Wiley.

Costabile, A., Smith, P. K., Matheson, L., Aston, J., Hunter, T., & Boulton, M. (1991). Cross-national comparisons of how children distinguish serious and playful fighting. *Developmental Psychology, 27*, 881–887.

Darwin, C. (1871). *The descent of man, and selection in relation to sex.* London: John Murray.

DiPietro, J. (1981). Rough-and-tumble play: A function of gender. *Developmental Psychology, 67*, 50–58.

Eaton, W. O., & Enns, L. (1986). Sex differences in human motor activity level. *Psychological Bulletin, 100*, 19–28.

Eaton, W. O., Enns, L., & Presseé, M. (1987). Scheme for observing activity. *Journal of Psychoeducational Assessment, 3*, 273–280.

Eaton, W. O., McKeen, N. A., & Campbell, D. W. (2001). The waxing and waning of movement: Implications for psychological development. *Developmental Review, 21*, 205–223.

Fagen, R. (1981). *Animal play behavior.* New York: Oxford University Press.

Fein, G. (1981). Pretend play in childhood: An integrative review. *Child Development, 52*, 1095–1118.

Fry, D. P. (2005). Rough-and-tumble social play in children. In A. D. Pellegrini & P. K. Smith (Eds.), *The nature of play: Great apes and humans* (pp. 54–88). New York: Guilford.

Gosso, Y., Otta, E., Morais, M., Ribeiro, F., & Bussab, V. (2005). Play in hunter-gatherer society. In A. D. Pellegrini & P. K. Smith (Eds.), *The nature of play: Great apes and humans.* New York: Guilford.

Gottlieb, G. (1998). Normally occurring environmental and behavioral influences on gene activity: From central dogma to probablistic epigenesis. *Psychological Review, 105*, 792–802.

Haight, W. L., & Miller, P. J. (1993). *Pretending at home.* Albany: State University of New York Press.

Harlow, H. (1962). The heterosexual affection system in monkeys. *American Psychologist, 17*, 1–9.

Hinde, R. (1980). *Ethology.* London: Fontana.

Humphreys, A., & Smith, P. K. (1987). Rough-and-tumble play, friendship and dominance in school children: Evidence for continuity and change with age. *Child Development, 58*, 201–212.

Krebs, J. R., & McCleery, R. H. (1984). Optimization in behavioural ecology. In J. R. Krebs & N. B. Davies (Eds.), *An introduction to behavioural ecology* (pp. 43–62). Oxford, UK: Blackwell.

Kujawski, J. H., & Bower, T. G. R. (1993). Same-sex preferential looking during infancy as a function of abstract representation. *British Journal of Developmental Psychology, 11*, 201–209.

Lewis, K. (2005). Social play in great apes. In A. D. Pellegrini & P. K. Smith (Eds.), *The nature of play: Great apes and humans* (pp. 27–53). New York: Guilford.

Lickliter, R., & Honeycutt, H. (2003). Developmental dynamics: Toward a biologically plausible evolutionary psychology. *Psychological Bulletin, 129*, 819–835.

Low, B. S. (1989). Cross-cultural patterns in the training of children: An evolutionary prespective. *Journal of Comparative Psychology, 103*, 311–319.

Maccoby, E. E. (1998). *The two sexes: Growing up apart, coming together.* Cambridge, MA: Harvard University Press.

MacDonald, K., & Parke, R. (1986). Parent–child physical play. *Sex Roles, 15,* 367–378.

Martin, P. (1982). The energy cost of play: Definition and estimation. *Animal Behaviour, 30,* 294–295.

Martin, P., & Caro, T. (1985). On the function of play and its role in behavioral development. In J. Rosenblatt, C. Beer, M.-C. Bushnel, & P. Slater (Eds.), *Advances in the study of behavior* (Vol. 15, pp. 59–103). New York: Academic.

Meaney, M., Stewart, J., & Beatty, W. (1985). Sex differences in social play: The socialization of sex roles. In J. Rosenblatt, C. Beer, M. C. Busnel, & P. Slater (Eds.), *Advances in the study of behavior* (Vol. 15, pp. 2–58). New York: Academic.

Neill, S. (1976). Aggressive and non-aggressive fighting in twelve-to-thirteen year old pre-adolescent boys. *Journal of Child Psychology and Psychiatry, 17,* 213–220.

Parke, R. D., & Suomi, S. J. (1981). Adult male infant relationships: Human and nonhuman primate evidence. In K. Immelman, G. W. Barlow, L. Petronovitch, & M. Main (Eds.), *Behavioral development* (pp. 700–725). New York: Cambridge University Press.

Pellegrini, A. D. (1988). Elementary school children's rough-and-rumble play and social competence. *Developmental Psychology, 24,* 802–806.

Pellegrini, A. D. (1989). Elementary school children's rough-and-tumble play. *Early Childhood Research Quarterly, 4,* 245–260.

Pellegrini, A. D. (1993). Boys' rough-and-tumble play, social competence, and group composition. *British Journal of Developmental Psychology, 11,* 237–248.

Pellegrini, A. D. (1995). A longitudinal study of boys' rough and tumble play and dominance during early adolescence. *Journal of Applied Developmental Psychology, 16,* 77–93.

Pellegrini, A. D. (2003). Perceptions and possible functions of play and real fighting in early adolescence. *Child Development, 74,* 1522–1533.

Pellegrini, A. D. (2004). Sexual segregation in childhood: A review of evidence for two hypotheses. *Animal Behaviour, 68,* 435–443.

Pellegrini, A. D., & Archer, J. (2005). Sex differences in competitive and aggressive behavior: A view from sexual selection theory. In B. J. Ellis & D. J. Bjorklund (Eds.), *Origins of the social mind: Evolutionary psychology and child development* (pp. 219–244). New York: Guilford.

Pellegrini, A. D., & Gustafson, K. (2005). Boys' and girls' uses of objects for exploration, play, and tools in early childhood. In A. D. Pellegrini & P. K. Smith (Eds.), *The nature of play: Great apes and humans* (pp. 113–138). New York: Guilford.

Pellegrini, A. D., Horvat, M., & Huberty , P. D. (1998). The relative cost of children's physical activity play. *Animal Behaviour, 55,* 1053–106.

Pellegrini, A. D., Kato, K., Blatchford, P., & Baines, E. (2002). A short-term longitudinal study of children's playground games across the first year of school: Implications for social competence and adjustment to school. *American Educational Research Journal, 39,* 991–1015.

Pellegrini, A. D., & Long, J. D. (2003). A sexual selection theory longitudinal analysis of sexual segregation and integration in early adolescence. *Journal of Experimental Child Psychology, 85,* 257–278.

Pellegrini, A. D., Long, J. D., & Mizerek, E. A. (2005). Sexual segregation in humans. In K. Ruckstuhl & P. Neuhaus (Eds.), *Sexual segregation in vertebrates* (pp. 200–220). Cambridge, UK: Cambridge University Press.

Pellegrini, A. D., & Smith, P. K. (1998). Physical activity play: The nature and function of a neglected aspect of play. *Child Development, 69*, 577–598.

Piaget, J. (1962). *Play, dreams, and imitation in childhood* (C. Gattengno & F. M. Hodgson, Trans.). New York: Norton. (Original work published 1951)

Piaget, J. (1967). *The psychology of intelligence*. London: Routledge & Kegan Paul.

Pitcher, E. G., & Schultz, L. H. (1983). *Boys and girls at play: The development of sex roles*. South Hadley, MA: Bergin & Garvey.

Schofield, J. W. (1981). Complementary and conflicting identities: Images and interactions in an inter-racial school. In S. R. Asher & J. M. Gottman (Eds.), *The development of children's friendships* (pp. 53–90). New York: Cambridge University Press.

Smith, P. K., Hunter, T., Carvalho, A. M. A., & Costabile, A. (1992). Children's perceptions of playfighting, playchasing and real fighting: A cross-national interview study. *Social Development, 1*, 211–229.

Stamps. J. (2003). Behavioural processes affecting development: Tinbergen's fourth question comes to age. *Animal Behaviour, 66*, 1–13.

Suomi, S. J. (2002, August). *Genetic and environmental contributions to deficits in rough-and-tumble play in juvenile rhesus monkey males*. Paper presented at the biennial meetings of the International Society for the Study of Behavioral Development, Ottawa, Canada.

Trivers, R. (1972). Parental investment and sexual selection. In B. Campbell (Ed.), *Sexual selection and the descent of man* (pp. 136–179). Chicago: Aldine.

Trivers, R. (1985). *Social evolution*. Menlo Park, CA: Benjamin/Cummings.

Whiting, B., & Edwards, C. (1973). A cross-cultural analysis of sex-differences in the behavior of children age three through 11. *Journal of Social Psychology, 91*, 171–188.

Wrangham, R. W. (1999). Why are male chimpanzees more gregarious than mothers? A scramble competition hypotheses. In P. Kappeler (Ed.). *Male primates* (pp. 248–248). Cambridge: Cambridge University Press.

III

SOCIAL/CULTURAL PERSPECTIVES OF PLAY AND DEVELOPMENT

5

On the Significance of Social Relationships in the Development of Children's Earliest Symbolic Play: An Ecological Perspective

Marc H. Bornstein
National Institute of Child Health and Human Development
National Institutes of Health
Department of Health and Human Services

Human beings inhabit a manmade world of symbolic thought, language, science, religion, money, art, and *play*. Cassirer (1951) defined man as an "animal symbolicum"; Kaplan (1961) saw symbolic activity as a characteristic feature of human existence; and von Bertalanffy (1968) viewed the evolution of symbolism as basic to anthropogenesis. The participant in symbolic interaction suspends, alters, or distorts current reality to take part in that which is depicted, heard, or read. On this argument, important features of human cognition and culture are linked to symbolism. Notably, one primary way children first enter the world of symbolism is through their pretense play. This chapter is concerned with the earliest emergence, manifestations, and developmental course of symbolic play in childhood and, more centrally, with how young children's symbolic play is fostered through their social relationships.

As Pieter Breugel so picturesquely portrayed in his 1560 *Children's Games*, the young of our species play in many unique and varied ways. Scientists have almost as many ways to conceive and parse children's play. Symbolic play has defied precise definition despite the efforts of numerous researchers and theorists, and theory and research have mostly served to make it clear that symbolic play is protean in nature and can be about "anything and everything" (McLane, 2003). The way I discuss children's earliest symbolic play in this chapter elaborates Piaget's (1962) seminal observations of play in his three young children—Jacqueline, Lucienne, and Laurent— and divides child play into two broad categories of exploratory and symbolic.

Child play changes dramatically during the first 2 years of life, developing from exploration and functional manipulation of objects toward sophisticated acts of increasingly differentiated pretense. In the first year, play is predominantly characterized by sensorimotor manipulation; infant play appears designed to extract information about objects, what objects do, what perceivable qualities objects have, and what immediate effects objects can produce. This form of play is commonly referred to as exploratory because children's play activities are tied to the tangible properties of objects. In the second year, children's play actions take on a nonliteral quality: The goal of play now appears to be symbolic and representational. Play is increasingly generative, as children enact activities performed by self, others, and objects in simple representational scenarios, pretending to drink from empty teacups, to talk on toy telephones, and the like. Symbolic play is a forum in which children may advance on their cognitions about people, objects, and actions, and construct increasingly sophisticated representations of the world and relations between symbols and their external referents.

This chapter addresses the following topics. In the first section, an ecological model is presented that focuses on antecedents of individual variation in child symbolic play: antecedents in the child, in the child's parent (or significant social others in the child's life), and in the child's society and culture. In the second section, the principal theories and mechanisms thought to underlie children's achievement of symbolic play are reviewed. Child play is a perennially "hot" topic in developmental science (see, e.g., Garvey, 1990; Howes, Unger, & Matheson, 1992; MacDonald, 1993; Papoušek & Von Gontard, 2003; Power, 2000; Roopnarine, Johnson, & Hooper, 1994); this chapter presents central ecological and theoretical considerations about the significance of social relationships in human children's earliest symbolic play.

AN ECOLOGICAL APPROACH TO UNDERSTANDING THE SIGNIFICANCE OF SOCIAL RELATIONSHIPS IN THE DEVELOPMENT OF CHILD SYMBOLIC PLAY

Children vary among themselves extraordinarily in their symbolic play. One of the central issues in developmental science is to explicate the sources of individual variation: What are the major contributors to individual differences in child symbolic play? Children also raise the level of their symbolic play when in interaction with more sophisticated play partners; their symbolic play becomes richer, more diverse, and sustained. What are the major contributors to this change in child symbolic play?

Figure 5.1 shows an *a priori* ecological model developed to show the main predictors of child symbolic play; it follows the general bioecological systems model of distal to proximal sources proposed by Bronfenbrenner (e.g., Bronfenbrenner & Morris, 1998). Most proximal to the child's manifestations of symbolic play is what the child himself or herself brings to symbolic play. Children's sociodemographic as well as individual characteristics might contribute to their play competence or performance. Next, children's parents, and significant others in the child's life, might contribute to children's symbolic play first and most significantly by their own symbolic play or by providing children's play experiences, models, scaffolds, or other mechanisms (more on this later). In turn, parents and others may be influenced in their play by their own individual characteristics (e.g., personality, intelligence, or parenting cognitions, such as knowledge, style, self-perceptions, and attributions). However, a singular focus on dyadic microsystem relationships involving partners and children disguises the extent to which partner–child relationships are themselves embedded in a mesosystem, exosystem, and macrosystem of broader contexts, like the family, school, and neighborhood; workplace and mass media; and values, social class, and culture that support, encourage, and reinforce patterns of interpersonal interactions and intrapersonal cognitions. These forces shape the short- and long-term goals parents and others have for children, their practices in attempting to meet those goals, and so the immediate play contexts and interactions experienced by children. Parental beliefs and behaviors about symbolic play reflect both distal (e.g., sociodemographic) and proximal (e.g., individual) influences; but, first, more about what the child brings to her or his own symbolic play development.

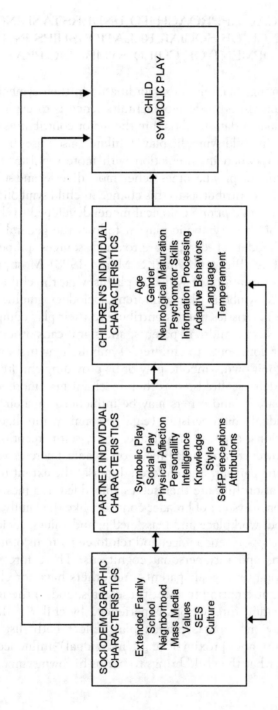

FIG. 5.1. An ecological model of child play: Expected predictive relations among child, mother, and sociodemographic characteristics on child symbolic play.

Contributions From the Child

Consider briefly multiple possible proximal contributions of the child to her or his own symbolic play development, about which Harris (1994) argued, "The stable timing of its onset in different cultures strongly suggests a neuropsychological timetable and a biological basis" (p. 256). Symbolic play in the child follows a rather fixed ontogenetic course. Tamis-LeMonda and Bornstein (1991) showed that children were significantly more likely to participate in pretense with age. Related to age considerations, nervous system maturation and integrity play a part. For example, heart rate variability and accelerations normatively develop across human gestation. We studied these cardiac functions in fetuses at multiple times prenatally, and later at 27 months postnatal age, we assessed symbolic play in the same children (Bornstein et al., 2002). Fetuses with higher heart rate variability and accelerations over gestation, and those with steeper growth trajectories, achieved relatively higher levels of symbolic play as children. It could be that individual variation in neurological development is stable, or it could be that efficient cardiac function positively influences development of the underlying neural substrate to enhance children's play.

Other biological characteristics of children, like their sex, appear to contribute to the expression of symbolic play as well: Girls show consistently more symbolic play than do boys of the same age (Bornstein, Haynes, O'Reilly, & Painter, 1996). It is well recognized that, generally speaking, girls may be more biologically mature than boys of the same age. Children's nutritional status also influences symbolic play development (Wachs, 1993) as does the growth of children's adaptive motor skills (Eisert & Lamorey, 1996).

Children's cognitive capacity is an important component of their symbolic abilities, and to explore this potential association we measured infant information-processing ability in longitudinal relation to child symbolic play (Bornstein, 1985, 1998). Habituation in infants has been interpreted as involving mental representation of stimulus information. Habituation is a stable individual-differences characteristic of infants. Notably, infant habituation predicts child symbolic play: Children who habituate more efficiently as infants engage in more symbolic play as toddlers, even when concurrent maternal stimulation is controlled (Tamis-LeMonda & Bornstein, 1989, 1993a).

Of course, not all biological characteristics of children contribute to symbolic play development: Spontaneous levels of infant vocal and exploratory activity (Tamis-LeMonda & Bornstein, 1993b) and hearing impairment (Bornstein, Selmi, Haynes, Painter, & Marx, 1999) apparently do not, for example. Furthermore, not all child contributions to child symbolic play capacity have direct effects: Sometimes antecedent child contributions to child symbolic play may be indirect, as, for example, through their effect on parent (McCune, Dipane, Fireoved, & Fleck, 1994).

Contributions From the Parent and Significant Others

Most mothers and fathers participate in pretend play with their children, and Haight, Parke, and Black (1997) reported that mothers and fathers alike generally characterize pretend play as an enjoyable activity and facilitative of children's cognitive development. American parents begin pretending with their infants within the first year (Haight & Miller, 1993; Tamis-LeMonda & Bornstein, 1991). Parents are not unique social partners in their scaffolding of children's symbolic play. Aureli and Colecchia (1996) found that children who attended day care played symbolically at a high level and with longer thematic units when in interaction with peers than children who did not attend day care.

Child symbolic play with a more sophisticated partner is more diverse, complex, and sustained than is child solitary symbolic play. For example, O'Connell and Bretherton (1984) observed that toddlers engaged in a greater number of different symbolic activities when in collaborative as opposed to independent play. Fiese (1990) showed that 15- to 24-month-olds spent a greater percentage of time in symbolic play, as opposed to exploratory play, during mother–child play compared to child-alone play. Bornstein et al. (1996) likewise reported that the degree to which mothers participated in and guided their children's symbolic play affected the level of their children's symbolic play. Children engaged in symbolic play more and for longer periods when in collaboration than when alone, and in collaborative play the proportion of child play that was symbolic increased from circumstances where children initiated play to ones where their mothers initiated the play. These kinds of results provide support for the hypothesis that social interaction enhances symbolic play. As a novice symbolic player, the child benefits from the presence of a more experienced play partner.

Individual Contributors. Social partners contribute to children's symbolic play in myriad ways. Consider, first, most proximally, actual partner play. When children are in collaborative play—as with their mothers or significant others, such as father, a peer, or an examiner—they may initiate their own symbolic play, or their partner may initiate children's symbolic play through demonstrations, where the more mature play partner provides the child with information about how to engage in particular symbolic activities, say, by modeling the activity, or through solicitations, where the more mature play partner places the onus for play on the child, say, by encouraging the child to execute specific play activities. Mothers engage in exploratory play with their children less over time, and engage in pretense more over time, and mothers tend to engage in solicitations more than demonstrations of symbolic play (Tamis-LeMonda & Bornstein, 1991). Furthermore, individual differences in mothers' symbolic demonstrations and solicitations of play are consistently stable in the short term (Bornstein, Haynes, Legler, O'Reilly, & Painter, 1997) and long term (Tamis-LeMonda & Bornstein, 1991), and stability in mothers' play is not contingent on child play (Tamis-LeMonda & Bornstein, 1991).

Presumably multiple individual factors motivate partner play behavior. Consider, first, intelligence and cognition. Maternal IQ predicts child symbolic play (Bornstein et al., 1996; Tamis-LeMonda & Bornstein, 1993b). What mothers know about child play and how play develops also predicts the degree to which they facilitate their children's play (Bornstein et al., 1999; Tamis-LeMonda, Damast, & Bornstein, 1994). Mothers recognize variation within child symbolic play, and some mothers possess more knowledge about child play than others. Mothers' orderings of the sophistication of child play match that established in the developmental literature; mothers are also stable in their knowledge of child play (Tamis-LeMonda, Chen, & Bornstein, 1998). These personological characteristics of parenting could reflect capacities that enable a mother to adjust her play behavior to her child's behavior so as to guide her child in play more effectively.

To explore this possibility, we investigated mother and child play in a study that had two goals: The first was to describe mothers' scaffolding behaviors in actual play interactions. Specifically, we examined the types of play mothers introduced in response to their 21-month-olds' play. The second goal was to examine the role of maternal knowledge about child play in their scaffolding (Damast, Tamis-LeMonda, & Bornstein, 1996). Sequential analyses addressed the first goal and revealed that mothers adjusted the level of their play to match or advance their children's play level. On the second, mothers who were more knowledgeable about the development of play responded to their children's play with more play at higher levels than their children's play. Haight, Parke, Black, and Trousdale (1993) found that the more importance parents assigned to play, the more parents engaged in episodes of pretend play with their children. Haight et al. (1997) further found that mothers' ratings of the importance of parental participation in symbolic play predicted the proportion of time they spent in symbolic play.

Additional examination of maternal play in direct relation to child play is telling in terms of the significance of dyadic coordination (Tamis-LeMonda & Bornstein, 1991). At each of two times in the second year (13 and 20 months), mothers who engaged in more symbolic play had children who engaged in more symbolic play. (By contrast, there was no relation, or an inverse relation, between mothers' exploratory play and their children's symbolic play, and between mothers' symbolic play and their children's exploratory play.) Moreover, these same general positive associations between mother and child symbolic play obtain in different cultures: Whether they are New Yorkers or Tokyo people or Buenos Aires Porteñas or Italians living in the north or south of their country, mothers who engage in more symbolic play with their children have children who engage in more symbolic play (Bornstein et al., 2002; Bornstein, Haynes, et al., 1999; Tamis-LeMonda, Bornstein, Cyphers, Toda, & Ogino, 1992; Venuti, Rossi, Spagnoletti, Famulare, & Bornstein, 1997; see also Unger & Howes, 1988). These cross-cultural findings point to a distinctive and perhaps universal attunement between mothers and children in symbolic play. Of course, conclusions about causality must be tempered because the findings are based on correlations. That said, analyzing sequential dependencies between maternal and child symbolic play reveals that, when children are engaged in symbolic play, their mothers are more likely to engage in symbolic play at or above the level of their child (Damast et al., 1996).

Further to this point, mother–child relationships in play, whether cognitive or behavioral, are characterized by mutual specificity. Mothers' knowledge about development in child language differs from their knowledge about development in child play (perhaps because of different societal emphases placed on the two domains), just as their play interactions with their children differ from their language interactions (Tamis-LeMonda & Bornstein, 1994). Likewise, in the United States, Argentina, and Italy, mothers' social play (their verbal and physical behaviors directed toward the child and intended to elicit an overt positive social response from the child), expressions of physical affection, and verbal praise are not directly related to their children's symbolic play (Bornstein et al., 2002; Bornstein et al., 1999; Venuti et al., 1997). In addition, mothers who are more responsive to their infants' play at 5 months have children at 13 months who are more advanced specifically in play, whereas mothers who are more responsive to their infants' vocalizations have children who are more advanced specifically in language, again without cross-domain effects (Tamis-LeMonda & Bornstein, 1994). When attempting to understand how adult–infant interactions shape child development, therefore, it is critical to assess relations within specific domains.

Ecological Approaches to Child Symbolic Play. With these several individual considerations in mind, we have examined multiple contributors to child play simultaneously from the perspective of a general ecological model (Fig. 5.1). The literature concerning endogenous and exogenous sources of influence on child symbolic play is rich. Typically, however, antecedents to child development have been studied in isolation, and few investigations have evaluated multiple influences simultaneously. Thus, the overlap of different antecedents vis-à-vis the unique contribution that any one may make to child play remains essentially unexplored. However, systems theorists emphasize the importance of considering the possible independence and interdependence of organismic and environmental or experiential concerns in predicting child development (see Belsky, Garduque, & Hrncir, 1984; Bornstein, 2002; Bornstein & Sawyer, 2005; Bronfenbrenner & Morris, 1998; Lerner, Rothbaum, Boulos, & Castellino, 2002).

In one such ecologically informed study, we included sociodemographic characteristics, individual characteristics, and behaviors of mothers and children in omnibus multivariate models. Maternal symbolic play and maternal individual characteristics were expected to exert direct effects on child play, and individual characteristics indirect effects through their influence on mothers' play. In turn, sociodemographic variables were hypothesized to stand most distal to and influence child symbolic play through maternal individual factors and actual play. Udwin and Shmukler (1981) found that socioeconomic status (SES) was a determinant of imaginative play in preschoolers, but parenting factors constituted key mediators. Three separate models were designed to predict mother-initiated child symbolic play, child-initiated child symbolic play, and solitary child symbolic play, respectively, at 20 months (Bornstein et al., 1996). To accomplish this analysis, we implemented structural equation modeling (SEM). SEM allows simultaneous testing of direct as well as indirect paths of influence of multiple variables in an effort to define a single integrative view. SEM evaluates each variable's effects controlling for the effects of all other variables in the model. SEM does not demonstrate causal relations among variables, but evaluates the fit of hypothesized relations in data and assigns statistical significance to individual paths within a model.

Figure 5.2 shows the final model for mother-initiated child collaborative symbolic play. This kind of child play was predicted directly by mothers' symbolic play and by child language competence. In addition, mothers' physical affection and verbal intelligence as well as child gender (girls more than boys) exercised small but statistically significant indirect effects on mother-initiated child symbolic play. Figure 5.3 shows the final model for child-initiated child collaborative symbolic play. This kind of child play was predicted directly by mothers' symbolic play and (negatively) by mothers' social play. In addition, mothers' physical affection and child gender (girls more than boys) exercised small but statistically significant indirect effects on child-initiated child symbolic play.

Play requires time, energy, resources, and intellectual commitment on the part of parents, and children appear to benefit cognitively from the experience. These two analyses clearly show that maternal play and individual characteristics are significant factors in promoting child symbolic play. How robust are the effects of maternal play? Surprisingly, not very. Figure 5.4 shows the final model of the influence of the original multivariate set of ecological factors on child solitary symbolic play. The direct antecedents of child solitary symbolic play are found principally in child gender and maternal verbal intelligence. When playing on their own, girls engage in more symbolic play than do boys, and children of mothers with higher verbal intelligence engage in more symbolic play. Maternal symbolic play influenced child collaborative symbolic play, but mothers' play itself was not an influential factor in child solitary symbolic play. In separate, but converging analyses, mothers' 13-month symbolic play did not predict their toddlers' 20-month symbolic play (Tamis-LeMonda & Bornstein, 1994). Tingley (1994), too, failed to find any longitudinal relations between mothers' symbolic play at 34 months and their children's symbolic play at 64 months. Indeed, Fein and Fryer's (1996) review underscored the lack of any lasting effects of mother play on child play.

It is unlikely that parental effects do not operate in any longitudinal dynamic, and it will challenge future investigation to untangle the reasons behind these outcomes. It may be that mothers find it difficult to help

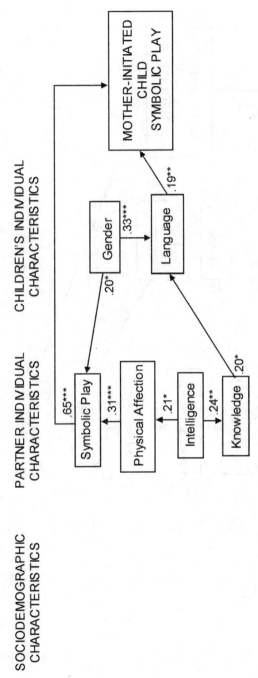

FIG. 5.2. Predictive relations between mother and child characteristics and mother-initiated child collaborative symbolic play. *$p < .05.$ **$p < .01.$ ***$p < .001.$

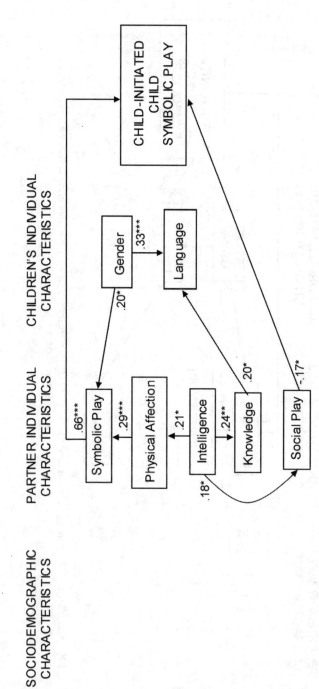

FIG. 5.3. Predictive relations between mother and child characteristics and child-initiated child collaborative symbolic play. *p < .05. **p < .01. ***p < .001.

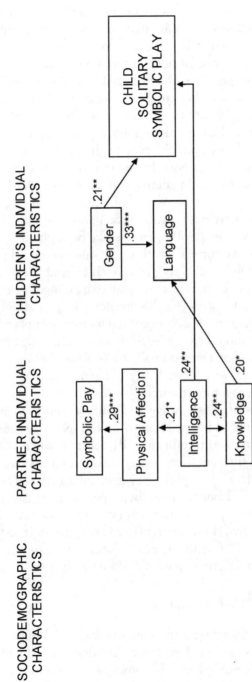

FIG. 5.4. Predictive relations between mother and child characteristics and child solitary symbolic play. *p < .05. **p < .01. ***p < .001.

113

children maintain symbolic understanding (DeLoache & Burns, 1994). Alternatively, mothers' symbolic play may be effective, but only to the extent that their play matches or challenges the child's own symbolic play level. That is, it may not be sufficient to assess how much or how long a mother's symbolic play is without considering the sophistication of her symbolic play relative to her child's symbolic play. Neither a mother who suggests symbolic play at levels below her child's baseline level nor a mother who solicits higher order symbolic play from a child who is only capable of rudimentary symbolic play might be expected to nurture her child's long-term achievements. In addition to considering the effectiveness of the form and level of maternal play, it may be critical as well to consider the timing and content of symbolic play with respect to children's ongoing symbolic activities (Bornstein & Tamis-LeMonda, 1997).

At the zero-order level, other factors like SES, physical affection, and maternal personality correlate with child symbolic play, but SEM shows that none uniquely or directly predicts child symbolic play. That said, other nonsymbolic features of child play (e.g., tempo) or other maternal personality characteristics (e.g., depression; Tingley, 1994), other attitudes toward parenting (e.g., about the importance of play; Haight et al., 1993), and other kinds of knowledge about children (e.g., specific knowledge about child play; Damast et al., 1996; Tamis-LeMonda et al., 1994) may relate directly to maternal or child symbolic play and should fall within the scope of future research.

The predictors of collaborative and solitary symbolic play in children clearly differ. What children bring to solitary play are their gender and their inherited (native) intelligence. By contrast, when children play in interaction with their mothers, whether they are responding to mother-initiated symbolic play by playing symbolically themselves or initiating symbolic play in collaboration, mothers' specifically engaging in symbolic play appears to be of paramount importance in promoting child symbolic play. Taken together, these differentiated analyses attest to how vital it is to assess multiple factors in the development and expression of individual differences in different types of child symbolic play.

Contributions From Culture

Some time ago, Slaughter and Dombrowski (1989) opined that, in the light of the anthropological evidence, "children's social and pretend play appear to be biologically based, sustained as an evolutionary contribution to human psychological growth and development" (p. 290). However, they also observed that, "Cultural factors regulate the amount and type of expression of these play forms" (p. 290). In its comprehensiveness, an ecological view of child symbolic play embraces more distal but still significant determinants, most notably culture. In addition to parents' unique life experiences, including interactions with their child, as well as those individual interests and strengths that shape their cognitions and practices, as members of a particular cultural community parents are presented with "cultural models" (Goodnow, 1988) of play through multiple converging sources, including intergenerational transmission, media, and "experts" such as teachers and pediatricians (Harkness & Super, 1986). Patterns of varying and meaningful dyadic effects in play (e.g., the specificity pointed to earlier) suggest that children's play is in some degree malleable and, by inference, that systematic cultural emphases in parental play could engender different patterns of play in children. Although human societies vary in the amount and type of such play, anthropological accounts attest that fully developed pretend play (including role play and sociodramatic play) appears to be universal. Play is therefore a common childhood activity across cultures, but at the same time play typically expresses concerns that are culture specific. In this sense, anthropologists have long agreed that play provides an important context for culture-specific learning (Schwartzman, 1978; Slaughter & Dombrowski, 1989).

The burgeoning contemporary literature on culture and play attests that distinctive cultural variation coexists alongside extant universals (e.g., Bornstein et al., 1996). In some cultures, mothers eschew play with children: Guatemalan, Indian, Indonesian, Italian, Kenyan, Korean, Mayan, and Mexican mothers reportedly attach no particular value to play, do not view play as especially significant in children's development, do not believe that it is important or appropriate to play with their children, and engage in relatively little pretense (see Farver, 1993; Farver & Howes, 1993; Farver, Kim, & Lee, 1995; Farver & Wimbarti, 1995; Gaskins, 1996; Harkness & Super, 1986; New, 1989, 1994; Rogoff, Mistry, Göncü, & Mosier, 1993; Rogoff, Mosier, Mistry, & Göncü, 1993). In other cultures, mothers consider play with children to be a central component of the parental role and take an active part in child play, although they may emphasize different aspects. Argentine, Chinese, European American, and Turkish parents, for example, think of themselves as appropriate play partners for their children and, consistent with such beliefs, promote and actively participate in pretend play with them (see Bornstein, Haynes et al., 1999; Haight, Wang, Fung, Williams, & Mintz, 1995; Rogoff et al., 1993). Notably, in research with cross-cultural samples, Farver (Farver & Howes, 1993; Farver & Wimbarti, 1995) found that mothers who valued play for its educational and cognitive benefits were more likely to encourage pretense by providing props and suggestions than were mothers who viewed play as amusement or imitation of adults.

From where do cultural differences in play arise? Leont'ev (1981a, 1981b) theorized that children's play varies from one context or community to another depending on how the context or community is structured, how play is defined, and the significance attributed to children's play. Göncü, Tuermer, Jain, and Johnson (1999) later asserted that understanding mother and child play requires appreciating how the economic structure of the community determines the availability of play, identifying community beliefs about the value of play, and analyzing how children are inculcated with community values about play. They contended that the development of play as characterized in Western theories is only one of many possible cultural models of play, and they emphasized economic (e.g., family income), physical (e.g., toys and play settings), and socioecological (e.g., adult beliefs and adult–child communication) aspects of children's lives in explaining the nature and role of play in context.

Play also varies within cultures that esteem it. We have examined and compared child-alone and child-with-mother play at several sites around the world, including, for example, Japan and the United States. Japan is a provocative base for comparison with the United States because these two countries maintain reasonably similar levels of modernity and living standards, and both are child-centered, but at the same time the two differ dramatically in terms of history, culture, beliefs, and childrearing goals, as well as the activities that mothers in each country emphasize in interactions with infants and young children. Notably, Japan is a "collectivistic" country, whereas the United States is "individualistic" (Greenfield & Suzuki, 1998). In general, American mothers promote autonomy and organize child-centered social interactions so as to foster physical and verbal assertiveness in children as well as their interest in the external environment, whereas Japanese mothers organize child-centered social interactions so as to consolidate and strengthen mutual dependence within the dyad (Tamis-LeMonda, Bornstein, et al., 1992; Toda, Azuma, & Bornstein, 1993). Japanese children in Tokyo engage in more symbolic play than do U.S. children in New York City. Japanese mothers engage in more symbolic demonstrations and solicitations than do American mothers; American mothers engage in more exploratory solicitations than do Japanese mothers. Thus, in line with the common cultural characterization, Japanese mothers encourage interactive (other-directed) pretense ("Feed the dolly"), whereas American mothers encourage self- and other-actualization at functional levels of play ("Push the bus"). For Americans, who promote interest in the environment and interpersonal independence supplemented by information-oriented verbal interactions, play and the toys used during play are more frequently the topic or object of communication; by contrast, the play setting and associated toys appear to mediate dyadic interaction among Japanese, who emphasize closeness and interdependency between dyad members. Comparative study of child and mother play in another collectivistic culture, Argentina, produced parallel findings (Bornstein, Haynes, et al., 1999).

Summary

In an ecological systems view, symbolic play development in the child can be expected to be the product of multiple antecedents that include economy, environment, and experience, as well as genetics and biology. Multivariate analysis brings to light some of the many direct and indirect contributions of the child, the child's parents and significant others, and the child's environment and culture to both nomothetic and idiographic expressions of children's earliest symbolic play.

THEORIES AND MECHANISMS IN THE CONTAGION AND TRANSFER OF SYMBOLIC PLAY THROUGH SOCIAL INTERACTION

Child play was historically studied from a structural point of view, as an activity primarily revealing internal cognitive modes of children's negotiating the world. Within that perspective, social influences on child play development were often neglected. A complementary approach is to study symbolic play as a reflection of individual cognitive growth in the context of interpersonal activity (Fein & Apfel, 1979; Fenson & Ramsay, 1980; Nicolich, 1977). Of course, children initiate pretend play, but in addition they learn from and imitate the pretense they see (e.g., Užgiris, Benson, Kruper, & Vasek, 1989), and they complete pretend scenarios begun by others (e.g., Dunn & Wooding, 1977). The fact that children's play that is symbolic increases from when children play alone to when they play collaboratively gives evidence for the importance of interpersonal interaction to more advanced expressions of symbolic play in the child.

It is not the mere presence of another in dyadic play interactions that facilitates greater play sophistication in children either. Of course, parents simply being nearby may set the occasion for rehearsal of practiced collab-orative play (Labrell & Simeoni, 1992), or children may feel heightened security in the presence of their mothers (Slade, 1987a, 1987b). Levine (1988) concluded that, when parents act as an audience, they can facilitate children's motivation to engage in symbolic play. Detailed analysis suggests, however, that just being with a child is insufficient by itself to enhance a child's play (O'Connell & Bretherton, 1984). Simply having a partner does not ensure cognitive gains (Gauvain & Rogoff, 1989; Rogoff & Gardner, 1984); rather, shared responsibility and joint problem solving are vital aspects of the novice–teacher relationship. Thus, mothers' timing and tuning their emotional displays appropriately to their children's emotional states during face-to-face exchanges in the first year of life predict children's symbolic play (Feldman & Greenbaum, 1997). Successful emotional sig-naling and responsiveness help to lay the foundation for later symbolic development (Bornstein & Tamis-LeMonda, 1997).

Theories

At least four theories suggest that symbolic play interactions with others should directly influence children's symbolic play. I discuss each theory briefly, and conclude with an equally short discussion of some specific mechanisms that have been identified in partner play that may motivate children's move to pretense.

Attachment. Maternal sensitivity, affection, and responsiveness are hypothesized to promote security in child attachments (e.g., Spieker & Booth, 1988) that, in turn, foster exploration and sophistication of play (Ainsworth, Blehar, Waters, & Wall, 1978; Baruch, 1991; Bowlby, 1969; Rubin, Stewart, & Chen, 1995; Slade, 1987a, 1987b). Vibbert and Bornstein (1989) found that mothers' affectionate social interaction style (in combination with didactic stimulation) predicted children's level of play sophistication. Furthermore, Bornstein et al. (1996) found that mothers' expressions of physical affection toward their children also exer-cised an indirect influence in child collaborative (but not solitary) play through their influence on maternal play. Families that are generally nur-turing tend to have children who express higher levels of competent play with adult caregivers, with peers, and with toys (Belsky et al., 1984; Howes & Stewart, 1987; Jennings & Connors, 1989; Slade, 1987b).

Scaffolding. According to Vygotksy (1978), higher mental processes appear first on the interpsychological (social) plane and only later on the intrapsychological (individual) plane. Vygotsky contended that, as a central feature of this transactional perspective, the more advanced or expert partner (the mother) raises the level of performance or competence of the less advanced or expert partner (the child), and the dynamic systems perspective posits that reciprocity between mother and child facilitates higher level forms of interaction (Thelen & Smith, 1998). In Vygotsky's (1978a) view, if children operate spontaneously and independently at some "actual developmental level," under adult guidance they may reach a higher level of "potential development" (p. 86). His notion of the zone of proximal development proposed that, through social interaction, the more advanced partner augments symbolic functioning in the less advanced partner. The parent is at a (much) higher level of physical and cognitive development than is the child and is thus able to structure and control the complexity of stimulation so that it is challenging and motivating to the child (MacDonald, 1993). Pretending is a prime candidate activity for parental scaffolding (Rogoff, 1990), and many parents' pretend behaviors seem aimed at scaffolding advances in children's understanding. As Vygotsky would predict, children perform above their spontaneous individual capabilities when supported by a more experienced partner. Indeed, Vygotsky fostered a major conceptual shift in the study of play, regarding it not solely as a solitary activity reflecting underlying cognitive schema that the child already possesses, but as a formative activity shaped through the child's social interactions with significant others (Smolucha & Smolucha, 1998).

Ethology. Parent–child play is an expression of high-quality parental investment in offspring (MacDonald, 1993). Certainly play provides a fun and enjoyable venue for parent–child interaction. Additionally, part of the parental effort to foster optimal development in offspring involves playing with children and, thereby, providing heterogeneous and enjoyable experiences to develop, practice, and fine-tune abilities that will promote adaptation to and coping with the physical and social world. Parental investment theory asserts that children constitute a resource drain on parents, but are net beneficiaries of parental resources (Trivers, 1986). The chief goal of parental investment is adaptiveness of offspring. Parental investment in young children can be expressed in many ways, most important among them the provision of physical protection, material resources, affection, and environmental and cognitive stimulation (Bornstein, 2002). Parent play is most frequently seen with the young, and is on this basis thought to be especially beneficial during early development. Notably, play is associated with increased brain size and particularly increased cortical size (Fagen, 1981). Thus, beyond its enjoyable and socially rewarding nature, play might promote cognitive sophistication and hence adapted fitness in offspring.

Stimulation, Modeling, and Training. Belsky, Goode, and Most (1980) hypothesized that parents might directly influence their children to explore the environment and play at higher levels. They conducted two studies. In the first cross-sectional correlational study, measures of maternal stimulation and infant exploratory (play) competence correlated at each of four ages; mothers who stimulated their babies more had babies who explored their environments and played more competently. In a follow-up experimental study, the investigators randomly assigned 1-year-olds to intervention or control groups. In the intervention, the investigators surreptitiously rewarded maternal attempts to stimulate children's exploratory competence. These rewards worked, and as a consequence mothers in the intervention group stimulated their toddlers more than mothers in the control group. Importantly, at the end of the study children in the intervention group scored higher on exploratory competence (play) than did children in the control group.

Another approach to assessing the effect of stimulation on symbolic play has been to use imitation tasks. Under structured play conditions, an experimenter models symbolic activities, such as pretending to eat or to feed a baby doll. Children are more likely to engage in more complex forms of symbolic play following such modeling (e.g., Bretherton, O'Connell, Shore, & Bates, 1984; Fein, 1975; Jeffree & McConkey, 1976; Watson & Fisher, 1977). In another direct training study on pretend play (Dockett, 1998), children were pre- and posttested on measures of shared pretense (from observations). One group of children received play training for 3 weeks; the control group experienced a normal curriculum without sociodramatic play. Analyses showed that, from an equal baseline, the training group significantly increased in frequency and complexity of pretense play relative to the control group.

Mechanisms

When children play with a more sophisticated partner, like their mother, they are furnished with models, stimulants, materials, and opportunities to perform at levels above those they may achieve on their own. The sophistication and specificity of partner symbolic play relative to child play may matter a great deal. As an example, two mothers could equate in the overall amount of symbolic play they engage in, yet the first mother might solicit sequences of higher level play from her child, and the second mother might solicit lower level play from her child. If the children to whom these play solicitations are directed are already capable of lower level symbolic play, the play prompts of the second mother will do little to challenge the child. By contrast, the first mother solicits play that advances on her child's baseline level, thereby inducing the child to represent mentally a more sophisticated scenario. In addition to considering the form and level of maternal play sophistication, it is critical also to consider the timing and content of partner play interactions with respect to children's ongoing activities. According to Fogel and Thelen (1987), interactional frames that are supportive as well as reciprocal serve a more facilitative function than frames that are directive and intrusive. Even though the partner may provide information through direction or instruction, intrusive interactions relate negatively to symbolic play and positively to more simple exploratory forms of play (Fiese, 1990).

At a macro level of behavioral analysis, Harding's choice construction model, based in part on an integration of Piaget's (1962) and Vygotsky's (1978a, 1978b) theories, proposes that certain behaviors initiated by a mother facilitate or inhibit a child's ability for behavior choice (Harding, Kromelow, Stilson, & Touris, 1995; Harding, Weissmann, Kromelow, & Stilson, 1997; Harding, Weissmann, Noll, Lynn, & Stilson, 2001). Stilson and Harding (1997) found that mothers' options-promoting (encouraging, affirming, or expanding on the child's activities) behaviors at 18 months significantly predict children's symbolic play at both 18 and 40 months. By contrast, options-limiting social interactions (disapproving, correcting, and replacing) significantly correlated with nonsymbolic play, leading Stilson and Harding to conclude that options-limiting social contexts may interfere with children's ability to engage in symbolic play, even when requisite cognitive abilities for symbolic play are present (see also Noll & Harding, 2003).

Actual partner symbolic play exercises a large and consistent influence over child symbolic play. Microlevel behavioral analysis shows that mothers alter their behaviors in ways that might signal pretense and so scaffold children's early pretense understanding. As Lillard and Witherington (2004) showed, mothers also enact certain behavioral modifications in pretense (as opposed to real situations) that assist young children in interpreting pretense acts *qua* pretense.

Summary

Play emerges in the child, but adults (or other more mature play partners) can influence its development in many ways, by provisioning the play environment, by modeling, by engaging children actively and symbolically, by responding to children's play overtures, and by scaffolding play at higher levels. Pretense play is generally less sophisticated when children play alone than when they play with their mother or others—and this change confirms important roles for children's more sophisticated play partners. During partner–child play, children are guided in the re-creation, expression, and elaboration of symbolic themes: Adults play in ways that children observe and learn from, they induce children to play, and they provide objects for child play. By actively participating in their children's play, parents and significant other senior players may structure experiences and enhance representational competencies in their junior partners. During play, children's partners may serve in several possible roles—as observer, facilitator, stage manager, mediator, scribe, or player—or they may pay little attention to play (Bornstein, 1975; Jones & Reynolds, 1992; Tamis-LeMonda, Katz, & Bornstein, 2002). It takes creativity and commitment to get down on the floor and attentively and actively engage a child in pretense; however, such investment pays rewards. Children's play is children's work, but parents' investment in child play also repays children welcome dividends.

CONCLUSIONS

The more we learn about what is happening inside the heads of children and what their actions mean, the clearer it becomes that development is a continuous process that intertwines a child's unique biological endowment with his or her unique experiential history. The role of biology cannot be explained without understanding how experiences influence its expression. The developmental achievements of the child both influence and are influenced by the style and the content of parent–child interaction and take place in larger cultural contexts. Thus, many tributaries contribute to the forceful flow of every construct, structure, function, or process in development—child symbolic play included—and the development of each in turn affects all other facets of the maturing, growing, sensing, thinking, speaking, feeling, and interacting child. Play is a guide to measuring the cognitive maturity and social growth of a child. Reciprocally, it is important for parents and significant others in the child's life to recognize the indelible significance of their play. Child symbolic play is ultimately the confluence of a social ecology of influences.

ACKNOWLEDGMENTS

This chapter summarizes selected aspects of my research, and portions of the text have appeared in previous scientific publications cited in the references. I thank S. Gaskins and A. Göncü for comments and S. Latif and C. Varron for assistance.

REFERENCES

Ainsworth, M. D. S., Blehar, M. C., Waters, E., & Wall, S. (1978). *Patterns of attachment: A psychological study of the Strange Situation*. Hillsdale, NJ: Lawrence Erlbaum Associates.

Aureli, T., & Colecchia, N. (1996). Day care experience and free play behavior in preschool children. *Journal of Applied Developmental Psychology, 17*, 1–17.

Baruch, C. (1991). *The influence of the mother–child relationship on the emergence of symbolic play*. Poster presented at the biennial meetings of the Society for Research in Child Development, Seattle, WA.

Belsky, J., Garduque, L., & Hrncir, E. (1984). Assessing performance, competence, and executive capacity in infant play: Relations to home environment and security of attachment. *Developmental Psychology, 20*, 406–417.

Belsky, J., Goode, M. K., & Most, R. K. (1980). Maternal stimulation and infant exploratory competence: Cross-sectional, correlational, and experimental analysis. *Child Development, 51*, 1163–1178.

Bornstein, M. H. (1975). Review of *Children in play therapy* by C. E. Moustakas. *Journal of Nervous and Mental Disease, 161*, 209–210.

Bornstein, M. H. (1985). Habituation of attention as a measure of visual information processing in human infants: Summary, systematization, and synthesis. In G. Gottlieb & N. A. Krasnegor (Eds.), *Measurement of audition and vision in the first year of postnatal life: A methodological overview* (pp. 253–300). Norwood, NJ: Ablex.

Bornstein, M. H. (1998). Stability in mental development from early life: Methods, measures, models, meanings and myths. In F. Simion & G. Butterworth (Eds.), *The development of sensory, motor and cognitive capacities in early infancy: From perception to cognition* (pp. 301–332). Hove, UK: Psychology Press.

Bornstein, M. H. (2002). Parenting infants. In M. H. Bornstein (Ed.), *Handbook of parenting: Vol. 1. Children and parenting* (2nd ed., pp. 3–43). Mahwah, NJ: Lawrence Erlbaum Associates.

Bornstein, M. H., DiPietro, J. A., Hahn, C.-H., Painter, K. M., Haynes, O. M., & Costigan, K. A. (2002). Prenatal cardiac function and postnatal cognitive development: An exploratory study. *Infancy, 3*, 475–494.

Bornstein, M. H., Haynes, O. M., Legler, J. M., O'Reilly, A. W., & Painter, K. M. (1997). Symbolic play in childhood: Interpersonal and environmental context and stability. *Infant Behavior and Development, 20*, 197–207.

Bornstein, M. H., Haynes, O. M., O'Reilly, A. W., & Painter, K. (1996). Solitary and collaborative pretense play in early childhood: Sources of individual variation in the development of representational competence. *Child Development, 67,* 2910–2929.

Bornstein, M. H., Haynes, O. M., Pascual, L., Painter, K. M., & Galperín, C. (1999). Play in two societies: Pervasiveness of process, specificity of structure. *Child Development, 70,* 317–331.

Bornstein, M. H., & Sawyer, J. (2005). Family systems. In K. McCartney & D. Phillips (Eds.), *Blackwell handbook on early childhood development* (pp. 381–398). Malden, MA: Blackwell.

Bornstein, M. H., Selmi, A. M., Haynes, O. M., Painter, K. M., & Marx, E. S. (1999). Representational abilities and the hearing status of child/mother dyads. *Child Development, 70,* 833–852.

Bornstein, M. H., & Tamis-LeMonda, C. S. (1997). Maternal responsiveness and infant mental abilities: Specific predictive relations. *Infant Behavior and Development, 20,* 283–296.

Bowlby, J. (1969). *Attachment and loss* (Vol. 1). New York: Basic Books.

Bretherton, I., O'Connell, B., Shore, C., & Bates, E. (1984). The effect of contextual variation on symbolic play: Development from 20 to 28 months. In I. Bretherton (Ed.), *Symbolic play: The development of social understanding* (pp. 271–298). New York: Academic.

Bronfenbrenner, U., & Morris, P. A. (1998). The ecology of developmental processes. In R. M. Lerner (Ed.) & W. Damon (Series Ed.), *Handbook of child psychology: Vol. 1. Theoretical models of human development* (5th ed., pp. 993–1028). New York: Wiley.

Cassirer, E. (1951). *The philosophy of symbolic forms.* New Haven, CT: Yale University Press.

Damast, A. M., Tamis-LeMonda, C. S., & Bornstein, M. H. (1996). Mother–child play: Sequential interactions and the relation between maternal beliefs and behaviors. *Child Development, 67,* 1752–1766.

DeLoache, J. S., & Burns, N. M. (1994). Symbolic functioning in preschool children. *Journal of Applied Developmental Psychology, 15,* 513–527.

Dockett, S. (1998). Constructing understandings through play in the early years. *International Journal of Early Years Education, 6,* 105–116.

Dunn, J., & Wooding, C. (1977). Play in the home and its implications for learning. In B. Tizard & D. Harvey (Eds.), *Biology of play* (pp. 45–58). Philadelphia: Lippincott.

Eisert, D., & Lamorey, S. (1996). Play as a window on child development: The relationship between play and other developmental domains. *Early Education and Development, 7,* 221–235.

Fagen, R. (Ed.). (1981). *Animal play behavior.* New York: Oxford University Press.

Farver, J. (1993). Cultural differences in scaffolding pretend play: A comparison of American and Mexican mother–child and sibling–child pairs. In K. MacDonald (Ed.), *Parent–child play: Descriptions and implications* (pp. 349–366). Albany: State University of New York Press.

Farver, J., & Howes, C. (1993). Cultural differences in American and Mexican mother–child pretend play. *Merrill-Palmer Quarterly, 39,* 344–358.

Farver, J., Kim, Y. K., & Lee, Y. (1995). Cultural differences in Korean and Anglo-American preschoolers' social interaction and play behaviors. *Child Development, 66*, 1088–1099.

Farver, J., & Wimbarti, S. (1995). Indonesian children's play with their mothers and older siblings. *Child Development, 66*, 1493–1503.

Fein, G. G. (1975). A transformational analysis of pretending. *Developmental Psychology, 11*, 291–296.

Fein, G. G., & Apfel, N. (1979). The development of play: Style, structure, and situations. *Genetic Psychology Monographs, 99*, 231–250.

Fein, G. G., & Fryer, M. G. (1996). Maternal contributions to early symbolic play competence. *Developmental Review, 15*, 367–381.

Feldman, R., & Greenbaum, C. W. (1997). Affect regulation and synchrony in mother–infant play as precursors to the development of symbolic competence. *Infant Mental Health Journal, 18*, 4–23.

Fenson, L., & Ramsay, D. (1980). Decentration and integration of the child's play in the second year. *Child Development, 51*, 71–178.

Fiese, B. H. (1990). Playful relationships: A contextual analysis of mother–toddler interaction and symbolic play. *Child Development, 61*, 1648–1656.

Fogel, A., & Thelen, E. (1987). Development of early expressive and communicative action: Reinterpreting the evidence from a dynamic systems perspective. *Developmental Psychology, 23*, 747–761.

Garvey, C. (1990). *Play.* Cambridge, MA: Harvard University Press.

Gaskins, S. (1996). How Mayan parental theories come into play. In S. Harkness & C. M. Super (Eds.), *Parents' cultural belief systems: Their origins, expressions, and consequences* (pp. 345–363). New York: Guilford.

Gauvain, M., & Rogoff, B. (1989). Collaborative problem solving and children's planning skills. *Developmental Psychology, 25*, 139–151.

Göncü, A., Tuermer, U., Jain, J., & Johnson, D. (1999). Children's play as cultural activity. In A. Göncü (Ed.), *Children's engagement in the world: Sociocultural perspectives* (pp. 148–170). New York: Cambridge University Press.

Goodnow, J. J. (1988). Parents' ideas, actions, and feelings: Models and methods from developmental and social psychology. *Child Development, 59*, 286–320.

Greenfield, P. M., & Suzuki, L. K. (1998). Culture and human development: Implications for parenting, education, pediatrics, and mental health. In I. E. Sigel & K. A. Renninger (Vol. Eds.) & W. Damon (Series Ed.), *Handbook of child psychology: psychology in practice* (5th ed., pp. 1059–1109). New York: Wiley.

Haight, W. L, Parke, R. D., & Black, J. E. (1997). Mothers' and fathers' beliefs about and spontaneous participation in their toddlers' pretend play. *Merrill-Palmer Quarterly, 43*, 271–290.

Haight, W., Parke, R., Black, J. E., & Trousdale, T. (1993). *Mothers' and fathers' beliefs about pretend play.* Unpublished manuscript, University of Utah, Salt Lake City.

Haight, W., Wang, X., Fung, H., Williams, K., & Mintz, J. (1995, April). *The ecology of everyday pretending in three cultural communities.* Paper presented at the meeting of the Society for Research in Child Development, Indianapolis, IN.

Haight, W. L., & Miller, P. J. (1993). *Pretending at home.* Albany: State University of New York Press.

Harding, G. C., Kromelow, S., Stilson, S., & Touris, M. (1995). First partnerships: The co-construction of intentional communication. *Early Child Development and Care, 3*, 19–33.

Harding, G. C., Weissmann, L., Kromelow, S., & Stilson, S. R. (1997). Shared minds: How mothers and infants co-construct early patterns of choice within intentional communication partnerships. *Infant Mental Health Journal, 18*, 24–39.

Harding, G. C., Weissmann, L., Noll, L., Lynn, L., & Stilson, S. R. (2001). *First choices: Parent–child communication as the first context for the development of intention*. Manuscript in revision for publication.

Harkness, S., & Super, C. M. (1986). The cultural structuring of children's play in a rural African community. In K. Blanchard (Ed.), *The many faces of play* (pp. 96–103). Champaign, IL: Human Kinetics.

Harris, P. L. (1994). Understanding pretence. In C. Lewis & P. Mitchell (Eds.), *Children's early understanding of mind* (pp. 235–239). Hove, UK: Lawrence Erlbaum Associates.

Howes, C., & Stewart, P. (1987). Child's play with adults, toys, and peers: An examination of family and child care influences. *Developmental Psychology, 23*, 423–430.

Howes, C., Unger, O., & Matheson, C. C. (1992). *The collaborative construction of pretend*. Albany: State University of New York Press.

Jeffree, D. M., & McConkey, R. (1976). An observation scheme for recording children's imaginative doll play. *Journal of Child Psychology and Psychiatry, 17*, 189–197.

Jennings, K. D., & Connors, R. E. (1989). Mothers' interactional style and children's competence at 3 years. *International Journal of Behavioral Development, 12*, 155–175.

Jones, B., & Reynolds, G. (1992). *The play's the thing: Teachers' role in children's play*. New York: Teachers College Press.

Kaplan, B. (1961). An approach to the problem of symbolic representation: Nonverbal and verbal. *Journal of Communication, 11*, 52–62.

Labrell, F., & Simeoni, F. (1992). *ZPD revisited: Parental presence may be enough*. Paper presented at the International Conference for Infant Studies, April Miami, FL.

Leont'ev, A. N. (1981a). *Activity, consciousness and personality*. Englewood Cliffs, NJ: Prentice-Hall.

Leont'ev, A. N. (1981b). The problem of activity in psychology. In J. V. Wertsch (Ed.), *The concept of activity in Soviet psychology* (pp. 37–71). Armonk, NY: M. E. Sharpe.

Lerner, R. M., Rothbaum, F., Boulos, S., & Castellino, D. R. (2002). Developmental systems perspective on parenting. In M. H. Bornstein (Ed.), *Handbook of parenting: Vol. 2. Biology and ecology of parenting* (2nd ed., pp. 285–309). Mahwah, NJ: Lawrence Erlbaum Associates.

Levine, J. B. (1988). Play in the context of the family. *Journal of Family Psychology, 2*, 164–187.

Lillard, A. S., & Witherington, D. C. (2004). Mothers' behavior modifications during pretense and their possible signal value for toddlers. *Developmental Psychology, 40*, 95–113.

MacDonald, K. (Ed.). (1993). *Parent–child play: Descriptions and implications*. New York: State University of New York Press.

McCune, L., Dipane, D., Fireoved, R., & Fleck, M. (1994). Play: A context for mutual regulation within mother–child interaction. In A. Slade & D. P. Wolfe (Eds.), *Children at play* (pp. 148–166). New York: Oxford University Press.

McLane, J. B. (2003). *"Does not." "Does too." Thinking about play in the early childhood classroom.* Chicago: Erikson Institute.

New, R. S. (1989). The family context of Italian infant care. *Early Child Development and Care, 50,* 99–108.

New, R. S. (1994). Child's play—*una cosa naturale*: An Italian perspective. In J. L. Roopnarine, J. E. Johnson, & F. H. Hooper (Eds.), *Children's play in diverse cultures* (pp. 123–147). Albany: State University of New York Press.

Nicolich, L. M. (1977). Beyond sensori-motor intelligence: Assessment of symbolic maturity through analysis of pretend play. *Merrill-Palmer Quarterly, 23,* 89–99.

Noll, L. M., & Harding, C. B. (2003). The relationship of mother–child interaction and the child's development of symbolic play. *Infant Mental Health Journal, 24,* 557–570.

O'Connell, B., & Bretherton, I. (1984). Toddlers' play, alone and with mother: The role of maternal guidance. In I. Bretherton (Ed.), *Symbolic play: The development of social understanding* (pp. 337–368). Orlando, FL: Academic.

Papoušek, M., & Von Gontard, A. (Eds.). (2003). *Spiel und Kreativität in der frühen Kindheit* [Play and creativity in growing children]. Munich, Germany: Pfeiffer bei Klett-Cotta.

Piaget, J. (1962). *Play, dreams and imitation in childhood.* New York: Norton.

Power, T. G. (2000). *Play and exploration in children and animals.* Mahwah, NJ: Lawrence Erlbaum Associates.

Rogoff, B. (1990). *Apprenticeship in thinking.* New York: Oxford University Press.

Rogoff, B., & Gardner, W. (1984). Adult guidance of cognitive development. In B. Rogoff & J. Lave (Eds.), *Everyday cognitions: Its development in social context* (pp. 15–27). Cambridge, MA: Harvard University Press.

Rogoff, B., Mistry, J., Göncü, A., & Mosier C., (1993). Guided participation in cultural activity by toddlers and caregivers. *Monographs of the Society for Research in Child Development, 58*(7, Serial No. 236).

Rogoff, B., Mosier, C., Mistry, J., & Göncü, A. (1993). Toddlers' guided participation with their caregivers in cultural activity. In E. A. Forman, N. Minick, & C. A. Stone (Eds.), *Contexts for learning: Sociocultural dynamics in children's development* (pp. 230–253). New York: Oxford University Press.

Roopnarine, J. L., Johnson, J. E., & Hooper, F. H. (Eds.). (1994). *Children's play in diverse cultures.* Albany: State University of New York Press.

Rubin, K. H., Stewart, S. L., & Chen, X. (1995). Parents of aggressive and withdrawn children. In M. H. Bornstein (Ed.), *Handbook of parenting* (Vol. 1, pp. 255–284). Mahwah, NJ: Lawrence Erlbaum Associates, Inc.

Schwartzman, H. (1978). *Transformations: The anthropology of children's play.* New York: Plenum.

Slade, A. (1987a). A longitudinal study of maternal involvement and symbolic play during the toddler period. *Child Development, 58,* 367–375.

Slade, A. (1987b). Quality of attachment and early symbolic play. *Developmental Psychology, 23,* 78–85.

Slaughter, D., & Dombrowski, J. (1989). Cultural continuities and discontinuities: Impact on social and pretend play. In M. N. Block & A. D. Pellegrini (Eds.), *The ecological content of children's play* Norwood, NJ: Ablex, 282–310.

Smolucha, L., & Smolucha, F. (1998). The social origins of mind: Post-Piagetian perspectives on pretend play. In O. N. Saracho & B. Spodek (Eds.), *Multiple perspectives on play in early childhood education* (pp. 34–58). Albany: State University of New York Press.

Spieker, S. J., & Booth, C. L. (1988). Maternal antecedents of attachment quality. In J. Belsky & T. Nezworski (Eds.), *Clinical implications of attachment* (pp. 95–135). Hillsdale, NJ: Lawrence Erlbaum Associates.

Stilson, S. R., & Harding, C. G. (1997). Early social context as it relates to symbolic play: A longitudinal investigation. *Merrill-Palmer Quarterly, 43*, 682–693.

Tamis-LeMonda, C. S., & Bornstein, M. H. (1989). Habituation and maternal encouragement of attention in infancy as predictors of toddler language, play, and representational competence. *Child Development, 60*, 738–751.

Tamis-LeMonda, C. S., & Bornstein, M. H. (1991). Individual variation, correspondence, stability, and change in mother and toddler play. *Infant Behavior and Development, 14*, 143–162.

Tamis-LeMonda, C. S., & Bornstein, M. H. (1993a). Antecedents of exploratory competence at one year. *Infant Behavior and Development, 16*, 423–439.

Tamis-LeMonda, C. S., & Bornstein, M. H. (1993b). Play, and its relations to other mental functions in the child. In M. H. Bornstein & A. W. O'Reilly (Eds.), *The role of play in the development of thought* (pp. 17–28). San Francisco: Jossey-Bass.

Tamis-LeMonda, C. S., & Bornstein, M. H. (1994). Specificity in mother–toddler language-play relations across the second year. *Developmental Psychology, 30*, 283–292.

Tamis-LeMonda, C. S., Bornstein, M. H., Cyphers, L., Toda, S., & Ogino, M. (1992). Language and play at one year: A comparison of toddlers and mothers in the United States and Japan. *International Journal of Behavioral Development, 15*, 19–42.

Tamis-LeMonda, C. S., Chen, L. A., & Bornstein, M. H. (1998). Mothers' knowledge about children's play and language development: Short-term stability and interrelations. *Developmental Psychology, 34*, 115–124.

Tamis-LeMonda, C. S., Damast, A. M., & Bornstein, M. H. (1994). What do mothers know about the developmental nature of play? *Infant Behavior and Development, 17*, 341–345.

Tamis-LeMonda, C. S., Katz, J. C., & Bornstein, M. H. (2002). Infant play: Functions and partners. In M. Lewis & A. Slater (Eds.), *Introduction to infant development* (pp. 229–243). New York: Oxford University Press.

Thelen, E., & Smith, L. B. (1998). Dynamic systems theories. In R. M. Lerner (Ed.) & W. Damon (Series Ed.), *Handbook of child psychology: Vol. 1. Theoretical models of human development* (5th ed., pp. 563–634). New York: Wiley.

Tingley, E. C. (1994). Symbolic play in the interactions of young children and mothers with a history of affective illness: A longitudinal study. In A. Slade & D. P. Wolfe (Eds.), *Children at play* (pp. 286–306). New York: Oxford University Press.

Toda, S., Azuma, H., & Bornstein, M. H. (1993). Juu-san ka getsu no asobi oyobi gengo ni oyobosu go ka getsu no hahaoya no hannō no eikyō [The effects of maternal responsiveness on infant play and language development at 5 and 13 months]. *Japanese Journal of Developmental Psychology, 4,* 126–135.

Trivers, R. (1986). *Social evolution.* Menlo Park, CA: Benjamin Cummings.

Udwin, O., & Shmukler, D. (1981). The influence of sociocultural, economic, and home background factors on children's ability to engage in imaginative play. *Developmental Psychology, 17,* 66–72.

Unger, O., & Howes, C. (1988). Mother–child interactions and symbolic play between toddlers and their adolescent or mentally retarded mothers. *Occupational Therapy Journal of Research, 8,* 237–249.

Užgiris, I. C., Benson, J. B., Kruper, J. C., & Vasek, M. E. (1989). Contextual influences on imitative interactions between mothers and infants. In J. J. Lockman & N. L. Hazen (Eds.), *Action in social context: Perspectives on early development* (pp. 103–127). New York: Plenum.

Venuti, P., Rossi, G., Spagnoletti, M. S., Famulare, E., & Bornstein, M. H. (1997). Gioco non simbolico e simbolico a 20 mesi: Comportamenti di gioco del babino e della madre [Nonsymbolic and symbolic play in children 20 months of age: Play behavior of the child and mother]. *Età Evolutiva, 58,* 25–35.

Vibbert, M., & Bornstein, M. H. (1989). Specific associations between domains of mother–child interaction and toddler referential language and pretense play. *Infant Behavior and Development, 12,* 163–184.

von Bertalanffy, L. (1968). *Organismic psychology theory.* Barre, MA: Clark University Barre Publishers.

Vygotsky, L. (1978a). *Mind in society.* Cambridge, MA: Harvard University Press.

Vygotsky, L. S. (1978b). Play and its role in the mental development of the child. In J. S. Bruner, A. Jolly, & K. Sylva (Eds.), *Play: Its role in development and evolution* (pp. 537–554). New York: Basic Books.

Wachs, T. D. (1993). Multidimensional correlates of individual variability in play and exploration. In M. H. Bornstein & A. W. O'Reilly (Eds.), *The role of play in the development of thought* (pp. 43–53). San Francisco: Jossey-Bass.

Watson, M. W., & Fisher, K. W. (1977). A developmental sequence of agent use in late infancy. *Child Development, 48,* 828–836.

6

Guided Participation: How Mothers Structure and Children Understand Pretend Play

Angeline Lillard

University of Virginia

Pretend play is a significant human invention. Despite occasional reports of other animals appearing to pretend, nonhuman animals clearly do not do what young children do, frequently using one object as if it were another, attributing imaginary properties to objects, and impersonating other characters. Several hallmarks of human civilization appear to arise from the same cognitive underpinnings as pretend play. The philosopher Walton (1990) claimed that all human art forms are rooted in pretend play. To create and appreciate art, drama, and music, one suspends the here and now. Hypothetical reasoning also shares this with pretending: In both, one temporarily suspends the present situation to imagine and partake in a different one (Harris, 2000). Language is also akin to pretending: In both genres, one entity (a word or object) represents another (Piaget, 1945/1962).

Understanding minds has also been related to pretending, because representing mental representations appears to underlie both abilities (Flavell, Flavell, & Green, 1987; Forguson & Gopnik, 1988; Leslie, 1987). On this account, children come to understand mental representation first in pretend, and then apply that understanding to more difficult mental states like belief. However, results from many experiments suggest that children do not understand mental representation in the pretense domain any earlier than they understand mental representation in the domain of belief (age 4). When presented with a troll who lacked a mental representation of a kangaroo (because he was from the faraway Land of the Trolls, and had never seen or heard of one), but who was nonetheless hopping like a kangaroo, 4-year-olds frequently claimed he was pretending to be a kangaroo (Lillard, 1993). Although when given nonconflicting situations children sometimes do evidence some appreciation of the mind's role in pretense (discussed in Lillard, 2001b), they generally do not seem to see mental representation or even the mind as essential to pretending (Berguno & Bowler, 2004; Lillard, 1996, 1998; Mitchell, 2000; Sobel, 2004; Sobel & Lillard, 2002). This work has suggested that young children view pretending more as an action than a mental representational state.

Pretending and understanding minds are empirically related: The frequency and level at which children pretend has been correlated with their passing theory of mind tasks, even when language abilities are controlled for (Astington & Jenkins, 1995; Lalonde & Chandler, 1995; Lillard, 2001a; Youngblade & Dunn, 1995). However, not all pretending is associated with theory of mind understanding: The relation is seen with social pretend play in particular (for further discussion, see Harris, 2000). One possibility is that social pretending leads children to engage in more perspective taking, which assists theory of mind (Lillard, 1998). Yet another possibility, perfectly compatible with this first one, is that the roots of the correlation lie even earlier, in the early pretend interactions that children have with their mothers (Lillard, 2001b). Perhaps part of the reason for the correlation between early pretend play and understanding mental representation stems from pretending sensitizing young children to certain observed behaviors (like looking and smiling) that then support theory of mind understandings.

Although once discussed primarily as a solitary activity (Piaget, 1945/1962), researchers are increasingly noting the social origins of pretending (Göncü, 1993; Göncü, Patt, & Kouba, 2004; Smolucha & Smolucha, 1998; Tomasello & Rakoczy, 2003). Mothers begin to pretend in front of children when they are as young as 8 months of age (Haight & Miller, 1993; Kavanaugh, Whittington, & Cerbone, 1983; Tamis-LeMonda & Bornstein, 1991). Early pretending between mothers and children can be seen in the context of intersubjectivity and shared meaning (Trevarthen & Hubley, 1978). Because pretending is an intersubjective act—something mothers do to share, not because they enjoy doing it on their own—mothers must somehow communicate meaning to their children when they pretend. How they do so poses an extremely interesting problem.

Take the case, for example, of a mother pretending to drink from a wooden block in front of her 18-month-old. What is the child to make of such an activity? If the child takes the activity literally, the interpretation should be, "Mother is drinking from a cup." Yet if the child's interpretation is literal, then his or her representation of what a cup is, and what a block is, should become confused (Leslie, 1987). Instead, the child must know to mark the activity as pretense, and temporarily keep the "cup" representation quarantined from its usual referents, applying it to the block only for this one session. Later, that same block could become a bed or a car. At issue is what signals to the child to keep events like this quarantined from representations of the real world, so that real-world representations and pretend ones do not become intermingled. This is an important issue, because if children did not keep pretend and real representations separate, their understanding of the real world could become seriously garbled by pretense. When their mother drank from a block, they might interpret that as a real and normal thing to do with blocks. When they were thirsty, they might go and get a block instead of a cup. This confusion obviously would not serve children well.

In this chapter, I discuss possible ways in which children could differentiate between pretend and real. I begin by discussing the potential contribution of content cues, but conclude that content cues alone could not suffice. I then review results from several experiments examining the potential contribution of pretender behavior to interpreting events as pretense. These experiments point out how pretend behaviors differ from real behaviors, and explore the extent to which those differences appear to cue observers of different ages to the fact that someone is pretending. Finally I discuss the potential contribution of three of the toddler's social cognitive skills to pretense interpretation: joint attention, social referencing, and reading intentions.

WRONG CONTENT AS A CUE TO PRETENSE

The easy and obvious answer to how a child can keep pretend representations separate from real ones is content: The child knows the event is pretense because he or she knows reality. In other words, he or she knows what a cup is, and knows what a block is, and knows the basic movements of drinking. Because an atypical object is involved in the event, the child automatically interprets the event as pretense. Clearly this is sometimes the case: Content cues can and surely do lead to some pretense interpretations. Miniaturization, for example, sometimes can cue pretense (Sutton-Smith, 1983). However, I would argue that content cues cannot act alone, and that in fact for very young children content cues often would not suffice to signal pretense.

Why are content cues insufficient to signal pretense? For one, young children's world knowledge is relatively limited. Young children frequently see new events, including familiar behaviors in which new objects are employed, but they do not take all such events to be pretense. If they did, their real-world representations would be jeopardized. The first time a young child saw someone drink from a mug instead of a cup, the child would assume the person was pretending. Logically, this could not generally happen, or children would learn very little about what is real.

Second, the people young children observe sometimes make mistakes, and if content alone signaled pretense, children would interpret such mistakes as pretense. Sometimes, although I have finished my coffee, I pick up my mug and try to drink a little more. I am not pretending. Pretending involves representing a situation one way, when one in fact knows it is another way. Mistakenly trying to drink from an empty mug is clearly different from pretending to drink coffee, and children need to learn to distinguish such events or they will overextend pretending.

Research has shown that even 18-month-olds understand failed intentions, and do not appear to interpret mistakes as pretending. When 18-month-olds observe mistakes, they in a sense fix them, by enacting the intended act instead of faithfully imitating the failed action (Meltzoff, 1995). Rakoczy and his colleagues provided an excellent example of this with somewhat older children. Two-year-olds watched an experimenter who was acting frustrated while trying to write with a pen that had a top on. When subsequently given the pen, these children removed the top and really wrote (Rakoczy, Tomasello, & Striano, 2004). Despite the content being wrong in this situation (because there was no ink coming out of the pen), children did not interpret the failed writing action as pretense. Instead, they correctly interpreted the actions as revealing a failed intention. Young children do not incorrectly interpret all failed acts (some of which are cases of wrong content, like the lack of ink in the pen or a lack of coffee in one's cup) as instances of pretense.

Given that children can correctly interpret some actions with wrong content as mistakes, and can also interpret actions with novel content, something besides content must assist pretense interpretations. Two less noted sources of information are pretender behavior and the child's own social cognitive skills. These might apply to a wider range of situations than content, in that (a) they can serve even when the content is new, and (b) they can help to differentiate pretense from mistaken action.

PRETENDER BEHAVIOR AS A SOURCE OF INFORMATION

Changes in pretenders' behavior when pretending are another potential source of information signaling pretense. The literature suggests some potential behavioral changes that might occur in when pretending. Among animals, the closest analog of pretending is play-fighting, which is, in a sense, pretending to have a fight. Play-fighting is not exactly pretending, in that it involves a relatively limited behavioral repertoire and (at least in animals) no substitute objects, but it does require a clear cue to the fact that one is playing, not fighting for real (Bateson, 1955/1972). Bateson pointed out that truncated actions, like a playful nip instead of an actual bite, could serve to signal play in animals. Sutton-Smith (1983) also noted that exaggerated actions and cyclical repetitions of actions might cue pretense. Bekoff (1995) identified particular movement patterns among dogs, baby wolves, and baby coyotes (a bow and head-shaking) that appear to be nonrandomly placed within play-fighting sequences (e.g., after a play bite). Such behaviors may indicate "This is play" to conspecifics.

Among chimpanzees and other nonhuman primates, a "play face" is exhibited (Eibl-Eibesfeldt, 1989; Symons & Symons, 1984; Van Hoof, 1972), apparently indicating nonaggression. Vocal signs of play have been noted among some mammals. Simonet (2001) tape-recorded a huffy, high-pitched noise among dogs apparently anticipating play, and others have recorded high-pitched noises among rodents particularly prior to play (Knutson, Burgdorf, & Panksepp, 1998). In sum, animals' movements, facial expressions, and vocalizations might serve to indicate that their pseudo-fighting actions are playful, not to be taken as the real actions for which they stand (Bateson, 1955/1972).

Among humans, the extension of activities that are considered pretense is much broader than play-fighting, but there has been little discussion of what behaviors might cue pretense. Piaget (1945/1962), in a study of the onset of pretending, claimed that, "the smile of the child is enough to show that [he/she] is perfectly conscious of pretending" (p. 32). Garvey and Berndt (1975) noted that pretense episodes are sometimes signaled by giggles, and studies of play-fighting in humans have suggested that laughter is often a cue that a fight is not real (Boulton, 1993; Smith, 1997). Others have examined vocal signals. In one study with 11- and 15-month-olds, parents varied the pitch and pitch range of their speech across pretend and instructional situations (Reissland & Snow, 1996). However, in this study the pretend situation involved a doll, whereas their real situation involved the child alone. Perhaps the pitch differences stemmed from how parents talk to dolls versus children. Sound effects are another potential cue to pretense in humans (DeLoache & Plaetzer, 1985), but whether they do cue pretense has not to my knowledge been formally studied.

Linguistic cues to pretending are the most researched topic in the area of how pretend differs from real, and this research has focused on preschool-aged children. For preschoolers, pretense is often accompanied by increases in the use of past-tense verbs, future auxiliaries, the subjunctive tense, modals, temporal expressions, formal proposals, and tags (Auwarter, 1986; Garvey, 1990; Garvey & Kramer, 1989; Giffin, 1984). Such means of signaling pretense seem unlikely to be effective with young children just learning language. Preschoolers also directly specify the pretend mode with the word "pretend," but not regularly until about 5 years of age (Lloyd & Goodwin, 1995; Schwartzman, 1978). Pinkham and I (Pinkham & Lillard, submitted) have been analyzing children's use of the word in the CHILDES database, and finding that the word first appears shortly before age 3, but is used mainly to direct action or make pretend–real contrasts. In one study examining how parents' verbal behavior changes when they pretend with toddlers, Reissland (1998) found that parents were particularly likely to use indirect methods of persuasion (i.e., "Do you think she's thirsty?") with 11- and 15-month-olds while operating in the pretense mode. Whether such linguistic changes help children interpret pretense as pretense is an open question; it does seem that such indirect constructions convey the open possibilities that characterize pretending.

In sum, the literature from animals and humans suggests that there may be behavioral cues to pretense. However, until recently we have known little about just what parents do when they are pretending with young children, which might serve to indicate that their actions should not be taken for real. This is a crucial issue, as without a means to discriminate pretend from real, young children's real-world representations would become very confused. Researchers have studied the linguistic means by which preschoolers designate pretending to other preschoolers, but there has been very little investigation of extralinguistic cues to pretending, and on the issue of how mothers signal pretending to young children. Several recent experiments in our laboratory have aimed to shed light on this problem. This work reveals how mothers' pretend behaviors differ from their real ones, and which of those behaviors appear to signal pretense.

How Pretend Behaviors Differ From Real Behaviors

To address how mothers' behaviors differ across real and pretend situations, we asked mothers to have a snack for real and for pretend with their 18-month-olds for 2 minutes each (Lillard & Witherington, 2004). This age was chosen because it is a pivotal age in the onset of pretense. Prior to that age, children only occasionally do something that might be considered pretense (like hold a spoon to a doll's mouth). From 18 to 24 months, such events occur with increasing frequency, and pretending is in full swing by age 2 (Haight & Miller, 1993; McCune, 1995). Which condition came first was counterbalanced across children, and no mother knew a pretend condition was coming until just before it began.

The snack implements were a metal serving bowl and pitcher, a napkin, and plastic cups and bowls for both mother and child. The only difference across conditions was the color of the plastic cups and bowls, and the presence of Cheerios and juice in the real condition. Tightly controlled situations allowed us to precisely measure how behavior differs across pretend and real contexts, not as a function of social partner, size of dishes, and so on, but solely as a function of pretense and real.

Mothers were filmed through one-way glass to minimize self-consciousness. We told them our primary interest was in social interaction, particularly in how babies respond to their parents' actions. A camera behind the mother captured the baby's behavior. In one experiment, the Flock of Birds motion monitor provided (x,y,z) coordinates of the mother's hand position at each millisecond; in another, the Computer Speech Laboratory provided estimates of the pitch and amplitude of mothers' voices throughout the sessions (Lillard et al., in press, Exp. 1). Videotapes of the mothers were coded and analyzed for condition differences in various aspects of smiling, looking, snack-related movements, and verbal and vocal behavior. Reliability coding was conducted on at least 20% of the sample in both conditions and levels of agreement were high (85%–94%).

Significant differences in pretend and real behavior were found across several experiments on almost every dimension we examined, revealing a wealth of linguistic and extralinguistic dimensions on which pretend behaviors differ from real ones. First, when mothers were pretending, they smiled more than when they had snacks for real. Mothers also smiled a lot when really having snacks with their toddlers, however, so smiling was not a unique cue to pretending.

Three additional aspects of smiling were particularly characteristic of pretense. For one, smiles in pretense lasted longer on average than real smiles did. In keeping with this, in pretense more of those smiles were over 4 seconds in length. The significance of this might lie in the smiles being signals, rather than expressions of pleasure. Ekman and his colleagues noted that faked facial expressions tend to last over 4 seconds (Ekman & Friesen, 1982). Many of mothers' pretend smiles may not be felt, but might instead be meant to serve as cues. Another difference in smiles was that pretense smiles were more frequently placed in particular places in the behavior stream. Being American, our mothers smiled frequently when their young children performed actions. However, smiles after their own actions were rare in the real condition, and much more common in the pretend condition. A common pattern in pretense was for mothers to look at the child, perform some pretend act (like pouring), then break into a pronounced grin. This sequence rarely occurred in the real condition. We interpret this behavior on the part of the mother as creating conditions for children to engage in social referencing, as an aid to how to interpret pretense acts. This possibility is discussed at the end of the chapter.

Looking behavior also varied across conditions. When mothers were pretending to have a snack, they spent a much greater proportion of time looking at the child than they did when really having a snack. The function of this looking is not yet clear. One might dismiss it as being due to task demands. Obviously in the real situation, task demands required more looking to the task: The mother had to be careful not to spill. However, the fact that any specific difference in pretense and real behaviors is required by the situation does not diminish the possibility that the difference could serve as a cue to pretense, and the difference is therefore still of interest. Why mothers looked more at babies when they were pretending and whether looking facilitates pretense interpretation are prime questions for further research.

In terms of verbal behavior, mothers used the word *pretend* on average about once in each session, but many mothers never used the word. Mothers talked more when pretending to snack than when snacking for real. This was not simply due to having food in the mouth: Mothers did not seem hesitant to talk at the moments when they were eating real Cheerios. Further, pretend eating also involved mouth movements that could make simultaneously talking difficult. Thus the increase in talking in pretense did not appear to be solely a function of not really eating.

What did they talk about? We had expected that mothers would talk more about Cheerios and juice, the imaginary objects, when those objects were not really there. In fact, the proportions of references to Cheerios and juice were equivalent across conditions. What increased (proportionately, to eliminate the confound with overall talking) was talking about the pretend actions and, to a lesser extent, the real objects involved in both conditions (cup, bowl). Perhaps by labeling the support structures for pretense that are real (cup, bowl) and that at least have much of the form of the real (eat, drink), mothers minimized the potential for "referential abuse" that would occur were pretend objects mislabeled (referring to juice when there is nothing there). Clearly some referential abuse occurs, and how children handle it is an interesting issue for further research.

We have also analyzed transcripts using Pennebaker and his associates' Linguistic Inquiry and Word Count program (Pennebaker, Francis, & Booth, 2001), which tallies words with reference to particular concepts. This analysis revealed that although parents talked even more in pretense, they used fewer unique words than in real snacks. Pretending was thus characterized by repetition of words. These repetitions appeared to be focused on providing verbal descriptions of pretense actions and reactions. In pretending there was also significantly more use of pronouns referring to "we" and "us," a verbal acknowledgment that pretending is a joint endeavor.

In terms of other vocal behavior, sound effects were very common in pretense, and close to nonexistent in real. When pretending, mothers mimicked the sounds of drinking, eating, juice pouring, and Cheerios falling into the bowl. Mothers also laughed a bit more in pretense, and used somewhat more comment noises ("mmm"), but these differences were not large.

Analyses of the Computer Speech Laboratory data, revealed, interestingly, that differences across pretend and real in terms of pitch were not particularly strong at 15 months, and were nonexistent by 24 months. This was surprising in light of the high-frequency noises involved in animal play-fighting, and in light of other studies of mother–baby pretense. Like Reissland and Snow's (1996) participants, our mothers did use a slightly higher pitch when pretending than when snacking for real with

15-month-olds, but by 24 months that difference had disappeared. However, mothers showed significantly more variation in pitch during pretense at all ages, suggesting that a sing-songy quality in one's voice is characteristic of pretense. In addition, mothers spoke more loudly when they were pretending, and there was more variation in the amplitude of their speech within pretend versus real sessions.

Mothers' snack-related movements showed several very interesting differences in pretend versus real modes. First, mothers engaged in more samples of each snack-related behavior in pretense: They poured more, drank more, ate more, and so on. Second, in pretense the timing of these actions was odd. Most actions occurred in too short a time. This could have been either because the path of motion was short (on a par with truncated actions), or because the mother moved too fast; results from the motion monitor showed it was the latter. This was not merely because pretending mothers were less concerned about correctly hitting targets like the mouth, because mothers even moved the hand away from the mouth (to no specific target) faster after pretending to eat. This also suggests it was not merely due to the tiny weight difference in moving an empty hand versus a hand carrying a Cheerio. Mothers appeared to get into a fast mode in pretense, which affected all action within the scenario. This may be related to time often speeding up in imagined realms. Children can bake a cake, get a full night's sleep, and age several years in a matter of minutes in the pretend realm. Likewise in movies and theater, years can pass within a few minutes. This freedom from the usual constraints of time may be what is reflected in the acceleration of mothers' actions in pretense.

One behavior was mistimed in the opposite way: When pretending to eat, mothers held their hand at the mouth significantly longer than they did when really eating. This long hold action was unique to pretense eating; pretend pouring and drinking both involved hold actions that were of shorter durations than they were in the real condition. Keeping the hand at the mouth while opening and closing the lips may be a conventionalized presentation of eating. If someone were miming eating, attempting to portray the action as it really occurs, the hand would not remain at the mouth during the chewing stage. We know little about when children learn such conventionalized gestures.

Spatial exaggeration of action in pretense was seen only for pouring, and was revealed in two ways. The motion monitor revealed that in pretending to pour, mothers moved the pitcher to a higher position above the cup than they did when pouring for real. The second indicator of spatial exaggeration in pouring was that mothers rotated the pitcher to a significantly greater degree when pretending to pour than when really pouring. Perhaps other movements did not show spatial exaggeration because they occurred within a defined space, for example the distance between bowl to mouth. Spatial exaggeration can only occur when there is additional space in which to move.

In other work, we have shown that mothers' behaviors in pretend versus real snack situations change very little as their children go from 15 to 24 months of age (Lillard et al., in press). This age span goes from when children have relatively little experience with pretending to when most children pretend daily. Mothers did not appear to adjust their pretense behavior in response to these developments, but instead presented a uniform picture of pretending across this span of time. This is consistent with the fact that mother behavior also did not vary as a function of children's level of experience with pretending in the experiments just described. This apparent lack of adjustment suggests that mothers were not attending to their child's level of understanding, but rather that they were simply presenting standard pretense behavior.

In sum, our research has revealed several reliable and hitherto-unidentified changes in mothers' behavior when they pretend in front of young children. Mothers do not simply tell children, "I am pretending." Instead, they vary their behaviors in all kinds of ways that might signal pretense: They smile more after their own actions, look at the child more, move faster and on larger trajectories, use more "we" talk and repetition in speech, and so on. A next logical question is which of these changes might assist pretense interpretation.

Adult and Child Interpretation of Pretense Acts

A second line of research in my laboratory has examined which of the changes in mothers' behaviors appear to assist pretense interpretations by adults, children, and toddlers (Lillard & Witherington, 2004; Lillard et al., 2006; Richert & Lillard, 2004).

Toddler Understanding in the Snack Scenario. In several experiments we have examined relations between mothers' behavior during the snack episodes and their children's apparent understanding of the pretense scenario, as indicated by the baby's smiles, laughs, and snack-related actions. This is, of course, an imperfect measure of understanding, and in other ongoing experiments we are using clearer measures (Ma & Lillard, 2006). Within the seminaturalistic snack scenario, this was the best available measure of understanding, and it corresponded to mothers' judgments of how they knew their babies followed pretense, maternal report of baby's experience pretending, and naive judgements of whether babies understood their mothers' pretense.

Across the experiments completed thus far, a remarkably consistent picture of what relates to baby understanding (by this measure) has emerged. For babies with a good deal of experience pretending, mothers' smiles, in terms of frequency, placement in the behavior stream, and overall time spent smiling were associated with pretense understanding. Of course, this might be simply due to affective mirroring: Mother smiles, then baby smiles. Two findings seem counter to a mirroring interpretation. For one, the relation is seen only in the pretend scenario, not the real one. If children were apt to engage in affective mirroring, it seems unlikely that one would see it in only one condition. Second, the relation was not seen for children without experience pretending to have a snack. Pretend experience should not impact the possibility that children engage in affective mirroring during pretense. More recent sequential analyses by Nishida are also against this interpretation, as described later.

The relative frequency of individual looks to the child (vs. the task) was also significantly related to apparent understanding for more experienced pretenders: Mothers who engaged in more "gaze checking" had children who appeared to understand pretend more, but only if the children had more prior pretend experience. Perhaps this gaze checking allowed mothers to time other signals when children were looking at them. For babies with less pretending experience, the overall amount of time mother looked at the child while pretending, rather than the frequency of individual looks, was associated with understanding. In other words, when children are less experienced with pretending, mothers' looking at them "all the time" was associated with understanding. These associations with looking and smiling both support the potential importance of joint attention and social referencing for pretense understanding.

Regarding movement, an interesting picture emerges. For younger, less experienced babies, mothers' normative changes in how they moved when pretending (generally faster) was associated with less understanding. For these children, better understanding was associated with mothers moving more slowly when they pretended to pour, drink, and bring food to the mouth. For older children, on the other hand, mothers' faster movements appeared to assist pretense understanding. Perhaps once children are more familiar with the canonical forms of eating and drinking, faster movements do cue pretense.

Interestingly, some cues that one would expect to be very helpful were not. For example, sound effects seem like a very obvious cue to pretending: They do not sound like the real sound, and they often emanate from the wrong source. However, babies whose mothers used a lot of sound effects were no more likely to understand pretending than were those whose mothers used few or no sound effects. The verbal differences observed in mothers also appeared unimportant to understanding, which seems significant given the near-exclusive research focus on verbal cues to pretense among preschoolers. Mothers saying "We're pretending now" to 18-month-olds had no impact on their apparent understanding.

It is important to note that the evidence from these experiments is also against the notion that content cues are all babies need to decipher pretense. All of the babies in these studies had full access to the fact that there were no Cheerios and juice from very early in the session, as soon as their mother began to pour juice or serve Cheerios (10 seconds into the session on average). If content cues are solely responsible for pretense interpretation, then because all babies had access to the content, all babies should have understood that their mother was pretending. Yet about half of the 18-month-olds appeared mystified, and received low understanding scores because they did not smile nor partake in the snack-related behaviors. Further, the understanding scores children obtained were associated with particular behaviors on the part of their mothers, suggesting that above and beyond content cues, pretender behaviors do impact pretense understanding. This is contrary to many people's intuition about how we discriminate pretense and real acts.

Pretense Understanding With Older Children and Adults. With development, people appear to be assisted in pretense interpretation by somewhat different cues. To examine how well, and on what basis, older children and adults can judge pretense, our initial experiments used pilot tapes from 9 mothers having pretend and real snacks with their children in the laboratory (Richert & Lillard, 2004). We selected, for each mother, two complete actions that occurred in both pretend and real form (e.g., a real and pretend drink, and a real and pretend pour). These actions were randomly ordered on stimulus videotapes and shown to adult and child participants, who were asked to judge if each was pretend or real, and how they knew.

Because of the literature showing that short splices of behavior can be as indicative for social perception as longer ones (Ambady & Rosenthal, 1992), and that quick judgments can be more accurate than more considered ones (Wilson & Schooler, 1991), we used very short (8–12 second) splices of behaviors. Second, although young children did not appear to be greatly assisted by content cues, adults surely could be. To avoid the boring result that adults judged pretense events perfectly based on lack of real content, and to ensure we were getting at what behavioral signals might better assist interpretation, content cues (e.g., the Cheerios, or where there would have been Cheerios if it were real) were blocked by video editing. Finally, to examine the impact of visual or auditory cues on pretense judgments, subsamples of participants were given only auditory ($n = 22$) or only visual ($n = 20$) information.

Across all conditions, undergraduates discriminated pretense and real events at above chance levels, despite the lack of content cues and the fact that they were seeing very short splices of behavior. Because coding was not yet completed for the experiments previously described (showing how mothers' behaviors change), systematic selection of clips portraying specific behaviors that we later knew differed was impossible. What we were able to do, post hoc, was examine features of clips on which participants were more likely to be correct.

By these analyses, the important behavioral cues to pretense for adults were looking longer at the child, moving more rapidly, holding the hand at the mouth longer while eating, and producing sound effects. The impacts of some potential cues, like the number of pretend acts and duration of smiles, could not be properly judged because the clips were selected to show only one behavior, and smiles did not always begin and end within a clip.

A next step was to see whether children could discriminate pretense and real given short splices and no content cues. Two groups of 17 children, ages 4 and 7, were tested, along with 28 more undergraduates. Because 36 clips taxed 4-year-olds in pilot testing, and we were interested in how well children would perform when good cues to pretense were provided, the 18 clips on which adults had performed best (over 80% correct) were used.

All participants performed better than chance, and there was a developmental trend of significantly better performance from age 4 (64% correct) to age 7 (78% correct). The 7-year-olds' performance was not statistically different from that of the adults (85% correct in this experiment). Thus even with content cues covered, and even from just 8- to 12-second splices of behavior, even 4-year-olds were able to discriminate pretense acts based on behavioral cues provided by the mother.

Because children do not encode information as quickly as adults (Chi & Ceci, 1987), in a further experiment we used longer (20-second) splices of behavior to see if children's performance would improve given longer encoding time. In addition, because by then we had completed enough coding to know what behaviors systematically vary across pretend and real situations, we were able to choose clips that did or did not show typical pretense behavior. The strategy of choosing previously filmed clips over creating new clips with actors intentionally providing a specific cue and no others was taken because efforts to produce clips in which only one cue was present resulted in unnatural-seeming stimuli.

Thirty 3- to 5-year-olds and thirty 9- to 10-year-olds watched twenty 20-second clips, 10 showing real and 10 showing pretend behaviors from the snack scenarios filmed previously. Eight clips of each type were selected to show, as far as possible, a good example of a cue (like sound effects) with all other cues muted or nonexistent, and a poor example of that same cue. "As far as possible" is important to note here: It was not possible to find really good examples for all cues. Two additional clips were "loaded," showing good or poor examples of all the cues. The four cues selected were smiles (in pretense: long, and following own action for the good ones; short, and prior to own action as the poor cues; in real, the opposite features), looks (more at the child for good pretend cues and at the task for poor ones), movements (a fast eat approach and long eat hold as good pretend cues), and sound effects (good cues to pretense). As in the prior experiment, content cues were always covered with videoediting.

The results of this experiment provided striking evidence that particular behavioral changes on the part of mothers, identified by our first series of studies, signficantly impact children's identification of pretense acts even when content cues are not available. Children were significantly more likely to correctly interpret pretense as pretense when it was accompanied by what our previous work had shown to be normative pretense behaviors. In addition, when real clips were characterized by features normally present in pretense, children more often misjudged real clips, thinking those clips showed pretense.

In terms of which cues were most helpful, children performed best on three types of clips: ones that were loaded with good cues, ones in which mothers looked more at the normative location (child in pretend, and task in real), and ones that involved normative movements (e.g., faster approach in pretend). They performed less well, but still better than chance, on the clips selected as good examples of sound effect cues.

Finally, although overall older children performed better than younger children, there was no interaction of age by cue type. Children seemed to rely on the same cues across both these ages, but became more adept at using them with age.

In sum, the pretender looking more at the play partner appears to have a meaningful impact on understanding of pretense for toddlers, older children, and adults. This particular cue to pretense interpretation has to our knowledge never been mentioned in the literature, and further study is needed to determine why looking at the play partner apparently enables pretense interpretation. Smiling appeared to be important mainly for toddlers who already had experience pretending. Given the common intuition (shared by Piaget) that smiling helps us to decipher pretense, it is surprising to find that in controlled experimental situations it appears to have little or no impact for most observers. Oddly timed movements— fast approaches and long eating holds—do not appear to influence young children's understanding of pretense; in fact, if anything, investigation of the data suggested that fast movements interfered with young children's understanding. However, by preschool and through to adulthood, oddly timed movements do appear to assist pretense interpretation. Finally, sound effects, an obvious cue to pretense for adults, appeared to have no impact at all on toddlers, and only some impact on slightly older children. As a cue to pretense, sound effects appear to be discovered quite gradually.

TODDLER'S SOCIAL COGNITIVE SKILLS AS CONTRIBUTORS TO PRETENSE UNDERSTANDING

We have seen that mothers' behaviors during pretense do vary, and that some but not all of these variations appear to assist pretense interpretation at different ages. A final source of information for understanding of pretense is a set of social cognitive skills that infants have by 18 months that might facilitate interpretation. These are the skills of coordinated joint attention, social referencing, and reading intentions.

Coordinated Joint Attention

Pretend play is not something mothers generally engage in by themselves, for themselves; they engage in it with babies, and with the intent that babies get the meaning of their actions. An activity on the part of babies that appears to be crucial for getting the meaning in social interaction is coordinated joint attention (Bruner, 1995). Coordinated joint attention occurs when a child looks back and forth between an object, event, or situation, and another person (usually the experimenter or the mother; Bakeman & Adamson, 1984). Coordinated joint attention builds on an earlier understanding that pointing signifies to other people attentional focus on third objects (Moore & Dunham, 1995). This earlier understanding, which comes in around 12 months of age, shows an appreciation of attention but falls short in terms of coordinating one's attention with another person's. Perhaps not coincidentally, the mean age at which notable increases are seen in coordinated joint attention (18 months; Bakeman & Adamson, 1984) coincides with the mean age at which we see notable increases in the production of pretend play (Haight & Miller, 1993; McCune, 1995). Increasing coordinated joint attention, in the context of clear cues from the pretender, might assist correct pretense interpretation. Making correct interpretations of others' pretense, in turn, likely leads to more engagement in pretense on the part of the child.

Social Referencing

Around 1 year of age, children begin to engage in social referencing behaviors. When faced with ambiguous objects or situations, they appear to adopt the same attitude to the object or situation that a trusted other adopts. In the classic social referencing experiments (e.g., with the visual cliff), the emphasis was on looking to the caregiver and visually reading his or her response to the situation (Sorce, Emde, Campos, & Klinnert, 1985). More recent studies suggest that information acquired through the auditory channel is important as well (Mumme, Fernald, & Herrera, 1996; Vaish & Striano, 2004). In addition, although social referencing has been found as early as 12 months of age in highly structured laboratory situations, it is seen even more reliably by 18 months of age (Sigman & Kasari, 1995).

Pretending presents an ambiguous situation for young children, in some ways similar to the ambiguity of social referencing situations in experiments. Why is mother "pouring" when nothing is coming out? Why is she "eating" when there is no food? The content alone did not appear to signal pretending in our snack paradigm: Many children appeared confused despite the availability of content cues. Instead, our data suggest that pretense interpretation may well be facilitated by looking and smiling, the same behaviors that are crucial in social referencing: The child sees the mother "pour," looks to her face, and sees her smile. If the mother was looking to the child when she smiled, she may have done so in order that the smile indicate to the child to interpret the pretense situation as not real, but silly.

Nishida and I have obtained preliminary evidence that is strongly supportive of this proposal (Nishida & Lillard, in press). Time-coded data on looking, snack-related behavior, and smiling, for both mother and child, were subjected to sequential analyses (Bakeman & Quera, 1995). We found that our indicators of baby understanding—smiling and snack-related actions—were significantly more likely to occur just after sequences of the mother's behavior would permit social referencing. Social referencing sequences were defined as sequences in which the child and mother were looking at each other while the mother engaged in a pretend act and then smiled (within a 4-second window), and then children smiled or engaged in a snack-related act. The frequency of these sequences was not simply because children mirrored their mothers' facial expressions, or imitated her behaviors. Such shorter sequences did occur, but not nearly as often as the full social referencing sequence. In addition, these sequences were rare in real snack conditions. These sequential analyses thus indicate that social referencing may well contribute to pretense understanding in young children.

Reading Intentions

Understanding pretense acts may involve reading intentions. For example, if a child sees someone pick up a stick and pretend to write, the child must at least implicitly understand the person as intending to portray writing. Indeed, this is what Rakoczy and his colleagues have shown for 3-year-olds (Rakoczy et al., 2004): 3-year-olds will copy a person pretending to write by pretending to write themselves. (An intention condition in this study was described earlier. Both 2- and 3-year-olds who watched someone try to write with a pen and fail because the pen's cap was on proceeded to remove the pen's cap and really write when given the pen.) Performance by 2-year-olds in the pretend condition was less clear. They really wrote, which could suggest they did not understand pretense. Alternatively, it may be the case that the real form of the pretense actions (e.g., really writing) was so strongly compelling for 2-year-olds that it masked pretense understanding.

We do know that outside of pretense scenarios, children correctly interpret real intentions by 18 months. Carpenter and her colleagues (Carpenter, Akhtar, & Tomasello, 1998) showed that when one performs an action and then makes a positive statement ("There!") children are significantly more likely to imitate it than when one performs an action and then makes a negative statement ("Whoops!"). By 18 months, children seem to understand that intended acts should be copied, and mistaken ones should not. Meltzoff (1995) went a step further, showing that

18-month-olds repair mistaken actions. After repeatedly watching someone fail at an intended act, such as trying and failing to pull apart the ends of a barbell, 18-month-olds carry out the intended action. By 18 months, then, children can read intentions into real actions. Whether they can do so in pretend cases is unclear, because experiments requiring children to reenact pretend events have involved particularly compelling real equivalents. Further work is needed to determine whether children's skills at reading intentions assist their early understanding of pretense.

In sum, three particular social cognitive skills may contribute to pretense understanding in young children. These are coordinated joint attention, needed to get the meaning of adults' pretense acts; social referencing, which is helpful in letting children know to adopt a silly attitude toward pretense events; and reading intentions, which allows children to "fill in" the missing components in pretense actions. Our looking data suggest that the joint attention behaviors are particularly influential, and it is within the context of joint attention that social referencing and reading intentions occur. In concert with content cues and changes in mothers' behavior when pretending, these skills may explain why young children do not generally become bamboozled when they observe pretense acts.

CONCLUSIONS

The issue of how very young children know when people are pretending is an important one, as without such knowledge young children's developing representations of the real world would be vulnerable to confusion. The research presented here shows that mothers do not merely tell children they are pretending. In fact, such verbal cues seem insignificant next to the array of nonlinguistic behaviors mothers engage in when pretending to have snacks. As compared to when they are really snacking, mothers who are pretending to snack engage in more snack behaviors, these behaviors are faster, and sometimes they are exaggerated in space. Mothers also look much more at their children when pretending, and they smile more and for longer, particularly after their own actions. Interestingly, these variations in behavior do not adjust to the age or the pretend experience of the child: Mothers pretend in the same way for all young children.

Young children may greet these pretend behaviors with social skills of their own: social referencing, joint attention, and the ability to read intentions. The first two skills interact particularly with looking and smiling, and indeed it is these behaviors on the part of mothers that seem most associated with children seeming to follow mothers' pretense. Perhaps part of the reason, then, that pretend play is associated with theory of mind is that early pretend play rests on attending to some of the same social behaviors—eye contact and smiles—that can facilitate understanding others' mental states. Mothers must communicate meaning to children during pretense, and what is inherent in this communication of meaning might help children to focus on social behaviors that later contribute in other ways to understanding minds.

REFERENCES

Ambady, N., & Rosenthal, R. (1992). Thin slices of expressive behavior as predictors of interpersonal consequences: A meta-analysis. *Psychological Bulletin, 111*, 256–274.

Astington, J. W., & Jenkins, J. M. (1995). Theory of mind development and social understanding. *Cognition and Emotion, 9*, 151–165.

Auwarter, M. (1986). Development of communcative skills: The construction of fictional reality in children's play. In J. Cook-Gumperz, W. Corsaro, & J. Streeck (Eds.), *Children's worlds and children's language* (pp. 205–230). New York: New Babylon.

Bakeman, R., & Adamson, L. B. (1984). Coordinating attention to people and objects in mother–infant and peer–infant interaction. *Child Development, 55*, 1278–1289.

Bakeman, R., & Quera, V. (1995). *Analyzing interaction: Sequential analysis with SDIS & GSEQ.* New York: Cambridge University Press.

Bateson, G. A. (1972). A theory of play and fantasy. In G. A. Bateson (Ed.), *Steps to an ecology of mind* (pp. 177–193). New York: Chandler. (Original work published 1955)

Bekoff, M. (1995). Play signals as punctuation: The structure of social play in canids. *Behaviour, 132*, 419–429.

Berguno, G., & Bowler, D. (2004). Understanding pretence and understanding action. *British Journal of Developmental Psychology, 22*, 531–544.

Boulton, M. J. (1993). A comparison of adults' and children's abilities to distinguish between aggressive and playful fighting in middle school pupils: Implications for playground supervision and behaviour management. *Educational Studies, 19*, 193–203.

Bruner, J. (1995). From joint attention to the meeting of minds: An introduction. In C. Moore & P. J. Dunham (Eds.), *Joint attention: Its origins and role in development* (pp. 1–14). Hillsdale, NJ: Lawrence Erlbaum Associates.

Carpenter, M., Akhtar, N., & Tomasello, M. (1998). Fourteen- through 18-month-old infants differentially imitate intentional and accidental actions. *Infant Behavior and Development, 21*, 315–330.

Chi, M. T. H., & Ceci, S. J. (1987). Content knowledge: Its role, representation, and restructuring in memory development. In H. W. Reese (Ed.), *Advances in child development and behavior* (Vol. 20, pp. 91–142). San Diego, CA: Academic.

DeLoache, J. S., & Plaetzer, B. (1985). *Tea for two: Joint mother–child symbolic play*. Paper presented at the biennial meeting of the Society for Research in Child Development, April, Toronto, Canada.

Eibl-Eibesfeldt, I. (1989). *Human ethology*. New York: Aldine de Gruyter.

Ekman, P., & Friesen, W. V. (1982). Felt, false, and miserable smiles. *Journal of Nonverbal Behavior, 6*, 238–258.

Flavell, J. H., Flavell, E. R., & Green, F. L. (1987). Young children's knowledge about the apparent–real and pretend–real distinctions. *Developmental Psychology, 23*, 816–822.

Forguson, L., & Gopnik, A. (1988). The ontogeny of common sense. In J. W. Astington, P. L. Harris, & D. R. Olson (Eds.), *Developing theories of mind* (pp. 226–243). New York: Cambridge University Press.

Garvey, C. (1990). The modals of necessity and obligation in children's pretend play. *Play and Culture, 3*, 206–218.

Garvey, C., & Berndt, R. (1975). *Organization in pretend play*. Paper presented at the meeting of the American Psychological Association, August, Chicago.

Garvey, C., & Kramer, T. L. (1989). The language of social pretend play. *Developmental Review, 9*, 364–382.

Giffin, H. (1984). The coordination of meaning in the creation of shared make-believe play. In I. Bretherton (Ed.), *Symbolic play* (pp. 73–100). Orlando, FL: Academic.

Göncü, A. (1993). Development of intersubjectivity in the social pretend play of preschool children. *Human Development, 36*, 185–198.

Göncü, A., Patt, M., & Kouba, E. (2004). Understanding young children's pretend play in context. In P. Smith (Ed.), *Handbook of social development*. New York: Oxford University Press.

Haight, W. L., & Miller, P. J. (1993). *Pretending at home*. Albany: State University of New York Press.

Harris, P. L. (2000). *The work of the imagination*. Oxford, UK: Blackwell.

Kavanaugh, R. D., Whittington, S., & Cerbone, M. J. (1983). Mothers' use of fantasy speech to young children. *Journal of Child Language, 10*, 45–55.

Knutson, B., Burgdorf, J., & Panksepp, J. (1998). Anticipation of play elicits high-frequency ultrasonic vocalizations in young rats. *Journal of Comparative Psychology, 112*, 65–73.

Lalonde, C. E., & Chandler, M. J. (1995). False belief understanding goes to school: On the social-emotional consequences of coming early or late to a first theory of mind. *Cognition and Emotion, 9*, 167–185.

Leslie, A. M. (1987). Pretense and representation: The origins of "theory of mind." *Psychological Review, 94*, 412–426.

Lillard, A. S. (1993). Young children's conceptualization of pretense: Action or mental representational state? *Child Development, 64*, 372–386.

Lillard, A. S. (1996). Body or mind: Children's categorizing of pretense. *Child Development, 67*, 1717–1734.

Lillard, A. S. (1998). Playing with a theory of mind. In O. Saracho & B. Spodek (Eds.), *Multiple perspectives on play in early childhood education* (pp. 11–33). New York: State University of New York Press.

Lillard, A. S. (2001a). Pretending, understanding pretense, and understanding minds. In S. Reifel (Ed.), *Play and culture studies* (Vol. 3, pp. 233–254). Westport, CT: Ablex.

Lillard, A. S. (2001b). Pretend play as Twin Earth. *Developmental Review, 21,* 1–33.

Lillard, A. S., Nishida, T., Vaish, A., Massaro, D., Ma, L., & McRoberts, J. (in press). *Mother's signs of pretense: New variables, ages, and paradigm.* Unpublished manuscript, University of Virginia, Charlottesville, VA.

Lillard, A. S., & Witherington, D. (2004). Mothers' behavior modifications during pretense snacks and their possible signal value for toddlers. *Developmental Psychology, 40,* 95–113.

Lloyd, B., & Goodwin, R. (1995). Let's pretend: Casting the characters and setting the scene. *British Journal of Developmental Psychology, 13,* 261–270.

Ma, L., & Lillard, A. (in press). Where is the real cheese: Young children's understanding of pretense. *Child Development.*

McCune, L. (1995). A normative study of representational play in the transition to language. *Developmental Psychology, 31,* 198–206.

Meltzoff, A. (1995). Understanding the intentions of others: Re-enactment of intended acts by 18-month-old children. *Developmental Psychology, 31,* 838–850.

Mitchell, R. W. (2000). A proposal for the development of a mental vocabulary, with special reference to pretense and false belief. In P. Mitchell & K. J. Riggs (Eds.), *Children's reasoning and the mind* (pp. 37–65). Hove, UK: Psychology Press.

Moore, C., & Dunham, P. J. (Eds.). (1995). *Joint attention: Its origins and role in development.* Hillsdale, NJ: Lawrence Erlbaum Associates.

Mumme, D. L., Fernald, A., & Herrera, C. (1996). Infants' responses to facial and vocal emotional signals in a social referencing paradigm. *Child Development, 67,* 3219–3237.

Nishida, T., & Lillard, A. S. (in press). *The informative value of emotional expressions: Social referencing behavior in mother–infant pretense.* Unpublished manuscript, University of Virginia.

Pennebaker, J. W., Francis, M. E., & Booth, R. J. (2001). *Linguistic inquiry and word count (LICW): A computerized text analysis program.* Mahwah, NJ: Lawrence Erlbaum Associates, Inc.

Piaget, J. (1962). *Play, dreams, and imitation in childhood* (G. Gattegno & F. M. Hodgson, Trans.). New York: Norton. (Original work published 1945)

Pinkham, A., & Lillard, A. (submitted). *Children's everyday use of the word pretend.* Unpublished manuscript, University of Virginia.

Rakoczy, H., Tomasello, M., & Striano, T. (2004). Young children know that trying is not pretending: A test of the "behaving as if" construal of children's understanding of "pretense." *Developmental Psychology, 40,* 388–399.

Reissland, N. (1998). Context dependency in parental speech. *British Journal of Developmental Psychology, 16,* 365–373.

Reissland, N., & Snow, D. (1996). Maternal pitch height in ordinary and play situations. *Journal of Child Language, 23,* 269–278.

Richert, R., & Lillard, A. S. (2004). Observers' proficiency at identifying pretense acts based on behavioral cues. *Cognitive Development, 19,* 223–240.

Schwartzman, H. B. (1978). *Transformations: The anthropology of children's play.* New York: Plenum.

Sigman, M., & Kasari, C. (1995). Joint attention across contexts in normal and autistic children. In C. Moore & P. J. Dunham (Eds.), *Joint attention: Its origins and role in development* (pp. 189–204). Hillsdale, NJ: Lawrence Erlbaum Associates, Inc.

Simonet, P. (2001, July). *Dog laughter*. Paper presented at the Annual Conference of the Animal Behavior Society, Corvallis, OR.

Smith, P. K. (1997). Play fighting and real fighting. In A. Schmitt, K. Atzwanger, K. Grammer, & K. Schäfer (Eds.), *New aspects of human ethology* (pp. 47–64). New York: Plenum.

Smolucha, L., & Smolucha, F. (1998). The social origins of mind: Post-Piagetian perspectives on pretend play. In O. N. Saracho & S. Bernard (Eds.), *Multiple perspectives on play in early childhood education* (pp. 34–58). Albany: State University of New York Press.

Sobel, D. M. (2004). Children's developing knowledge of the relationship between mental awareness and pretense. *Child Development, 75*, 704–729.

Sobel, D. M., & Lillard, A. S. (2002). Children's understanding of the mind's involvement in pretense: Do words bend the truth? *Developmental Science, 5*, 87–97.

Sorce, J. F., Emde, R. N., Campos, J. J., & Klinnert, M. D. (1985). Maternal emotional signaling: Its effect on the visual cliff behavior of 1-year-olds. *Developmental Psychology, 21*, 195–200.

Sutton-Smith, B. (1983). Piaget, play, and cognition, revisited. In W. F. Overton (Ed.), *The relationship between social and cognitive development* (pp. 229–250). Hillsdale, NJ: Lawrence Erlbaum Associates, Inc.

Symons, D., & Symons, D. (1984). *Play and aggression: A study of rhesus monkeys*. New York: Columbia University Press.

Tamis-LeMonda, C., & Bornstein, M. (1994). Specificity in mother–toddler language-play relations across the second year. *Developmental Psychology, 30*, 283–292.

Tomasello, M., & Rakoczy, H. (2003). What makes human cognition unique? From individual to shared to collective intentionality. *Mind & Language, 18*, 121–147.

Trevarthen, C., & Hubley, P. (1978). Secondary intersubjectivity: Confidence, confiding and acts of meaning in the first year. In A. Lock (Ed.), *Action, gesture, and symbol: The emergence of language* (pp. 183–229). New York: Academic.

Vaish, A., & Striano, T. (2004). Is visual referencing necessary? Contributions of facial versus vocal cues in 12-month-olds' social referencing behavior. *Developmental Science, 7*, 261–269.

Van Hoof, J. A. R. A. M. (1972). A comparative approach to the phylogeny of laughter and smiling. In R. A. Hinde (Ed.), *Non-verbal communication* (pp. 209–237). Cambridge, UK: Cambridge University Press.

Walton, K. L. (1990). *Mimesis as make-believe*. Cambridge, MA: Harvard University Press.

Wilson, T. D., & Schooler, J. W. (1991). Thinking too much: Introspection can reduce the quality of preferences and decisions. *Journal of Personality & Social Psychology, 60*, 181–192.

Youngblade, L. M., & Dunn, J. (1995). Individual differences in young children's pretend play with mother and sibling: Links to relationships and understanding of other people's feelings and beliefs. *Child Development, 66*, 1472–1492.

7

Children's Play as
Cultural Interpretation

Artin Göncü
Jyoti Jain
Ute Tuermer
University of Illinois at Chicago

Children's play continues to puzzle us despite the significant advances we have made in our effort to understand it during the last three decades. As we untangle some aspects of play, we discover its new features. As a result, we continue to expand its conceptualizations. A quick glance at different perspectives from which play has been conceptualized illustrates this. One line of earlier theory and research conceptualized play on the basis of the psychological processes involved in it such as cognition, affect, or communication. A second line conceptualized play as a psychological construct such as power (cf. Sutton-Smith, 1983, 1995), and a third line emphasized play's performance features and named play accordingly; for example, play-as-improvisation (e.g., Sawyer, 1997). Finally, a fourth line of work focused on the contributions of play to children's development and education (e.g., Göncü & Becker, 1992; Nicolopoulou, chap. 11, this volume).

We maintained this tradition of calling play something when we described children's play as a cultural activity (Göncü, Tuermer, Jain, & Johnson, 1999). There are two reasons for this: First, we wanted to emphasize that play is only a partially understood activity, the meaning of which varies as a result of the perspective from which it is examined.

Therefore, we need to make sure that the activity has the same meaning for everybody involved when we engage in discussion about play. The second reason for referring to play as a cultural activity was substantive and emerged as a corollary of the first. Disturbed by the characterizations of low-income and non-Western children's play as inadequate from a Western middle-class perspective, we brought to the developmental psychologists' attention that these children's play may not be inadequate. Rather, the economical, value, and communicative structures in low-income communities may influence the occurrence of children's play in ways that may not be obvious to the middle-class Western scientific community. Therefore, we need to learn to look at children of different cultures from their points of view to make sense of the occurrence and meaning of their play before we reach judgments about its adequacy.

This chapter extends our previous work on both conceptual and empirical grounds (cf. Göncü et al., 1999): We begin with a brief historical overview of how previous characterizations of low-income children's pretend play as inadequate led us to adopt a cultural approach. Then, we present an expansion of our previous conceptualization by advancing that children's play is a cultural activity not only in terms of its occurrence but also as an interpretative activity and expression, arguing that only when we consider play as a form of cultural expression would we be able to discover its varying manifestations and assure that its conceptualizations reflect this richness. Against this background, we present a study that describes the conditions in which low-income and non-Western children's play develops, as well as the ways in which it is expressed, supporting the proposal that play is best conceptualized as a form of cultural expression. We conclude the chapter with a call for future work to search for different cultural manifestations of children's play and conceptualize this variability to provide a fair and accurate picture of children's play in different communities.

JUSTIFYING A CULTURAL STANCE TO THE STUDY OF CHILDREN'S PLAY

The reason to conceptualize children's play as a cultural activity germinated in reaction to a research tradition that began with Smilansky's (1968) work characterizing children in low-income and non-Western cultures as not playing as imaginatively as their Western counterparts. It was claimed that low-income children needed intervention to achieve optimal levels of symbolic functioning as did their middle-income counterparts. Researchers interpreted increases in children's symbolic representation observed in some intervention work only as an indication of development, among other possible interpretations (e.g., children's ability to adjust to experimenters' requests) and used it as a justification for considering the low-income children's play as inadequate.

In our view, intervention research suffered from the lack of cultural validity as evidenced in three sets of problems and, in turn, led us to conceptualize play as a cultural activity. First, in previous experimental research, low-income children were pulled out of their classrooms by unfamiliar adults and were requested to pretend in unfamiliar settings such as mobile research laboratories. As Schwartzman (1978) stated, the fear induced by exposing young children to an unfamiliar setting rather than children's inability could be the reason for the relative absence of symbolic play, rendering intervention meaningless. Second, previous work did not consider the possibility that low-income and non-Western children's play may be influenced by the social and economical conditions as well as adult values that are different from those of the Western and middle-class world. Finally, influenced by the dominant developmental theorists who focused almost exclusively on pretend play (e.g., Leont'ev, 1981; Piaget, 1945; Vygotsky, 1978), researchers followed suit. Without entertaining the possibility that low-income children may have play kinds that may not have been identified in Western theory and research, previous work yielded potentially ethnocentric information.

In view of these criticisms we developed a model to serve as a framework for a fair description of children's play in different communities. In the following paragraphs, we first summarize the features of this model, stating that children's play is influenced by the economical, value, and communicative contexts of their communities (Göncü et al., 1999), and then discuss in greater detail its new feature that claims play as a cultural interpretation. As well, we reiterate the methodological premise of the model that a holistic stance to the study of children's play requires adoption of an interdisciplinary methodology.

Regarding the influence of the economical context, previous research illustrated that the material wealth influences the degree of engagement in play of both the caregivers and the children. For example, in contrast to the findings that the middle-class Western parents value and participate in children's play (e.g., Dunn, 1988; Göncü, Mistry, & Mosier, 2000; Haight & Miller, 1993), research with non-Western families states that adults do not participate in children's play largely due to their work load (e.g., Göncü et al., 2000; Martini, 1994). Furthermore, in rural communities children's engagement in play may be less than that of Western children due to their work load both in and outside the home. Therefore, people's involvement in play may vary across cultures as a function of their responsibilities and not as a result of differences in their abilities.

Concerning the influence of value context on play, there is evidence that caregivers' values influence the nature of children's engagement in play (cf., Gaskins, Haight, & Lancy, chap. 8, this volume). For example, Chinese caregivers consider pretend play as a medium of teaching children culturally accepted forms of conduct, whereas Irish American parents see play as meeting their children's needs and supporting their interests (Haight, 1999). Even in the same nation and at similar economical levels parents may not share the same values about play. As an extension of many factors such as their ethnicity, parents may attach different values to play. For example, middle-class European American mothers think of play as a learning experience whereas Korean American mothers con-sider it as primarily amusement for children (Farver, 1999). These find-ings indicate that cultural variations in children's play may be due to variations in adults' constraints imposed on children's activities rather than to differences in children's assumed inherent ability or motivation to play.

Regarding the influence of communication context on play, we do not yet have sufficient information about how caregivers, teachers, and child-care workers communicate their values to children. However, the few existing studies suggest that to understand variations in the occur-rence of children's play we need to understand how adults communicate their values to children. Even in the Western middle-class world where play is valued, adults encourage some and discourage other kinds of play through certain types of messages. For example, Göncü and Weber (2000) were told by a preschool teacher in an affluent community that pretending to be a house pet was prohibited in her classroom because either unpopular children became house pets or children who became house pets were low-ered in status in the classroom. When the teacher saw a child adopt this role she explicitly terminated this activity although she did not express her approval or disapproval when children assumed other pretend roles, tacitly informing the children that pretend would come to an explicit halt only when it involved potential injury. These observations suggest that we need to take into account the communication about and occurrence of a given type of play in relation to the broad system of values and communicative contexts in which children's activities are embedded in reaching judgments about the adequacy of children's activities.

As for conceptualizing play as a cultural activity of interpretation and expression, if we agree that play is a cultural as well as a developmental phenomenon, it becomes plausible to argue that cultural communities may vary in their preferred form of expression in play. It may be that in some communities pretend play is an extension of expressive cultural traditions, whereas in other cultures it is not. Therefore, focusing on pretend play by ignoring other forms of play would be privileging pretend play and its specific manifestations and the communities that encourage it (Slaughter & Dombrowski, 1989).

Some authors argued that play is an activity of interpretation (e.g., Corsaro, 1997; Schwartzman, 1978); however, only a few stated that cultural traditions find their expression in children's play. For example, Sutton-Smith and Brice-Heath (1981) argued that certain of the cultural differences in pretend play can be connected to varying levels of modernity and technology across cultures. They stated that in technologically advanced Western cultures where schooling is common and therefore functioning on the basis of decontextualized skills (e.g., literacy) is a requirement, pretend play will occur more frequently than in rural cultures where functioning relies on concrete tools of daily life (e.g., features of oral traditions such as storytelling). In addition, they noted that due to their increasing ability to work with decontextualized symbols, children of the Western world incorporate fantastic roles (e.g., fairy tale characters) into their play, whereas the rural children with oral traditions base their play on themes of domestic life (e.g., mother–baby role play).

In a study informing the present research, Goldman (1998) agreed with Sutton-Smith and Brice-Heath that play is an expressive system reflecting children's cultural traditions. However, in disagreement with them, Goldman showed that in non-Western rural cultures children incorporate decontextualized symbolic representations into their play as seen in the play of 4- to 11-year-old Huli children in the Southern Highlands Province of Papua New Guinea. Goldman illustrated that through metaphors, rhyming, motherese, and proverbs, adults presented to children the possibility that features of language can be manipulated to signify the meaning of events, people, and objects. In addition, Goldman observed that Huli children used pretend play as an interpretive activity in which they tested their understanding of the particular symbols of Huli myth such as "ogre" and "trickster."

In summary, in view of the previous literature on the significance of economical, value, and communicative contexts as well as conceptualizing play as an expressive system, we came to the conclusion that for us to describe fairly the play of low-income and non-Western children we need to go beyond the existing play theory and research methods in psychology. We need to adopt an interdisciplinary stance by which we flexibly adjust our theory and methods according to the priorities of children's cultures so that we can see play as a form of cultural expression, and interpret its developmental significance in relation to the community structure in which it is embedded. As we illustrate in the next section, we were able to describe play in low-income communities by building on the psychological theory as we also drew from education, anthropology, and sociology.

DESCRIBING THE PLAY OF LOW-INCOME AFRICAN AMERICAN, EUROPEAN AMERICAN, AND TURKISH CHILDREN

This study was designed to describe children's play in relation to the conditions of poverty in an African American city community, in a semirural European American community, and in a Turkish peasant community. The choice of these three communities was not arbitrary. Inclusion of an African American community was the result of the fact that a large majority of U.S. children of color live in poverty and are the recipients of intervention as those who need improvement (cf., McLoyd, 1982, 1998). The working-class European American community was included as a result of the recognition that research on low-income children excludes poor White children (cf., McLoyd, 1998) with few exceptions that focus primarily on the development of language (e.g., Brice-Heath, 1983; Miller, 1982). Finally, this work includes a peasant Turkish community as a rural non-Western community because the limited amount of research that focuses on rural Middle Eastern children through the lenses of Western theory describes their activity also as inadequate (McLoyd, 1982).

Against this background, we embarked on this study in consideration of the following principal expectations. Our first expectation was that the three low-income communities would value and make provisions for children's play. This expectation stemmed from the shared conviction that poverty itself cannot be an inhibitor of children's play and it found conceptual strength in our recent analysis of pretend play as a lifespan activity (Göncü & Perone, 2005). Our analyses revealed that adult play is common in many Western and non-Western communities and is necessary for their functioning (Geertz, 1976; Goldman, 1998; Sawyer, 2003a; 2003b; Spariosu, 1989; Sutton-Smith, 1997; Turner, 1982). Given this fact, we expected that like their middle-class and

Western counterparts, low-income and non-Western adults will value play and encourage children's engagement in it.

Second, we expected that children's primary play partners would be other children, siblings, and friends in all three communities. However, in the U.S. communities, teachers and caregivers would also participate in children's play due to factors including recognition of play as an important educational medium and parents' possible exposure to media and educational resources on the role of play in child development. The Turkish village caregivers would value play but see it primarily as children's activity due to their work load and values that adult–child play is not appropriate when children begin to construct relationships with their peers. Thus, the Turkish adults would not make a concerted effort to be a part of children's play.

Third, we expected that poverty would influence the occurrence of play in various forms depending on children's communities. We thought that one cultural difference would emerge in the types of activities that compete with children's play. In the U.S. communities, children's schooling along with possible engagement in household chores would compete or cooccur with their play, whereas in the Turkish village children's contributions to the workforce and household chores would compete with the opportunities afforded for their play.

We also expected that poverty would influence the ecological features of children's play. Because African American children lived in a community with a high level of violence, we expected that they would receive supervision during their play more than the European American and Turkish children, whose communities did not involve violence. In addition, we felt that in all communities with high economical need, children might have limited access to toys.

Fourth, we expected that low-income children and their partners would engage in the kinds of play that reflect their cultural traditions. When children are observed in their daily settings and activities in which they are distracted minimally as part of data collection procedures, their engagement in all kinds of play including pretend play will be evident. More substantively, however, based on previous language (e.g., Brice-Heath, 1983; Miller, 1982) and play research (e.g., Goldman, 1998; Goodwin, 1990) illustrating that children's activities reflect common cultural practices, we expected that children would engage in play forms that reflect traditions that may be present predominantly in the non-Western and low-income communities, such as oral traditions, and thus not identified in the developmental literature.

The Communities and Families

The African American community lived in an economically impoverished neighborhood in Chicago where over 98% of the residents in the community were African American. A large proportion of residents received public assistance. The participating families lived in small apartments in multiple-family dwellings. Some of the buildings had a backyard in which children could play but the fronts of the buildings were off limits to children due to violence.

Fourteen children (7 girls), their caregivers, and teachers participated in the study. The age range was between 4 years and 5 years, 9 months with mean age of 4 years, 9 months. Two children came from homes with two parents, and 12 children came from homes with one parent. The primary caregivers of 13 children were their mothers. Mothers' years of schooling ranged from elementary to college education, and their work experiences included entry-level jobs in the food, service, and factory industries.

The children attended a state prekindergarten program housed in a public school building to assist with the education of "at-risk" children. A wide range of factors such as delays in social, cognitive, or language development as determined by standardized tests, as well as other factors such as low family income and being a language minority child contribute to the determination of at-risk status. The children were taught by two teachers, a White lead teacher and an African American assistant teacher whose child had attended the program previously.

Our work in this community began as part of a university-initiated project before we collected data for the study reported in this chapter. Göncü had worked with a community organizer and children's teacher for over a decade. This collaboration led to the children's teacher serving as a mentor for the preservice teachers from the university and assisting us in the present project.

The European American community came from a 98.1% European American semirural town, outside of Chicago, in which less than 2% of families lived below the poverty line. However, our sample represented some of the poorest families in this community. This community afforded play spaces for the children such as parks, playgrounds, and yards. The homes of children varied from an apartment in a complex to a single-family dwelling. The parents were not concerned about violence in the community. Our entry to this community was made possible by a graduate of the early childhood program at the University of Illinois who was involved in the Head Start program.

Fifteen children (7 girls), their caregivers, and teachers participated in the study. There were three sets of 2 children who were siblings, with two sets being twins. The age range was between 4 years, 2 months and 5 years, 7 months with a mean age of 4 years, 11 months. Nine children had both parents living with them. The primary caregivers of 13 children were their mothers and 2 children's primary caregivers were both parents. The education level of caregivers ranged from being barely literate to having some college education. Eight children's mothers stayed at home to take care of their children, and the others worked either part or full time. Mothers' employment included jobs in the service and factory industries.

The children were attending a Head Start center that served low-income children. The center was in an independent, spacious building with its own facilities and a big yard. The center was similar to the state prekindergarten in the African American community in many regards: For example, just like the teachers of the African American children, one of the teachers was an experienced teacher and the other one got involved in the Head Start first as a parent, then in the parent council as a member, and eventually as a teacher.

The Turkish community was established on the foothills of a mountain in western Turkey. It was near other villages and a municipality. Only one road led to the village off the highway and it ended in the village plaza, prohibiting car traffic through it. The plaza was surrounded by homes, the mayor's office, a mosque, and a café where only men gathered. Children also used the village plaza for play. There was a small convenience shop on the main road near the village plaza.

Families lived in small houses. It was common for kin to live in compounds of two or more homes that were attached to one another. Some families had relatives in nearby villages. There was only one pair of divorced parents in the village. There was only one elementary school with two teachers. During the time of the data collection (i.e., summer), the school was closed.

Fourteen children (8 girls) and their families participated in the study. Three sets of 2 children were siblings. The families did not often remember children's birthdays. According to parents' reports children's ages were between 4 and 6 years. All the children in the sample lived with their mothers and fathers. Ten children and their families lived in extended families and 4 children lived with only their siblings and parents. The primary caregivers were the mothers for all 14 children.

The level of mothers' schooling ranged from being illiterate to having some high school education. All the mothers reported that they did not work outside of homes except that most of them worked in the cotton fields during the season, gardened, or took care of animals. The fathers had an elementary school education. The fathers worked in the cotton fields, did animal husbandry, or worked as day laborers. Not all fathers were employed during the data collection.

The researchers were introduced to the villagers by the mayor and his family, whom Göncü met through mutual friends. Throughout the data collection, the researchers stayed in the mayor's house and with his family. This enabled the researchers and the villagers to establish rapport easily and engage in an ongoing dialogue. In the course of this, one daughter of the mayor emerged as a research assistant, introducing us to the villagers who participated in the study enthusiastically.

Data Collection and Analyses

In keeping with the model of conceptualizing play as a cultural activity of interpretation, we examined children's play in relation to the economical resources of children's communities and adult values. To this end, we used census information and adults' responses to our inquiries during an interview conducted with them. In our effort to obtain sufficient representation of children's play, we interpreted children's play both in the classroom and in their neighborhood in the two U.S. communities. We observed Turkish children's play only in the village as there was no school available for preschool-age children.

In the two U.S. communities, we interviewed both children's caregivers and their teachers, whereas in the Turkish community the interviews were conducted only with the caregivers. The interviews with the teachers inquired about a range of issues from their ideas about children's play and their participation in it to their knowledge about the community and the families. The interviews with the caregivers focused on children's daily routines, caregiving and social network, children's play and games, adults' values about and provisions for children's play, and adults' conceptions of children's play in comparison to other activities such as chores, economical activity, and schooling. In all communities the interviews were conducted primarily with the mothers, but 9 fathers and some relatives and neighbors were present during the interviews in the Turkish village due to communal living. The interviews were transcribed and then coded according to the criteria described in the Results section.

In the classroom, each child was videotaped during the free activity period. In the neighborhood, each target child was observed in a setting in which he or she frequently played. Depending on the community, the location of neighborhood play varied from a playground, a yard, or inside the house, to village mountains. The only changes in children's daily routines during data collection were the cameras and a portable microphone that was attached to their collar. Children were introduced to the video equipment before data collection by the researchers. They quickly got used to it and, indeed, sometimes used it as part of their play.

Children's play videotapes were transcribed verbatim and the transcriptions went through several transformations before they were used for data analyses. First, we described all the participants' actions and utterances in a narrative fashion. Then, we extracted play segments and described them in greater detail, including the participants' pauses, inflections of the voices, and changes in body posture, along with our interpretations of the story line. During this phase, the transcriptions went through several local revisions until they reflected children's play activities as fully as possible. The end products were so detailed that they could be used as screenplays by someone who has never seen the videotapes. The play segments were later coded according to several sets of criteria such as children's play partners and kinds.

RESULTS

The Value of Children's Play

Our first expectation that low-income communities would value play received support. We determined this by examining the caregivers' and teachers' responses to our interview questions. We first summarize our results obtained in the interviews with the caregivers in the U.S. communities. After that we describe teachers' responses jointly in both communities due to great similarities between two sets of responses. Then, we summarize the results from the Turkish village.

Our interviews with the caregivers led us to determine their values about play in two ways. One involved examining whether or how the caregivers addressed our interview questions and to what extent they provided answers to them. A second way involved examining directly the caregivers' answers to our questions about the value of play. Regarding the first issue, the caregivers in both U.S. communities addressed our questions in the way we posed them, revealing that they were in tacit agreement with us that children's play was worthy of inquiry regardless of their substantive values about play. However, the Turkish caregivers expressed some surprise at a scholar's curiosity to do a study about children's play. Both during the interviews and at other times, the caregivers stated that play is something children do among themselves, and, therefore, it was not worth adults' while to spend time talking about it. As a result, the adjustments required asking fewer questions, as some questions appeared redundant. Despite their explicit surprise, however, the Turkish peasant caregivers expressed curiosity and interest in the study and offered valuable information about children's play.

Our second way of determining the extent to which caregivers valued play involved examining whether or not they thought play was good for children and encouraged or discouraged it, as well as identifying their knowledge about children's play kinds, settings, and rules. Although caregivers' reports about children's play partners provide another indication of their values about children's play, we address that issue in the discussion of our second expectation.

In the African American community, almost all of the caregivers (13)[1] reported that play was a good activity that made contributions to children's development and education. When asked why they thought children's play was good, caregivers stated that play contributes to the development of cognition and academic understandings and skills ($n = 8$); play is a natural and appropriate activity of childhood and thus, play indicates healthy and normal growth ($n = 6$); play prepares children for life by allowing them to imitate adults ($n = 4$); it enables communication and cooperation with peers as well as sharing ($n = 3$); and it provides physical exercise ($n = 2$).

In response to our question about whether or not they encourage play, the majority of the African American caregivers said yes ($n = 10$), and some ($n = 4$) reported that children do not need to be encouraged (2 of these parents added that they thought that children played too much). When asked whether or not they discourage play, some caregivers ($n = 6$) reported that they discouraged play to take care of other tasks such as dressing, with 2 of these caregivers stating that they discouraged play to encourage schoolwork, such as reading a book.

An additional indication that low-income caregivers valued play emerged in their keen observations of the kinds of play in which children were engaged. The African American parents reported that children's

---

[1]The numbers in parentheses indicate the numbers of children whose caregivers' responses fell in that given category out of a possible 14.

play included physical play (n = 13), pretend play (n = 11), games (n = 8), and language play (n = 1), which were identified in the previous developmental play literature. Also, the caregivers reported that children engaged in sound and rhythm play (n = 8), informing us of a new play form that was not identified in the extant developmental literature. As we discuss later, the caregivers' reference to sound and rhythm play led us to create a new category of play for consideration in these present analyses.

The play settings and times identified for the African American children were inside and outside the home before or after school (n = 14), during eating (n = 8), dressing (n = 6), bathing (n = 4), and during bedtime (n = 4). Outside, children played in a park or on a playground (n = 10), on the way to school (n = 8), in a backyard or courtyard (n = 7), church (n = 6), and other locations such as the zoo, the beach, or a picnic ground (n = 7). The off-limits areas included playing in the kitchen (n = 5), hallways and stairwells (n = 4), bathroom (n = 3), living room (n = 2), everywhere other than their own room (n = 2), and grandmother's room (n = 1).

Regarding the rules, some caregivers prohibited excessive physical activity such as running and playing basketball inside the house and fighting (n = 4), and some talked about not allowing physical or verbal aggression (n = 2). As we discuss later in reference to community poverty, outside play took place under supervision (n = 14). Five caregivers reported that there were no areas off-limits inside the house because they felt that children should have all the freedom they could have inside the house because they could not play outside.

All the European American mothers said play is good for children and provided explanations like their African American counterparts. For example, they said that play is an important activity promoting cognitive growth and contributing to children's learning (n = 8)[2] and that as an activity of imagination, creativity, and fun, play is necessary for optimal development of children (n = 6). As well, they said that play contributes to the development of sharing, turn taking, and learning to respect others (n = 8); it prepares children for life by teaching them social roles (n = 5), and that play is a form of energy release and physical exercise (n = 2).

All but 1 European American caregiver said they encourage play. For that 1 mother, her child did not need any encouragement. When asked

---

[2]The numbers in parentheses refer to the numbers of children whose caregivers' responses fell under the given categories out of a possible 15. We interviewed 12 caregivers. However, because the caregivers of siblings did not make distinctions for individual children, we used the same three interview data twice, yielding 15 data points.

whether or not they discouraged play, 10 mothers told us that they discouraged play to take care of chores or when children's play appeared dangerous.

In the European American community, children were reported as engaging in pretend play ($n = 15$), games ($n = 15$), physical play ($n = 12$), and sound and rhythm play ($n = 4$). Their indoor play settings and times were the home (before and after school; $n = 15$), and such home play could occur in the bathtub ($n = 5$), during meal ($n = 2$), and bedtime ($n = 1$), and during dressing ($n = 1$). The outside play occurred in the backyard ($n = 15$), in a park or playground ($n = 10$), at parents' workplace ($n = 2$), on the school bus ($n = 2$), at church ($n = 1$), and in other different locations such as the babysitter's house, the zoo, museums, shopping, bowling centers, and amusement parks ($n = 10$). All 15 caregivers reported that there were off-limits aeas. These spaces were streets and driveway ($n = 9$); bathroom ($n = 8$); parents' ($n = 6$); or sister's bedroom who had a disability ($n = 1$); creeks, baby birds, and trees ($n = 4$); drawers and closets ($n = 3$); basement ($n = 2$); stairs and hallway ($n = 2$); kitchen ($n = 2$); and other children's homes or yards ($n = 2$). Regarding the rules, they mentioned no hitting or hurting ($n = 10$), playing only in certain sections of the house ($n = 8$), no excessive physical activity such as running and jumping ($n = 7$), no bad words ($n = 4$), sharing ($n = 3$), responding to mother's call ($n = 2$), no writing on the walls ($n = 2$), or hurting self ($n = 1$).

As far as teachers' values are concerned, it was clear that both the state prekindergarten and the Head Start center gave utmost significance to children's play. In both schools, the teachers saw play as a significant activity through which children explored their world and learned the important tools of their culture such as literacy and math. Therefore, the teachers made space and time provisions in their schools. Further, the teachers used play as a form of instruction in which they guided children's learning by following children's leads rather than subscribing to a practice in which they established the agenda in a didactic manner. In keeping with this view, the teachers engaged in play with children when they had the opportunity.

In the Turkish community, parents of 7[3] children either did not address the questions on whether or not play is a good activity with contributions

---

[3]Similar to the analyses of the interview data in the European American community, we considered the data from the caregivers of siblings twice, yielding 14 data points although we conducted 11 family interview in total.

to children's development or whether they encouraged play. For the other 7 children, the caregivers expressed important insights about children's play, emphasizing that play is good but it is something children do on their own. They expressed opinions indicating that play is what is expected of children, it prepares children for life by allowing opportunities to imitate adults, and it provides opportunities for learning. In this respect, the most striking was an answer that came from a grandmother during one of the interviews when she said, "Playing with mud is good; children learn how to cultivate the earth that way."

The Turkish caregivers reported that children engaged in pretend play ($n = 9$), physical play ($n = 9$), sound and rhythm play ($n = 5$), and games ($n = 2$). Children's play occurred inside the house and these settings and times included dressing ($n = 9$), mealtime ($n = 4$), bedtime ($n = 2$), and bathing ($n = 1$). Children's play outside the house occurred in various places in the village. The rules and off-limits areas included no hurting or fighting ($n = 7$), no playing with sharp objects such as tin cans and knives ($n = 5$), no playing with mud ($n = 3$), not going too far away from the home ground ($n = 3$), not bringing in garbage from outside ($n = 2$), and no play during mealtime or inside the house ($n = 2$).

Children's Play Partners

Caregivers' reports about children's partners provided further support that they valued children's play as it also offered information in favor of our expectation. As we expected, the African American caregivers reported that children played with their mothers ($n = 13$), cousins and relatives ($n = 13$), neighborhood children ($n = 10$), siblings ($n = 8$), children at church ($n = 6$) and fathers ($n = 5$). Similarly, the European American children played with mothers ($n = 14$), neighborhood children ($n = 14$), fathers ($n = 13$), siblings ($n = 12$), relatives and cousins ($n = 11$), and animals ($n = 4$). In the Turkish community, the play partners were mostly other children including siblings and peers ($n = 14$), reflecting adults' value that play was children's activity, although mothers ($n = 5$) occasionally play with their children also.

An additional test of our expectation was the observation of the degree to which adults and children participated in play with the target children during the time when we videotaped their play. As Table 7.1 indicates, more U.S. adults, both caregivers and teachers, played with the children than the Turkish caregivers, and in the U.S. communities caregivers were play partners almost to the same degree as the children.

TABLE 7.1
The number of African American, European American,
and Turkish children who played with other children and adults

| | Partners | | |
Community and Setting	Children	Adults	n
African American			
Classroom	14	5	14
Neighborhood	10	10	13
European American			
Classroom	15	12	15
Neighborhood	13	12	15
Turkish	14	6	14

Poverty and Children's Activities

One of our goals was to get a sense of whether or how community and family poverty influenced children's engagement in play, schooling, and economic activity. Our analyses revealed three kinds of insights. First of all, we found that the three communities differed in the degree of safety they afforded for children's play activities. In the African American community, children's safety was threatened by violence. Therefore, children were not allowed to be outside or they went out only under supervision. In contrast, the European American children's play was not constrained by community violence, although they received guidance about safety. The Turkish children freely roamed about the village, playing around their houses, in the gardens, on paths, and in the cotton fields. Because there was only one paved road for an occasional vehicle to pass through in the entire village, children did not experience the daily types of safety hazards that are common in urban or suburban Western communities.

In contrast to community poverty, family poverty had only limited influence on U.S. children's play. Despite their poverty, the caregivers made time and monetary provisions to provide play opportunities for the children. Although they were not provided with the kinds of play environments of the affluent families described by Haight and Miller (1993), all of the U.S. children had some toys. There were fewer toys in the Turkish village and 11 children were reported to have toys. Turkish children were encouraged to play with household objects and to make toys from objects such as tree branches and chewing gum wrappers. It was common for children to make objects with mud ($n = 12$).

Our second set of analyses focused on the significance attributed to play relative to children's schooling. To this end, we asked the U.S. caregivers if they thought play was as good as schoolwork The caregivers' responses indicated that there were differences between the African American and European American communities in their emphasis. In the African American community, two kinds of responses emerged as dominant with reference to this question; some caregivers ($n = 6$) said play was as good as schoolwork, whereas others said that play was not as good as schoolwork ($n = 5$) and 1 believed that play was more important than schoolwork. Finally, 2 caregivers said play was sometimes as good as schoolwork, indicating that each activity has its place in the child's development and education. In the European American community, the majority of the mothers reported that play was as good as schoolwork ($n = 9$), and for others ($n = 2$) play was more important than schoolwork. For 2 children, play was reported not to be as good as schoolwork. One mother did not differentiate play and schoolwork from one another, and 1 mother did not address this question.

Third, we found out that what describes childhood in all three of these communities is not only play and schooling. The caregivers in all of the communities noted that children actively participate in taking care of certain chores. All 14 African American children do some chores such as cleaning the house ($n = 8$), cleaning up after themselves ($n = 7$), dishes ($n = 5$), care for house pets ($n = 2$), and laundry ($n = 1$). Similarly, all 15 European American children did some chores, including cleaning the house ($n = 13$), cleaning up after themselves ($n = 11$), helping with a sibling ($n = 8$), dishes ($n = 4$), making their beds ($n = 4$), caring for animals and helping with yardwork ($n = 4$), and picking up mail ($n = 2$). Of the 14 children in the Turkish community, 11 children contributed to the maintenance of their households. The children did a wide variety of chores around their homes. These involved cleaning ($n = 5$), cooking ($n = 4$), helping with child care ($n = 4$), doing the laundry ($n = 3$), dishes ($n = 2$), and shopping ($n = 1$). Unlike the U.S. children, 4 children did work that made some direct or indirect contribution to the economic well-being of their households. These children helped their parents in construction, animal husbandry, or the cotton fields. In summary, in keeping with our expectation, the caregivers' reports indicate that play is only one of the activities as emphasized by caregivers, and children are expected to focus on their schooling and their chores, and to some extent work activities.

Children's Play Kinds

To address our last expectation that broad cultural traditions would reflect themselves in children's play activities, we first conducted qualitative analyses. Guided by the previous literature (e.g., Goldman, 1998; Sutton-Smith & Brice-Heath, 1981) as well as the caregivers' descriptions, we sought to identify the types of play that would reflect oral traditions in children's play activities. After doing so, we established the numbers of children who engaged in the types of play identified in the qualitative analyses.

Our qualitative analyses provided support for our expectation. We found three examples of play that appeared as childhood versions of oral traditions in all three communities. These are sound and rhythm play, language play, and teasing. Sound and rhythm play refers to playing with music and rhythm. Examples included singing songs made up of nonsense syllables (e.g., a boy claps his hands and jumps as he sings "bla-pa"), playing an instrument (e.g., a boy hits on a cart with his drumsticks keeping in rhythm with two other boys who are singing and playing the xylophone) and improvising the logo of a radio station (e.g., "WGCI, dot that 'i'. Ha ha ha. WGCI dot that 'i'. Dot that 'i'. Dot that 'i'.").

The most notable examples in this category were songs and chants children brought to their play from their lives, as exemplified in the following gospel song. Diana and her sister are standing next to each other on a platform and Diana pretends that she is holding a microphone. Diana starts singing, "I know somehow, I know somewhere, we gonna make it." Diana laughs, claps her hands, and gets off the stage. The girls continue to sing together by clapping their hands and moving their bodies to the beat. A little later Diana sings "Amen!" and she claps her hands, laughs, and drops on her knees on the side of the platform. Her sister approaches her as she gets back on her feet. Diana declares, "Let's do church," and she starts singing and dancing around on the platform. Saying "OK, do like this," the sister demonstrates to Diana how she should move. Diana jumps off the platform and starts tap dancing on the floor, then she stops and laughs. Her sister jumps off the platform as well. Children carry on this fun-filled activity of playing church and improvising music and action as Diana starts to walk around the room. Her sister follows her as Diana sings, "Hallelujah! Hallelujah! Hallelujah!"

The second play kind was language play. Although it has been identified in the literature (Garvey, 1990), language play has not received much attention. Language play involved manipulating units of language such as the sound system, words, and sentences with the purpose of having fun. This category is different from sound and rhythm play, in that language play does not involve playing with actual music and rhythm. A wide variety of activities fell under the category of language play such as rhyming words (e.g., "We're making cookies. Cookie, boogie, ride a monkey"), making up words (e.g., one child used the word *scripiscrap* in referring to the "writing" of another child), repeating one another's words with or without variation in conversation, and creating sound effects.

The third type of play we identified was teasing. Although language development researchers focused on teasing as part of language socialization (e.g., Miller, 1986), playful teasing has never been included in play research in developmental psychology. Teasing is defined as having fun in terms of playful threats, insults, and mocking. Teasing is a form of pretend play in which the behaviors are expected to be interpreted for what they represent rather than what they actually denote. Teasing could occur in verbal or nonverbal ways. A nonverbal example for mocking involved a boy who turned to a girl and started making faces at her. She stuck her tongue out at him in response. This exchange went on for a few seconds and then he started laughing loudly. A verbal example for playful threat is directed by one child to another in the statement, "I'ma cut you with a knife."

The other three kinds of play we observed in all three communities— physical play, pretend play, and games—have been the subject of inquiry in work with middle-class Western children in developmental psychology. Consistent with previous work (e.g., Garvey, 1990; for a review see Pellegrini, chap. 4, this volume), we defined physical play as playing with motion that took various forms such as gymnastics (e.g., rollovers), organized sports (e.g., basketball), games involving physical activity (e.g., jumping rope, playing double dutch), or simply tumbling and jumping up and down. We defined pretend play as play in which children used a symbol to represent the meaning of an object or an experience (Fein, 1981). Children used either their language or a feature of the physical environment to represent a wide variety of experiences through a diverse means of symbolic representations from object substitutions to role play. Finally, the sixth major category was games which included both conventional (e.g., Simon Says) and invented activities involving rules such as routinized turn taking. Activities involving an element of playful competition were also coded as games.

The numbers of children who engaged in the six kinds of play in their classrooms and neighborhoods are presented in Table 7.2. These results

TABLE 7.2

The Number of African American, European American, and Turkish Children Who Engaged in the Six Kinds of Play in Their Classrooms and Neighborhoods

Community and Setting	Pretend	Physical	Teasing	Sound & Rhythm	Language	Games	n
African American							
Classroom	14	14	7	10	9	6	14
Neighborhood	9	13	2	9	7	9	13
European American							
Classroom	14	11	4	6	12	5	15
Neighborhood	12	13	4	3	9	9	15
Turkish	12	9	8	8	10	5	14

indicate that low-income children in all three communities included in their play activities both the new kinds of play identified in this study and those included in previous research.

CONCLUSIONS

The work reported in this chapter provides significant substantive information on the play of low-income and non-Western children. When we considered the adult values, caregivers' and teachers' alike, as well as the numbers of children who engaged in the kinds of play included in these analyses we found that play is a supported activity of childhood in the low-income communities. The low-income children provided examples of pretend play as they also engaged in the types of play that have not been used in previous descriptions of the middle-class children's play activities. Children and sometimes the adults around them played with the music, words, threats, symbols, motion, and rules, and they did so in carefully designed contexts of safety and instruction. On theoretical grounds, this work illustrates that a scientific approach to the study of play is influenced by personal knowledge like many other aspects of our lives. In view of these results, the previous dominant scientific approach to children's play that privileged pretend play and its experimental investigation emerges as Western and middle class. When play is examined in natural contexts of living with minimal intervention and from the "other" perspectives, both what is known and what is not known in the middle-class world is found in communities that are low income or non-Western. Thus, it is plausible now to state that theories of children's play should be situated in children's context, taking into account unique dimensions of children's specific communities as they seek to establish universals.

Adopting a cultural approach enabled us to identify similarities and differences among the three low-income communities included in this study. The community poverty and adult responsibilities and values made a difference in children's play activities. Where the U.S. children benefited from a great deal of play opportunity with their peers and learned through instruction provided in play in their schools, the absence of early schooling did not allow such an opportunity for the Turkish children. It also appeared that the African American and European American communities differed from one another in the emphasis they put on play relative to children's schooling; whereas the former qualified the significance of play with respect to children's schooling, the latter embraced play as an instructional device.

Significant cultural differences emerged in the ecology of children's play. As the African American and European American children had other children, their caregivers and, to some extent their teachers, as their play partners, the Turkish children played mostly with other children. Whereas the Western children had access to toys despite their poverty, this was not the case for the Turkish children. All the children took care of chores but the Turkish children also had work responsibilities. Finally, whereas the African American children's play was confined to indoors or adult supervision when outside, the European American and especially the Turkish children freely played in their communities.

In view of these results, we identify the following tasks for future research. First, in exploring class and cultural differences we must study play in relation to other activities of childhood. These results should be extended to determine the degree to which children's schooling, work, and chores influence their play. Second, we must be sure to include both the means of having fun that are universal (e.g., pretend play) and those that are culture specific in providing fair and accurate descriptions. Thus, it follows that future research on cultural and class differences should compare the meaning and function of children's play activities from their perspectives in reaching judgments about the (in)adequacy of their performance. Third, we must be more careful about making judgments about the developmental significance of a given play form and privileging it in our work. The analyses here indicate that representational play is not limited to pretense, as other play forms such as teasing also involve representations. Therefore, in assessing the development of symbolic functioning we must carefully consider different forms of representations.

ACKNOWLEDGMENTS

The research reported in this chapter was supported by the Spencer Foundation. We extend our appreciation to the children, caregivers, teachers, and community members for their enthusiastic participation in this project. We thank Mamie Shorter, Adell Brock, Linda Fitzgerald, and Virginia Cannella for their help in data collection in the African American community; and Iskender Savasir, Sumer Atak, and Ali and Devrim Yalcin for their help in locating the Turkish village and data collection there, and Beverly Elmore and Marilyn Brink for locating the European American community, as well as Cathy Healy and Linda Sorensen for their help during data collection there. Finally, we acknowledge Danielle Johnson and Hulya Adak for assisting us in transcribing the play data.

REFERENCES

Brice-Heath, S. B. (1983). Ways with words: Language, life, and work in communities and classrooms. New York: Cambridge University Press.

Corsaro, W. (1997). The sociology of childhood. Thousand Oaks, CA: Pine Forge.

Dunn, J. (1988). The beginnings of social understanding. Cambridge, MA: Harvard University Press.

Farver, J. A. M. (1999). Activity setting analysis: A model for examining the role of culture in development. In A. Göncü (Ed.), Children's engagement in the world: Sociocultural perspectives (pp. 99–127). New York: Cambridge University Press.

Fein, G. (1981). Pretend play in childhood: An integrative review. Child Development, 52, 1095–1118.

Garvey, C. (1990). Play. Cambridge, MA: Harvard University Press.

Geertz, C. (1976). Deep play: A description of the Balinese cockfight. In J. S. Bruner, A., Jolly, & K. Sylva (Eds.), Play: Its role in development and evolution (pp. 656–74). New York, Basic Books.

Goldman, L. (1998). Child's play: Myth, mimesis, and make-believe. New York: Berg.

Göncü, A., & Becker, J. (1992). Some contributions of a Vygotskian approach to early education. International Journal of Cognitive Education & Mediated Learning, 2, 147–153.

Göncü, A., Mistry, J., & Mosier, C. (2000). Cultural variations in the play of toddlers. International Journal of Behavioral Development, 24, 321–329.

Göncü, A., & Perone, A. (2005). Pretend play as a life-span activity. Topoi. 24: 137–147.

Göncü, A., Tuermer, U., Jain, J., & Johnson, D. (1999). Children's play as cultural activity. In A. Göncü (Ed.), Children's engagement in the world: Sociocultural perspectives (pp. 148–170). New York: Cambridge University Press.

Göncü, A., & Weber, E. (2000). Preschoolers' classroom activities and interactions with peers and teachers. Early Education and Development, 11, 93–107.

Goodwin, M. H. (1990). He-said-she-said: Talk as social organization among Black children. Bloomington: Indiana University Press.

Haight, W. L. (1999). The pragmatics of caregiver–child pretending at home: Understanding culturally specific socialization practices. In A. Göncü (Ed.), Children's engagement in the world: Sociocultural perspectives (pp. 128–147). New York: Cambridge University Press.

Haight, W., & Miller, P. (1993). Pretending at home: Early development in sociocultural context. Albany: State University of New York: Press.

Leont'ev, A. N. (1981). Activity, consciousness, and personality. Englewood Cliffs, NJ: Prentice-Hall.

Martini, M. (1994). Peer interactions in Polynesia: A view from the Marquesas. In J. Roopnarine, J. Johnson, & F. Hooper (Eds.), Children's play in diverse cultures (pp. 73–103). New York: State University of New York Press.

McLoyd, V. (1982). Social class differences in sociodramatic play: A critical review. Developmental Review, 2, 1–30.

McLoyd, V. C. (1998). Children in poverty: Development, public policy, and practice. In W. Damon (Series Ed.) & I. Sigel & K. A. Renninger (Eds.), Handbook of child psychology: Vol. 4. Child psychology in practice (5th ed., pp. 135–208). New York: Wiley.

Miller, P. (1982). *Amy, Wendy, and Beth: learning language in South Baltimore*. Austin: University of Texas Press.

Miller, P. (1986). Teasing as language socialization and verbal play in a White working-class community. In B. B. Schieffelin & E. Ochs (Eds.), *Language socialization across cultures* (pp. 199–212). Cambridge, UK: Cambridge University Press.

Piaget, J. (1945). *Play, dreams, and imitation in childhood*. New York: Norton.

Sawyer, R. K. (1997). *Pretend play as improvisation: Conversation in the preschool classroom*. Mahwah, NJ: Lawrence Erlbaum Associates, Inc.

Sawyer, R. K. (2003a). *Group creativity: Music, theater, collaboration*. Mahwah, NJ: Lawrence Erlbaum Associates, Inc.

Sawyer, R. K. (2003b). *Improvised dialogues: Emergence and creativity in conversation*. Westport, CT: Ablex.

Schwartzman, H. (1978). *Transformations: The anthropology of children's play*. New York: Plenum.

Slaughter, D., & Dombrowski, J. (1989). Cultural continuities and discontinuities: Impact on social and pretend play. In M. N. Bloch & A. D. Pellegrini (Eds.), *The ecological context of children's play* (pp. 282–310). Norwood, NJ: Ablex.

Smilansky, S. (1968). *The effects of sociodramatic play on disadvantaged preschool children*. New York: Wiley.

Spariosu, M. (1989). *Dionysus reborn: Play and the aesthetic dimension in modern philosophical and scientific discourse*. Ithaca, NY: Cornell University Press.

Sutton-Smith, B. (1983). Piaget, play, and cognition, revisited. In W. F. Overton (Ed.), *The relationship between social and cognitive development* (pp. 229–249). Mahwah, NJ: Lawrence Erlbaum Associates, Inc.

Sutton-Smith, B. (1995). Conclusion: The persuasive rhetorics of play. In A. Pellegrini (Ed.), *The future of theory: A multidisciplinary inquiry into the contributions of Brian Sutton-Smith* (pp. 275–295). Albany: State University of New York Press.

Sutton-Smith, B. (1997). *Ambiguity of play*. Boston: Harvard University Press.

Sutton-Smith, B., & Brice-Heath, S. (1981). Paradigms of pretense. *Quarterly Newsletter of the Laboratory of Comparative Human Cognition*, 3(3), 41–45.

Turner, V. (1982). *From ritual to theatre: The human seriousness of play*. New York: Performing Arts Journal Publications.

Vygotsky, L. S. (1978). *Mind in society*. Cambridge, MA: Harvard University Press.

8

The Cultural Construction of Play

Suzanne Gaskins
Northeastern Illinois University

Wendy Haight
University of Illinois at Urbana-Champaign

David F. Lancy
Utah State University

Play is most commonly conceived of as an intrinsically motivated, universal behavior of children, not only present but also qualitatively similar in all cultures. This conception of play has limited play theory because of the tendency to see the play of children of highly educated Euroamericans as representative of all children's play (Gaskins & Göncü, 1992; Lancy, submitted). This chapter presents an alternative conception that play is a culturally structured activity that varies widely across cultures (as well as within them) as a result of differences in childrearing beliefs, values, and practices. It is argued that play varies across cultures not only in its content, in the types of social interactions experienced during play, and in the resources that are made available for play (including material objects, space, and time), but also in the relation play has to other everyday activities. Ultimately, to the extent that both the quantity and quality of play varies across cultures, one must question the role of play in promoting universal developmental outcomes.

To demonstrate the variation in play, three case studies of children's play are presented here, based on our in-depth observations of children in their everyday lives, as well as the meanings the participants ascribe to the observed behaviors. These three examples differ dramatically on one factor that strongly influences the role of play in children's everyday lives—the role of adults in permitting, facilitating, and participating in children's play. Within educated, urban, middle-class families in the United States and Taiwan, play is highly cultivated by adults, whereas among the Kpelle play is accepted but not cultivated by adults, and among the Yucatec Mayan play is curtailed to encourage participation in productive activity.

Most of the individual findings reported in this chapter have been reported in more detail in each author's previous publications. The contribution of this chapter is to place the individual cultural perspectives along a single dimension—the value of play for adults—that captures a primary organizing principle for play in each of the cultures and thereby provides a principle for comparison that does not diminish the ethnographic understanding of each of the cultures. When children's play is compared across these examples that differ on the amount of adult tolerance for and involvement in play, a more accurate understanding of potential universals and potential cultural specifics is achieved. The integrative analysis increases our understanding of the inherent nature of children's play and the richness of its variety. Comparing children's play across multiple cultures also allows us to raise more focused questions about the impact of cultural variation on the role of play in human development.

CULTURALLY CULTIVATED PLAY

The most extensively studied type of play is found in cultures in which adults typically invest heavily in children's play. Haight and her colleagues have focused on pretend play in two such contexts: urban, educated, middle-class, Euroamerican and Taiwanese families. They also have some pilot data on pretend play in traumatized at-risk families in the United States involved with the public child welfare system. These data provide a context for considering what children may learn from adult involvement in pretend play.

Pretending in Euroamerican Families

The complex picture that emerges in urban, middle-class, Euroamerican families is one in which children's pretend play typically is highly supported by adults (Haight & Miller, 1992, 1993; Haight, Parke, & Black, 1997; Haight, Wang, Fung, Williams, & Mintz, 1999). Euroamerican parents often emphasize individuality, independence, and self-expression (e.g., Greenfield, 1994). Many families also prioritize the development of their children's self-esteem and individual potential through focused attention from the parent (e.g., Mintz, 1998). Parent–child pretending is one context, but not the only context, in which such attention can occur and children's uniqueness and self-expression may be promoted. Mothers and fathers generally argue that pretend play supports children's cognitive, social, and emotional development, but other contexts do as well. They believe that "play is the child's work." They typically view parents' support and active participation in young children's pretending as appropriate and desirable.

Consistent with their cultural beliefs, Euroamerican caregivers typically provide support for pretending, beginning before the child begins to pretend spontaneously. They provide toys specialized for pretending, and physical space for play. They also participate directly in children's pretend play. With infants, parents may pretend for the child, for example, by making a stuffed animal or doll talk, even before the child has displayed independent pretend play. With very young children, parents serve as active play partners. They initiate pretend play with their toddlers and elaborate on their children's early imaginative forays. As children become increasingly competent pretenders, they share equally with parents the responsibility for initiating pretending.

By early childhood, Euroamerican children generally are highly active and assertive play partners capable of elaborating complex, imaginative scenarios with their partners, including other children. They particularly enjoy playing with toy miniatures (Haight & Miller, 1992), such as action figures, and enacting fantasy themes (Farver & Shin, 1997), like superheroes and fairies. Parents continue to provide many toys and physical space for pretending, and to fill in as play partners if other children are not available. They also increasingly capitalize on children's interests and skills to lead them into other, culturally appropriate interactions. For example, a mother suggested that she and her bored, tantruming preschooler "have a parade." Another mother challenged her young son to a pretend race to maintain his cooperation in picking up toys.

The relation between parents' beliefs about pretend play and participation with their children in pretend play, however, is complex and illustrates that specific childrearing beliefs and practices must be viewed within a broader cultural context. For example, although most middle-class Euroamerican mothers and fathers hold positive beliefs about pretend play, and participate with their young children in pretend play, the relation between parenting beliefs and practices varies with parent gender. Mothers', but not fathers', beliefs about the developmental importance of pretend play and the importance of their own participation are related to the amount of time in which they actually engage in pretend play with their children. Fathers', but not mothers', personal preference to engage in pretend play relative to other activities is significantly related to the amount of time they spend pretending with their children. One explanation of these findings is that maternal roles within middle-class, Euroamerican communities are more culturally mandated, whereas paternal roles are more discretionary (Parke, 1996). Hence, mothers have greater responsibility than fathers for ensuring that young children participate in everyday activities viewed as facilitative of development (Haight et al., 1997).

In addition to their childrearing beliefs and values, other contextual factors may contribute to adult mediation of pretend play in middle-class, Euroamerican families. The bulk of the data on children's pretend play in Euroamerican families has been collected from small families living in urban neighborhoods. In urban contexts, young children must be closely supervised by adults when playing outside of the home. In small families, adults also may need to fill in as play partners when there are no older siblings, or they are away at school. Further, urban adults who have had relatively little exposure to young children may be highly motivated to encourage what may be, to them, a novel and charming expression of early childhood. Clearly, more research needs to be conducted on adult mediation of pretend play in other Euroamerican families, including rural families, larger families, and families with fewer economic resources to devote to childrearing.

Pretending in Taiwanese Families

The picture that emerges in many middle-class Taiwanese families is one in which children's pretend play also is supported. Many Taiwanese mothers are influenced by Confucian thought: They generally emphasize harmonious social interaction obtained through obeying, respecting, and submitting to elders; adherence to rules; and cooperation (e.g., Fung, 1994). They typically do not expect their children to interact with them as equals and, relative to Euroamerican mothers, are heavily didactic in their interactions with their children. They extensively expose their children to explicit models of proper conduct, often focusing on the acquisition of those values and behaviors necessary for group acceptance and participation (Fung, 1994; Wang, Goldin-Meadow, & Mylander, 1995).

They generally view pretend play as facilitative of development and endorse maternal participation. Pretend play is one vehicle, but not the only vehicle, through which Chinese mothers may teach proper conduct to young children. Indeed, Confucian thought has emphasized "playing rites" in which children enact social roles to learn social rules and adult customs (Pan, 1994).

Consistent with these beliefs, Taiwanese caregivers participate in pretend play with their young children (Haight et al., 1999). In addition, contextual factors also may support adult mediation of pretend play. Like Euroamerican families, the Taiwanese families studied by Haight and colleagues live in urban communities in which children need to be closely supervised by adults when outside of the home, and families are quite small. Although young children in both Taiwanese and Euroamerican families are equally active pretenders, other potentially important contextual factors differ, possibly shaping their play. For example, Taiwanese families from Taipei live in compact apartments, and the children have a very modest number of possessions relative to Euroamerican children. Their collections of toy miniatures, rather than filling a room, fill a shelf. Not surprisingly, caregivers and children use many fewer toy miniatures in their play and, overall, fewer objects than do Euroamerican children. They do, however, make extensive use of ritualized, social exchanges. These well-practiced routines may serve a similar scaffolding function to toys in the Euroamerican children's pretending.

In contrast to Euroamerican caregivers, but consistent with their own beliefs about appropriate adult–child relations, Taiwanese caregivers continue to lead the play and initiate most of the episodes, even as their children's initiations of pretend play and abilities to elaborate play themes increase over the preschool years. Like Euroamerican mothers, as their children become more competent pretenders, Taiwanese mothers begin to use pretend play to fulfill other nonplay functions. For example, Taiwanese mothers use pretend play to practice proper conduct with their young children. Play themes of Taiwanese mothers and children revolve not around fantasy, but around everyday social routines with nonkin adults, such as appropriately addressing and responding to a teacher, or interacting with a vendor.

Discussion of Culturally Valued and Adult-Mediated Play Contexts

Although in both contexts just described adults support play, considerable cross-cultural variation was observed in how caregivers and children participate in, shape, and communicate within pretend play. This variation appears related to culturally specific resources, values, and socialization goals. In summary, Euroamerican children interact with their caregivers as peers during pretend play, and caregivers focus on helping children to elaborate their pretend themes. The play revolves around toys, particularly toy miniatures, and focuses more on fantasy themes. In Taiwan, caregivers lead the pretending and use it to teach socially appropriate behavior especially with adults. The play revolves around social routines, not objects, and focuses on proper conduct.

It is also important to point out that there is considerable variation within cultural groups. Not all parents from a given community value or enjoy pretend play to the same degree, and not all parents are equally comfortable or skilled with pretending. Some parents prefer other types of interactions that may serve equivalent developmental functions. For example, some of the Euroamerican parents preferred involving their children in stories, visual arts, or household chores to pretend play (Haight et al., 1997). In these families, parent–child pretend play was not the richest or most complex or elaborated context for parent–child interaction.

Life circumstances, as well as individual preference, also may shape intracultural variation in parent–child pretend play. Research on parent–child pretend play in the United States has focused almost exclusively on economically privileged, apparently well-functioning families with no known history of trauma. Some pilot data are available with impoverished, at-risk families involved with the public child welfare system (Haight, Jacobsen, Black, & Sheridan, in press). In these families, both mothers and children have experienced multiple traumas resulting from some combination of domestic violence, substance abuse, homelessness, or unmet parent mental health or health needs. In addition, all mothers and children were experiencing separation because of children's placement in foster care and saw one another only during brief, weekly, supervised visits. Most children expressed intense distress when separated from the mothers at the close of these visits. The childrearing beliefs of mothers in this traumatized sample did not vary greatly from other U.S. families. Furthermore, spontaneous pretend play was a frequent parent–child activity during visits. In some instances, pretend play became a venue through which mothers comforted their distraught young children by reminding them of mundane, everyday routines. For example, some dyads repeatedly enacted bedtime routines and family dinners using toy replicas and addressing family members no longer present. Not all parent–child pretend play, however, necessarily was reassuring or soothing to the child, or socialized values and practices tolerated by the mainstream. For example, one mother introduced into the play themes of interpersonal violence distressing to her child.

This brief example of pretending in traumatized families suggests variation in parents' sensitivity to their children's emotional well-being during pretend play and the themes elaborated within the play. In the hands of a skillful and sensitive parent, parent–child pretend play may well support children's well-being and resilient recovery from trauma. In the hands of a distressed parent with an extensive history of complex and unresolved trauma, parent–child pretend play may be another venue for the intergenerational transmission of violence and psychopathology.

What Children May Learn From Parent–Child Pretend Play

In both Euroamerican and Taiwanese families, parent–child pretend play is a venue for socialization. Through pretending with their parents, many children elaborate strategies for pretending; for example, how to indicate pretend play and how to elaborate it with another person. In pretending with their parents, children also reflect on and elaborate broader cultural values and beliefs. Euroamerican children are given the opportunity to elaborate on the importance of play and creativity. Taiwanese children are given the opportunity to elaborate on the importance of respect and cooperation.

There also is variation within communities, stemming from individual preferences, life experiences, and circumstances. For some, but not all, families, pretend play is an enjoyable and stimulating context for elaborating the parent–child relationship. Parents also vary in their general sensitivity to their children and in their beliefs. For example, not all of the themes parents elaborate with their children necessarily support or reflect mainstream values. It is important not to overlook these and other within-cultural complexities in parent–child pretend play, even as we construct generalizations about the cultural value of play in these societies. The danger is that, because of our cultural values about the importance of play, we can become overzealous in advocating particular ways of interacting with children to promote their development and well-being.

CULTURALLY ACCEPTED PLAY

A second type of cultural context for play is found in cultures in which adults typically expect and even value children's play but invest little in it. Lancy's (1996) work provides an elaborate case study of this type through his research on the Kpelle. The Kpelle are a numerous population of slash-and-burn horticulturalists, occupying much of the interior of Liberia. Tidy villages, headed by a "chief," range up to 500 persons in size. The unit of production is the household, and these can also vary greatly in size. The staple, dryland rice, requires enormous inputs of labor that put a premium on senior males' ability to acquire wives and other dependents. In spite of civil war, public education, roads, and modernization, the majority of Kpelle live as their ancestors did. Lancy's principal research site, Gbarngasuakwelle, had no public school and very limited access to the outside world (Lancy, 1975). If anything, the task of enculturating children has become less complex over time as forest resources are so depleted that foraging skills have been, effectively, deleted from the "curriculum" of subsistence tasks children are expected to learn.

As is true through much of the world, infants are "tethered" closely to their mothers until toddlerhood. Unless the mother is doing very strenuous work, the infant is attached to her back or hip with a *lappa* or length of cloth. The infant may be temporarily lodged with another adult female or an older (female) sibling or in a hammock-like sling. *Allomothering*, a concept borrowed from the literature on primates (e.g., Hrdy, 1999), where older female siblings relieve their mothers of some of the burdens of infant care while learning to be effective caretakers, is very much in evidence. At night, the infant sleeps within reach of the mother's breast.

At the end of the workday, babies are passed around a circle of adults—including males—and played with. Contented, attractive, fat babies are a great source of pride and pleasure. They are never put on the ground to explore independently except during a fairly brief period just prior to the onset of walking and then only in areas inside and immediately adjacent to the house that have been cleared of snakes, insects, and vermin. In other words, play and exploration are seen as potentially harmful to the child and the tendency for infants to crawl and to mouth objects they discover is troubling to the Kpelle, as it reinforces the animal-like and uncontrolled character of the not-yet-person. In addition, there is no sense that the child needs "stimulation" or that its development requires adult intervention other than basic care. Adults do not talk to babies or try and teach them words.

Toddlers develop under the watchful gaze of a large number of relatives of various ages. However, there is little opportunity or incentive for any but the youngest of these relatives to pay much attention to the child; everyone else is too busy. Only siblings in middle childhood have both a responsibility and an incentive (recruiting and training a potential playmate) to spend a lot of time with young children. The "tether" is lengthened somewhat. Toddlers are free to play but they must remain "on the mother-ground," a cleared area in the village or farm that is within the scanning range of adults (Lancy, 1996), who will intervene if they perceive the child to be at risk. Toddlers must remain in the company of their sibling caretakers. As Harris (1998) pointed out, "sibling rivalry" is lessened, if not eliminated, in societies where older siblings are expected to dominate younger ones.

Sutton-Smith (1977), commenting on a study by Weisner and Gallimore (1977) that found, in a sample of more than 100 societies, that 40% of infants and 80% of toddlers are cared for primarily by someone other than their mother, noted:

> Maximal personal and social development of infants is produced by the mother (or caretaker) who interacts with them in a variety of stimulating and playful ways. [For a case study, see Haight, 1999.] Unfortunately the intelligence to do this with ever more exciting contingencies is simply not present in child care-takers. It is difficult enough to impart these ideas of infant stimulation even to mothers. As the review demonstrates so well, children as major caretakers maintain social life at a much lower level. (p. 184)

Sutton-Smith's comment reflects an assumption on his part, typical of developmentalists, that the ideal and universal goal of infant socialization is to maximally stimulate infants through focused social interaction. In fact, his concern does not apply to the Kpelle (or parents in most of the other societies, either) because they are not worried about "maximal personal and social development" for their children. Their attitude is much more conservative, as they do not want to lose their genetic and personal investment in the child. On the other hand, they do not want to "waste" a lot of their time caring for the child, either. As many scholars have noted (e.g., Hausfater & Hrdy, 1984), the parent must always weigh the trade-offs of investment in living offspring versus preserving their own well-being and future reproductive potential.

For the Kpelle, it makes perfectly good sense to utilize 6- to 10-year-old girls as child-minders as they do not yet have sufficient strength and endurance to contribute much to food procurement and processing, and they are capable of approximating the adults' conservative style of caretaking. Bock (2002) noted that, in subsistence societies, most of the important skills are simply not available to children because of their limited size and strength. It is likely that the Kpelle would agree with the theoretical argument that play keeps children busy and out of the way until they are old enough to be useful (Lancy, in preparation).

Between 4 and 5, a subtle change occurs. The tether lengthens yet again. The child must remain under the eye of a young caretaker but may travel beyond the mother ground, including visits to other areas of the village or even short hikes into the bush to gather mushrooms or snails. The children gain "sense" (*haYYillo* in Kpelle); that is, they are now capable of listening, following directions, and learning. They begin to take on chores, including fetching water from the stream—in a group—and delivering goods and messages to extended family members or between village and outlying farm. There is clearly a sense of apprenticeship as younger children closely observe and imitate their elder siblings and neighbors. Playgroups may be of mixed age—especially if the play includes singing, dancing, make-believe, and stories. Or, there may be fairly large same-age playgroups—especially in larger households.

In research on play in various human societies and among highland gorilla troops, playgroup composition and size is a critical variable that determines the extent and complexity of play, especially games. Mixed-age groups are constrained to play games that are no more taxing than can be handled by the youngest member (Lancy, 1983). In Euroamerican society, enormous investments are made to ensure that children have opportunities to play with peers of similar abilities, thereby maximizing the potential of individual competitors to improve. In Kpelle society, the primary function for play is "keeping kids busy and safe." Some degree of conflict was often witnessed when younger charges created a "ceiling effect" on play complexity. However, a child caretaker who abandoned his or her charge to pursue an exciting play opportunity would be severely punished.

Pretend play takes up a disproportionate share of the child's play time beginning at age 4 or 5. This can range in complexity from piling up a mound of dirt (the mortar) to drive a stick (the pestle) into over and over (as women do when they husk rice), to a thoroughly scripted and appropriately cast "playlet" (which is as faithful to the source as children can make it). Two vivid examples replicate the setting of the blacksmith's forge (Lancy, 1980a) and town chief's court (Lancy, 1980c). A nontrivial amount of Kpelle childhood is taken up with a two-step process of observing adult activity and then incorporating these scenes and the accompanying actions and speech forms into realistic pretend play episodes. However, it should not be assumed that such play is necessary for the successful acquisition of adult competencies. In spite of admonitions from

Schwartzman (1978) and Corsaro (1997), among others, to seek evidence of children constructing novel and even critical versions of the culture in their play, this does not appear likely for the Kpelle or similarly conservative societies. Pretend play for the Kpelle remains grounded in what the children have observed in their daily lives.

Again at 8 to 10 years of age, Kpelle childhood shifts direction slightly. The tether for girls is actually shortened because they now become indispensable helpmates for their mothers. They are "on call" and beginning to undertake near-adult tasks. For example, they will husk rice in a mortar each afternoon but the mortar and pestle will be scaled down to fit. Boys have fewer responsibilities, chiefly to roam over the ripening rice plots chasing away birds. However, this is play–work, where games of tag and sling-shot competitions get the job done just fine. Girls certainly bring a playful attitude toward their work, as well, preferring, whenever possible, to gather in pairs or larger groups to complete their chores. Games with rules and storytelling ("fairy tales") are popular at this age, and boys' game play and storytelling is, as a consequence, more varied and extensive than that of girls, who are free to play only during the hour or so at twilight. The Kpelle themselves would see some value in this play at preparing boys for the cut and thrust of argument and strategy that characterizes Kpelle political and legal affairs, in which men predominate.

Of course, there is considerable intravillage variation. If a boy has no 6- to 10-year-old sister, he takes on what would have been her responsibilities. Children in smaller households work more and play less than those in larger households. Indeed, village children are subject to many of the same social class effects as children in industrialized societies.

The "folk" repertoire in the typical Kpelle village is large. Dozens of songs, dances, folk tales, and games with rules exist. An analysis of this repertoire linked, at least tentatively, these play activities with corresponding adult socioeconomic skills. That is, these play forms appeared to serve to enculturate children (Lancy, 1996). However, this assertion must be immediately qualified by the fact that many, if not most, children actually went through only fragments of this play curriculum. Yet, in spite of this high rate of noncompletion, there were few conspicuous "failures" among young men and women.

Two points can be made, one obvious and one less so. First, there must be alternative means for children to learn how to be Kpelle—play activities are not the only pathway. Second, becoming a Kpelle adult is not all that demanding. The core skills are common to human beings everywhere: the ability to participate in group processes and the ability to carry out rather simple subsistence chores. This generalization was apparent in Gbarngasuakwelle and also in several of the communities in Papua New Guinea (Lancy, 1983). It is not that the Kpelle do not have craft skills, but rather, very few young people elect to learn these skills; they are entirely optional. One sees little obvious impact of play on the acquisition of most core adult attributes.

In conclusion, although play among Kpelle children may, on the surface, look similar to that found in a typical U.S. school playground, its extent and complexity are more limited. Parents and other adults are missing from the picture and, most important, it is not heavily programmed to exploit the potential to maximize the child's development. Play, in this view, ends up as an almost infinitely flexible and elastic "utility" that societies use for their children for varying periods of time and varying purposes. Kpelle children play a lot but, to their parents, although play is accepted, it is unimportant and almost invisible.

CULTURALLY CURTAILED PLAY

The third type of cultural context of play is found in cultures in which play is curtailed because adults will tolerate only minimal amounts of play. A Yucatec Mayan village in Mexico provides the third case study. It is dominantly a peasant farming village, and adults' and children's everyday lives are still structured around traditional patterns of household work (Gaskins, 2003). The village has about 1,200 inhabitants who live in compounds distributed around a main square, with slash-and-burn agricultural lands carved out of the surrounding forest. An average compound is 50 square meters and might have one or two houses built in it.

Most of the time, young children stay within the household compound. From age 3 or 4, they leave the compound to run errands within the village, to accompany their father or mother when they go out to work or visit, and, during the school year, to attend school. Directly around the house within the compound is an open area that is used as living space. It is here, within earshot of their mother, where children are most likely to be found playing and doing the rest of their daily activities (Gaskins, 1999).

This one fact—that daily life occurs primarily among family members within the compound walls—significantly influences the nature of play. First, the opportunities for play are restricted by the physical and social resources available in the compound. The physical environment of play consists of space that is shared with other ongoing activities and objects that no longer serve a useful purpose. One's playmates are largely determined by what other children live in the compound—siblings, cousins, or young aunts or uncles. Children are discouraged or prohibited from playing in adjacent compounds to avoid disputes with their neighbors. Play therefore usually takes place not among a range of same-age peers but among age-stratified relatives who live together, and the players remain the same day after day (Gaskins, 1999).

Second, play is inherently integrated into the daily activities of the compound (Gaskins, 1999). Play is never a privileged activity. Children are never out of earshot and therefore never beyond the responsibility of responding to their mother's call to do some chore. Also, play is never a socially exclusive activity. Play must include all those resident children who want to play, despite their character flaws or their age-limited capacities. Conversely, because all players are free to go do other activities, keeping all players engaged and content is essential for the play to continue on course. Finally, play takes place with the same people with whom children live the rest of their daily life, so secrets are less likely to be exchanged and risks are less likely to be taken (Gaskins & Miller, 2002).

There are also cultural constraints and affordances, including norms for social interaction; values placed on work, play, and other activities; and cultural beliefs, including those about children's development and learning. These are all reflected in how adults structure and mediate the daily activities of the children. Those that are particularly relevant for how play is mediated are mentioned here (see Gaskins, 1996, for a more complete discussion of Mayan parental ethnotheories).

The Yucatec Maya consider development to be primarily a process of unfolding of inner abilities and character, with little input from the environment. The one exception is in children's ability to learn to work and take responsibility. This must be taught as children develop more capacity by engaging them regularly in participating in the household work activities, thereby getting them to accept that they share responsibility for the household's production. They also believe that specific learning of skills occurs primarily through careful observation and eventually imitation, both of which are intrinsically motivated. Thus, children are not guided through activities before they are competent, are not praised for successes, and are criticized for mistakes only when it is judged that they should know better. Adults believe that children should not be stimulated; they come with their own inner energy and curiosity, sometimes too much. As the child grows older, that energy should be directed increasingly toward productive work.

In Mayan society, every person is an independent agent, responsible for his or her own actions. Young children are allowed to make many of their own decisions to the extent they do not put themselves, others, or valuable property in great danger, even when their choices are at odds with adult preferences. At the same time, adults expect that the age hierarchy of older sibling responsibility and younger sibling obedience (Gaskins & Lucy, 1987) will never be suspended, including during play.

Specific cultural beliefs about play and pretense limit the importance of children's play even further. Play is seen as serving little purpose beyond being a distraction for children when they cannot help with the work to be done and as a signal that the children are healthy (Gaskins, 1996). Equally important, children should not make more work for their mothers by getting dirty unnecessarily. Finally, extensive pretense in particular is of questionable appropriateness. Adults believe that one should not lie even in jest, and fiction, written or oral, is not a valued genre.

Taken together, these values give little support to children's play. The primary focus of every day in a Mayan home is to get the necessary work done for that day (Gaskins, 1999), and all family members, including children, are expected to contribute according to their ability. Children like to work. It allows them to feel proud of their competence and includes them in the ongoing social life of the household. Those too young to contribute are actually discouraged from participation, so most young children have some time to play by default, not by the design of the parents. Parents do not provide play materials or ideas, do not mediate ongoing play, and do not participate in play. Both adults and children, even very young children, understand and accept that play occurs on the sidelines of work. Although children enjoy playing they are almost always happy to drop their play when they are called to do an errand.

Yet, even under these curtailed conditions, children play. Children between the ages of 0 and 2 spend about 25% of their time in play. That rises between years 3 and 5 to almost 40% of their time playing. Between the ages of 6 and 8, there is a precipitous drop in play, back to 25% of their time, as work becomes more important. That decline continues in children 9 to 11 and older, who play only 15% of their time (Gaskins, 2000). For all ages, pretend play is never the dominant form of play. Children spend more time in large or small motor play or games with rules. Whereas in general children between the ages of 3 and 5 spend the most time in play, children between 6 and 8 spend more time in pretend play than at any other age (Gaskins, 2000). Although children in most families show a fairly similar cultural pattern in the amount of play, a few families have children who play somewhat more than other children, and in these families, more time is also spent in pretend play (Gaskins, 2001).

The position play holds for these children in their daily lives can be understood better when we look at what other activities they engage in (see Gaskins, 1999). Mayan children spend much of their time at work (Gaskins, 2000). By the ages of 3 to 5, children spend over 15% of the day working, and even more remarkably, about 40% of that work is done because the children volunteer to do it. This suggests that the extensive time they spend in playing is not an indication that they value play above work, but rather that their work abilities remain marginal and they turn to play when they are excluded from work. From 6 to 8, children spend 35% of the day working, and still 25% of that work is self-initiated. By 9 to 11, children spend the most time working of children of any age—50%. They are taught during this time many of the skills they need by being assigned chores of increasing difficulty. The proportion of volunteer chores to total daily activity remains high at this age (20% of their work time). This means that children 9 to 11 who spend half their time at hard work during the day are still volunteering to do much of it. As children get older, the increase in the amount of their work is offset by an almost equal decrease in the amount of their play.

A third kind of activity in which Mayan children engage is tuning in to other people, either by actively interacting with them or by observing them (Gaskins, 1999). Mayan children at all ages spend more time watching people than interacting with them, reflecting that observation is valued as the primary way a child can learn (Gaskins, 2000). During the years that children are active players, from 3 to 11 years of age, they are also watching people between 10% and 15% of the time and interacting with them very little. Observation, which is focused on learning skills and patterns of social interaction, is more common than pretend play. The fourth, and final, kind of activity in which Mayan children engage is maintenance activities of various kinds, including eating, sleeping, and grooming (Gaskins, 1999). This kind of activity occurs between 20% and 40% of the time and rounds out the allocation of time to 100% for all children (Gaskins, 2000).

Given the amount of volunteering that the children are doing in the work domain, and the amount of time they spend watching others, one can argue that the children are voluntarily reducing their own engagement in play so that they can increase their engagement in household work (rather than the parents pulling the children unwillingly away from play and forcing them to work). Thus, although play is a significant activity in children's lives, it is not the most highly valued, even for children as young as 4.

Not only are Yucatec Mayan children's motivations for play different than that for urban, middle-class Euroamerican children, but their play itself looks somewhat different. Large and small motor play and a few games with rules take up the majority of playtime for these children (Gaskins, 2000). These types of play are based on few objects designed to facilitate such play, as Yucatec Mayan children have almost no store-bought or homemade toys. All of these play activities must be able to adapt to a wide age range and a limited and frequently changing number of participants. All will be played within or just outside the compound, and all will be played with exactly the same people who played them yesterday and will play them tomorrow (Gaskins, 1999). Young children in particular must always be kept happy, because older children have a responsibility for the well-being of younger ones (Gaskins & Lucy, 1987). There is no adult supervision, mediation, encouragement, or participation; there may, however, be adult-imposed termination at any time if work needs to be done, play becomes too noisy or rambunctious, or a younger player begins to cry.

Pretense usually occurs clearly outside of these other types of play. Most of the time, the theme and roles are decreed by the most senior players and represent a generalized reenactment of adult daily life that the children have directly observed or participated in. Themes are chosen from a list of perhaps six to eight themes the players have developed; it is not an open list and does not change greatly over time. Roles are also fairly predictable. The oldest one or two children take the dominant roles and apportion out the others according to the players and their abilities. Despite the predictability, there is a sense of excitement in the planning and negotiation. Older children not only choose the plot, but often feed actual lines to the younger children. The children never cease to monitor the real world while playing, reengaging in play only when a real-world intrusion has passed.

There are a number of significant differences between the pretend play in the Yucatec Maya compound and the pretend play in an Euroamerican nursery school or home setting. The players are not peers, but older and younger siblings. The older children not only take charge of the content of the play, but they are concurrently in charge of the real well-being and happiness of the other players. The themes are repetitive and reflect real adult life rather than fantasy. The children always enact the play themselves, not through dolls or figures. And, like almost all Mayan social interaction, pretend play is never a private, exclusive activity between chosen partners, but rather an activity for anyone present to participate in or observe.

CULTURAL VARIATION IN THE DEVELOPMENTAL
FORCE OF PLAY

Cultivated, accepted, and curtailed play differ in how play is viewed by adults, and how it is used by children in their daily lives. Such cultural variation in the quantity and quality of children's play brings into question the universality of the developmental consequences of play. Two general findings have an impact on any developmental claims. First, although children of all ages are found to engage in play, pretend play in particular appears to peak as an important kind of play at different ages in different cultures. For example, for Euroamerican children, pretend play is most prevalent between the ages of 3 to 6, whereas for Yucatec Maya children, it is most prevalent between the ages of 6 and 8. It is unlikely that it will have the same developmental force at these different ages. Second, the social context of the play also is likely to influence its developmental functions. That is, what children will be offered and will be able to take from play will differ depending on whether that play is with parents (with high levels of cultivation), with mixed-age groups of children (with hierarchies of responsibility and authority), or with same-aged peers (with presumptions of equality of knowledge and status). If the social system of the culture makes it more likely that play occurs in one of these social situations more than the others, that alone is a powerful determinant of the developmental force of play, independent of any specific cultural beliefs or values.

Play has been theorized to have an impact on each of the four domains of child development—physical, cognitive, social, and emotional development. The three case studies presented in this chapter provide a useful basis for suggesting what research needs to be done to determine the extent to which the developmental force of play is universal in these four areas.

In terms of physical development, play has been argued to be an activity for both small-motor and large-motor skill development at all ages, and children in all the case studies engage in such play. However, the opportunity for children to do similar activities in nonplayful settings differs across the case studies. The cultures differ also in the number of specialized play objects that might encourage such development. Thus, although play appears to be a promising universal candidate as a domain where small- and large-motor skills are developed, it differs across cultures in whether or not it is a privileged domain for this developmental task.

In terms of cognitive development, a number of claims have been made that need to be questioned given the ethnographic reports given in this chapter. Piaget (1954) argued that the infant's "construction of reality" is solidified through practice play in which children repeat the production of phenomena that demonstrate their emerging understanding of relationships and causation in the physical world. This type of play is found to vary in the case studies given in this chapter. For Yucatec Maya infants, it is known that their object play is less complex than that of white American infants (Gaskins, 1990), even though they are free to explore, and for the Kpelle, infants are actively discouraged from playing with objects.

Vygotsky (1934/1987) gave a critical role to early symbolic expression using objects. He argued that this behavior separates the signifier from the signified for the young child, thus distinguishing the word from the thing for which it stands. This appears to be a candidate for a universal behavior. It is seen in cultures where play is highly cultivated (e.g., Euroamerican) and where it is curtailed (e.g., Yucatec Mayan). However, in the Mayan home, early symbolic expression is not mediated, celebrated, or expanded by adults as it is likely to be in the Euroamerican home. It is not clear how such differences in support of this symbolic expression might influence the child's cognition.

Vygotksy (1978) also attached significance to more complex symbolic play in older children as a way of learning about and reflecting on social roles and scripts. Reality-based pretend does occur among children in many if not all cultures, but it varies both quantitatively and qualitatively. There are differences in the age when children pretend the most, whether or not young children have primary or secondary control over themes, roles, and plot (depending on their social partners) and the amount of creative expression used in developing scripts and roles. Again, the importance of such differences for development is not clear.

In terms of social development, theorists suggest that through play, children can learn how to communicate and negotiate with other children in dyads and in larger groups. In the case studies provided here, play occurs in radically different social environments, including who children have for playmates, the relationships the playmates have in everyday life, the amount of adult involvement in the play, the amount of separation between play and the real world, and the opportunities for social interaction outside of play. Thus, although play is undoubtedly one kind of activity that teaches children about how to interact with one another in every culture, it is not offering universal social experiences. In many cultures, where children participate in more real-world activities, is it not the dominant or unique social opportunity for children to interact with one another. Where it is perhaps unique in all cultures is that it gives children, through pretend, a chance to enact (and therefore conceptualize, reflect on, and comment on) adult roles together.

Finally, play may also have an important role in emotional development. Piaget (1962), Vygotsky (1978), and Freud (1950) all suggested a cathartic potential in pretend play for children to rewrite the world to be more to their liking. In these case studies, one sees a wide variation in the amount of such emotional expression in children's play. In both Euroamerican and Taiwanese play, there seems to be significant opportunity for expressions of emotions, but it seems to be absent in Kpelle and Yucatec Mayan play. What does seem to be universal is an expression of joy and pleasure, demonstrated by smiling and laughing during most kinds of play. The children are interpreted to be happy while playing in all these cultures, but it is not universally a cathartic moment.

CONCLUSIONS

Three cultural approaches to play have been presented: cultivated, accepted, and curtailed play. In all three, children do spend time playing, their play takes varied forms, and it is clearly an enjoyable activity. However, the developmental power that play has seems to decline along the continuum of cultural support. Play is a more significant activity in children's lives in cultures where it is highly valued and adults spend a lot of resources in supporting and extending it. It is less significant if it is just accepted and taken for granted. It assumes somewhat minimal significance in the lives of children from a culture where it is curtailed as children spend a lot of their time working and observing others. Across these different cultures, play does not take up an equal amount of the children's time; it is not equally as complex, varied, and creative; and it does not seem to serve equally many important developmental functions.

Although these generalizations are drawn from the examples developed in this chapter, it is clear that cultural investment is not the only source of variation in play. Both the Euroamerican and the Taiwanese children are growing up in cultures where play is heavily cultivated, but the particular values and lessons from play are strongly influenced by specific values and beliefs in each culture. Likewise, within each of the cultures described here, there is variation in individuals' experiences with play. This intracultural variation serves as a cautionary reminder that although cultural understandings provide a general blueprint for childhood experience, they do not preclude individual or subgroup differences from developing.

There are at least four reasons why play is less valued, less cultivated, and less extensive in some cultures than in others. First, children in some cultures are engaged in meaningful activities outside of play, including the everyday activities of adults, that offer opportunities to practice and learn many skills that are often attributed to play. Development is a process that is characterized by redundancy, because it is so important that a child succeeds. A great variety of experiences can trigger many developmental accomplishments. It is not surprising if play is not necessary for important developmental achievements when other activities are present in abundance.

Second, it is possible that children in some cultures need to learn less through play because they are being socialized to enter into worlds that are less complex and less open-ended. From this perspective, such skills as creativity and inventiveness, which seem to be particularly supported in play, are not necessarily needed or even valued in all cultures. In addition to the Kpelle and the Yucatec Maya discussed here, researchers of several other cultures have also made this claim (Bird & Bird, 2002; Bock, 2002; Blurton Jones & Marlowe, 2002; Kramer, 2002). Lengthy training or preparation, through play or other activities, is probably not essential for adult skills in these societies. In contrast, in most postindustrial societies, both the complexity of skills and the flexibility to learn throughout the life span may be responsible for the large increase in adult management of children's experiences, including the intense mediation of play.

Third, when play is not seen as intrinsically valuable to children, as is the case with the Kpelle, parents may deliberately curtail their children's play if they see it as endangering the child itself, others, or property (Lancy, 2001). Children's play may also be halted by obligations imposed by the parent (work, church attendance, service to kin) that the parent considers of greater value, as seen in the Yucatec Maya. If play is not seen as having a value, then often the cost of play is considered too high.

Fourth, to the extent that one conceives of play as compensation, children in some cultures may need to play less because they are not required to cope with high demands made of them. In many cultures, children are not asked to do things before they know how, they do not interact often with strangers or in novel environments, they do not negotiate rigorously with caregivers over daily activities, and they do not regularly experience extreme emotional peaks and valleys. Cultural expectations are clearly communicated to them, and their behavior is less carefully scrutinized and structured. Under such circumstances, children may need to rely on play less to cope.

Finally, although all of children's play has been seen as theoretically interesting, the role of pretense and symbolic play in children's development has been privileged. However, the distinction between fantasy and reality-based pretend play has usually been ignored. Vygotsky (1978) articulated the cognitive value for older children of exploring real-life roles and scripts in pretense, and that type of pretense is found in all of the cultures discussed here. On the other hand, theorists argue that it is fantasy pretend play that provides the emotional value of addressing children's frustrations and desires. In the descriptions of children growing up in Taiwanese, Kpelle, and Yucatec Maya cultures, children appeared to engage in little true fantasy play. This finding raises the question of whether reality-based pretend and nonrealistic fantasy might have distinct developmental functions, one more universal, the other culturally specific. For instance, fantasy could encourage the development of a cognitive capacity to deny reality in favor of internal representations, constructed models, abstractions, and counterfactuals that could never be true, and an emotional capacity to be comfortable with such a stance. This stance may prepare children for the out-of-context learning that occurs regularly in Western school contexts and discovery in the arts and sciences. At the same time, it may also result in being egocentric and out of contact with reality. Whatever the strengths and weaknesses of engaging in fantasy play, we need to incorporate its cultural nature into our efforts to understand better the sources and consequences of this kind of play.

Even though, as we have seen, the value and cultural resources assigned to play vary widely across cultures, play does appear to serve a universal immediate function of giving the children something enjoyable to do when their immaturity and lack of skills prevent them from being engaged fully in adult activities. In this sense, play has a proximal payoff, that is, players may experience "flow" (Csikszentmihalyi, 1990) or "optimal stimulation" (Lancy, 1980b) in play at a time when they are not able to so in other activities. It may also have at least two universal distal payoffs, by improving children's competence and, ultimately, their fitness to participate in adult society. First, it may have an important function for physical development and skill building, especially for large-motor skills. Second, reality-based pretend play in particular may help children to understand better the roles and scripts of adults that they increasingly have to respond to and enact. In addition, there might be a universal payoff to the society in keeping children occupied and out of the way until they can participate effectively in adult work.

At the same time, it appears that cultures have different levels of investment in play, and it is not always a privileged and unique activity in children's lives. Even among those cultures that cultivate play, the specific value of play varies, as was seen with the Euroamericans and the Taiwanese. Recognizing that play is a culturally constructed activity allows us to pose some intriguing new research questions about children's play: What cultural values lead to play being privileged as the principle for structuring and cultivating children's daily activities? What are the specific developmental outcomes—positive and negative—of privileging play over other activities, or for privileging particular kinds of play, such as fantasy? Rephrasing our questions in this manner allows us not only to recognize the cultural nature of children's lives, including the form and substance of their play, but also to develop a more complete picture of the complexities of the developmental process.

REFERENCES

Bird, R. B., & Bird, D. W. (2002). Constraints of knowing or constraints of growing?: Fishing and collection by the children of Mer. *Human Nature 13*, 239–267.

Blurton Jones, N., & Marlowe, F. W. (2002). Selection for delayed maturity: Does it take 20 years to learn to hunt and gather? *Human Nature, 13*,199–238.

Bock, J. (2002). Learning, life history, and productivity: Children's lives in the Okavango Delta, Botswana. *Human Nature, 13*, 161–197.

Corsaro, W. (1997). *The sociology of childhood*. Thousand Oaks, CA: Pine Forge.

Csikszentmihalyi, M. (1990). *Flow: The psychology of optimal experience*. New York: Harper & Row.

Farver, J., & Shin, Y. (1997). Social pretend play in Korean- and Anglo-American preschoolers. *Child Development, 68*, 544–556.

Freud, S. (1950). *Beyond the pleasure principle*. New York: Liveright.

Fung, H. (1994). *The socialization of shame in young chinese children*. Unpublished doctoral dissertation, University of Chicago.

Gaskins, S. (1990). *Exploration and development in Mayan infants*. Unpublished doctoral dissertation, University of Chicago.

Gaskins, S. (1996). How Mayan parental theories come into play. In S. Harkness & C. Super (Eds.), *Parents' cultural belief systems*. New York: Guilford.

Gaskins, S. (1999). Children's daily lives in a Mayan village: A case study of culturally constructed roles and activities. In A. Göncü (Ed.), *Children's engagement in the world* (pp. 25–61). New York: Cambridge University Press.

Gaskins, S. (2000). Children's daily activities in a Mayan village: A culturally grounded description. *Journal of Cross-Cultural Research, 34*, 375–389.

Gaskins, S. (2001, February). *Ignoring play—Will it survive?: A Mayan case study of beliefs and behaviors*. Paper presented at the annual meetings of the Association for the Study of Play, San Diego, CA.

Gaskins, S. (2003). From corn to cash: Change and continuity within Mayan families. *Ethos, 31, 2.*

Gaskins, S., & Göncü, A. (1992). Cultural variation in play: A challenge to Piaget and Vygotsky. *Quarterly Newsletter of the Laboratory of Comparative Human Cognition, 14*(2), 31–35.

Gaskins, S., & Lucy, J. (1987, December). *Passing the buck: Responsibility and blame in the Yucatec Maya household.* Paper presented at the annual meeting of the American Anthropological Association, Philadelphia.

Gaskins, S., & Miller, P. (2002, February). *The cultural roles of emotions in pretend play.* Presented at the annual meetings of the Association for the Study of Play, Santa Fe, NM.

Greenfield, P. (1994). Preface. In P. Greenfield & R. Cocking (Eds.), *Cross-cultural roots of minority child development* (pp. 1–39). Hillsdale, NJ: Lawrence Erlbaum Associates, Inc.

Haight, L. (1999). The pragmatics of care-giver–child pretending at home: Understanding culturally specific socialization practices. In A. Göncü (Ed.), *Children's engagement in the world* (pp. 128–147). New York: Cambridge University Press.

Haight, W., Jacobsen, T., Black, J., & Sheridan, K. (in press). Pretend play and emotion learning in traumatized mothers and children. In D. Singer, R. Golinkoff, & K. Hirsh-Pasek (Eds.), *Play = learning.* New York: Oxford University Press.

Haight, W., & Miller, P. (1992). The development of everyday pretend play: A longitudinal study of mothers' participation. *Merrill-Palmer Quarterly, 38,* 331–349.

Haight, W., & Miller, P. (1993). *Pretending at home: Development in sociocultural context.* Albany: State University of New York Press.

Haight, W., Parke, R., & Black, J. (1997). Mothers' and fathers' beliefs about and spontaneous participation in their toddlers' pretend play. *Merrill-Palmer Quarterly, 43,* 271–290.

Haight, W., Wang, X., Fung, H., Williams, K., & Mintz, J. (1999). Universal, developmental, and variable aspects of young children's play: A cross-cultural comparison of pretending at home. *Child Development, 70,* 1477–1488.

Harris, J. R. (1998). *The nurture assumption: Why children turn out the way they do.* New York: Free Press.

Hausfater, G., & Hrdy, S. B. (1984). Comparative and evolutionary perspectives on infanticide: Introduction and overview. In G. Hausfater & S. B. Hrdy (Eds.), *Infanticide: Comparative and evolutionary perspectives.* New York: Aldine.

Hrdy, S. B. (1999). *Mother nature: Maternal instincts and how they shape the human species,* (pp. i–xxxix). New York: Ballantine.

Kramer, K. L. (2002). Variation in juvenile dependence: Helping behavior among Maya children. *Human Nature, 13,* 299–325.

Lancy, D. F. (1975). The social organization of learning: Initiation rituals and public schools. *Human Organization, 34,* 371–380.

Lancy, D. F. (1980a). Becoming a blacksmith in Gbarngasuakwelle. *Anthropology and Education Quarterly, 11,* 266–274.

Lancy, D. F. (1980b). Play in species adaptation. *Annual review of anthropology, (vol. IX,* pp. 471–495).

Lancy, D. F. (1980c). Speech events in a West African court. *Communication and Cognition, 13,* 397–412.

Lancy, D. F. (1983). *Cross-cultural studies in cognition and mathematics*. New York: Academic.

Lancy, D. F. (1996). *Playing on the mother ground: Cultural routines for children's development*. New York: Guilford.

Lancy, D. F. (2001). Cultural constraints on children's play. *Play and Culture Studies, 4*, 53–62.

Lancy, D. F. (in press). Nurture redefined as nature: Accounting for variability in mother-child play. *American Anthropologist, 108*(2).

Mintz, J. (1998). *The socialization of self in middle-class, Irish American families*. Unpublished doctoral dissertation, University of Chicago.

Pan, H. (1994). Children's play in Taiwan. In J. L. Roopnarine, J. Johnson, & E. Hooper (Eds.), *Children's play in diverse cultures* (pp. 31–50). Albany: State University of New York Press.

Parke, R. (1996). *Fatherhood*. Cambridge, MA: Harvard University Press.

Piaget, J. (1954). *The construction of reality in the child*. New York: Basic Books.

Piaget, J. (1962). *Play dreams and imitation in childhood*. New York: Norton.

Schwartzman, H. (1978). *Transformations: The anthropology of children's play*. New York: Plenum.

Sutton-Smith, B. (1977) Commentary. *Current Anthropology, 18*, 184–185.

Vygotsky, L. S. (1978). *Mind in society: The development of higher mental processes*. Cambridge, MA: Harvard University Press.

Vygotsky, L. S. (1987). *Thinking and speech*. In. R. W. Rieber & A. S. Carton (Eds.), *The collected works of L. S. Vygotsky: Vol. 1. Problems in general psychology of education* (N. Minick, Trans., pp. 39–285). New York: Plenum. (Original work published 1934)

Wang, X., Goldin-Meadow, S., & Mylander, C. (1995, March). *A comparative study of Chinese and American mothers interacting with their deaf and hearing children*. Paper presented at the meeting of the Society for Research in Child Development, Indianapolis, IN.

Weisner, T., & Gallimore, R. (1977). My brother's keeper. *Current Anthropology, 18*, 169–180.

IV

APPLIED PERSPECTIVES OF PLAY AND DEVELOPMENT

9

Hard Work for the Imagination

Paul L. Harris
Harvard University

If we look back at the history of child psychology, we can identify two opposing views of the development of the imagination. According to one account, early childhood is the high season for the imagination as reflected in the time that children spend in pretend play. On this view, as children get older, they adopt a more sober and objective stance and the role of the imagination declines. According to the second view, the imagination is not especially characteristic of early childhood. It is a capacity that contributes to cognitive development and to normal adult functioning. Although it is true that pretend play declines, this particular type of imaginative activity can be seen as just one early manifestation of a wide-ranging and sustained capacity.

In this chapter, I examine the historical origin of these different views of the imagination by way of a brief biographical sketch of Sabine Spielrein, a Russian psychoanalyst and educational psychologist. In the course of her professional life, she encountered, and in some cases collaborated with, the key proponents of each view. I then offer three lines of evidence to suggest that the second view of the imagination is plausible and important. I conclude by discussing the wider implications of our lifetime dependence on the imagination.

PIAGET, VYGOTSKY, AND SABINE SPIELREIN

In 1904, 19-year-old Sabine Spielrein left her native city of Rostov-on-Don. Her parents took her to the internationally renowned Burghölzli psychiatric clinic in Zürich. The clinic was directed at that time by Eugen Bleuler, the first psychiatrist to identify schizophrenia as a distinct syndrome. Bleuler assigned the new patient, apparently suffering from hysteria, to one of the young clinicians in residence, Carl Jung, who was pioneering the clinical application of psychoanalysis at the Burghölzli. Her treatment continued into 1905 but she eventually made a recovery, and registered in Zürich for a degree in medicine. In 1911, having completed a doctorate on schizophrenia under Bleuler's supervision, which was duly published in the *Yearbook for Psychoanalytic and Psychopathological Research*, Spielrein visited Vienna and for a while became a member of Freud's inner circle.

In the course of the next dozen years, she married, gave birth to the first of two daughters, worked as a clinician, and wrote various research papers on child development. In 1923, she returned to Russia where she became a researcher at the Psychoanalytic Institute in Moscow. She came into contact with Luria, who at that point in his career had a deep interest in psychoanalysis. Via Luria, it is highly probable that she also met Vygotsky (Kerr, 1994). By 1933, psychoanalysis was condemned as a bourgeois science under Stalin's rule. No longer able to earn her living as a practicing analyst, Spielrein returned to Rostov-on-Don where she continued to work as an educational psychologist. In 1942, she refused to leave the stricken city. Being Jewish, she was arrested and shot by the invading Nazis.

Spielrein's dramatic and tragic life story links together many of the individuals and competing ideas that shaped early theories of the imagination—the ideas of her two mentors Freud and Bleuler, and those of two younger men destined to dominate the study of cognitive development for most of the 20th century, Vygotsky and Piaget. Piaget's early ideas about development, particularly with respect to play and imagination, were profoundly influenced by his early interest in psychoanalysis. Like Spielrein, Piaget also studied in Zürich. He went there in 1918, immediately after World War I, where he attended lectures by Jung and Bleuler. Especially important for Piaget's subsequent views on pretend play and the imagination was his exposure to Bleuler's concept of autistic thinking (Harris, 1997). From 1919 to 1921, he undertook cognitive developmental work with children in Paris. During that same period, he accepted an invitation from Simon to give an introductory lecture on psychoanalysis—a relatively unknown theory in France at that time—to the assembled members of the Binet Society.

In the early 1920s Piaget deepened his knowledge of psychoanalysis by entering into analysis himself. His analyst was Sabine Spielrein, then living in Geneva, and working as a clinician and researcher. The analysis was brief and Piaget subsequently wrote of it—somewhat disingenuously perhaps—as an intellectual exploration rather than a therapeutic experience. However, Piaget also shared another interest with Spielrein, namely the development of children's language (Spielrein, 1923) and it is very likely that on her return to Moscow in 1923 she carried information about Piaget's views on language and thought to members of the Psychoanalytic Institute in Moscow, including Vygotsky. Certainly, as is well known from his subsequent classic *Thought and Language*, first published in 1934 but several years in the making, Vygotsky (1934/1986) was deeply familiar with Piaget's ideas and their relationship to those of Bleuler, Spielrein's former adviser.

In 1922, with Freud in the audience, Piaget presented a paper at the 7th International Congress of Psychoanalysis in Berlin. Piaget's paper is a fascinating blend of ideas that he had encountered in Zürich and his own emerging ideas on the constructive and rational nature of cognitive development. Borrowing from psychoanalytic theory, and more specifically from Bleuler's concept of autistic thinking, Piaget proposed that the infant's thought is prerational, and dominated by association and wish fulfillment. He also claimed—on the basis of his experimental findings in Binet's former laboratory in Paris and more recently in Geneva—that rationality and objectivity increasingly dominate children's thinking as they get older. Effectively, Piaget outlined a developmental transformation from a period of early autism to later logic. On this account, pretend play belongs to the earlier stage and is marked by some of the negative features of so-called autistic thinking as described by Bleuler: free association, wish fulfillment, and the setting aside of objective reality.

Explicitly departing from Piaget's views, Vygotsky developed a more positive account of the status of pretend play. He also borrowed from Bleuler but, unlike Piaget, he paid careful attention to Bleuler's caution that autistic thinking in general—and pretend play in particular—is not to be regarded as an unsophisticated or primary mode of thought (Vygotsky, 1934/1986). Rather, the conjuring up of alternatives to reality presupposes a certain knowledge of reality. Moreover, again in agreement with Bleuler, Vygotsky supposed that the capacity for entertaining such alternatives is not suppressed as the child moves toward cognitive maturity. To varying degrees and at different moments, adults entertain imaginary states of affairs when they daydream, plan, speculate, or hypothesize. Such thinking only becomes problematic when it dominates consciousness, as in the case of the schizophrenic with delusions of grandeur or paranoia. Vygotsky's critique of Piaget and his misconstrual of Bleuler is set out forcefully in the second chapter of *Thought and Language*—alongside his better known reanalysis of the role of egocentric speech. Indeed, at a structural level, Vygotsky's argument on these two topics runs in parallel: Piaget, he said, too readily identified a psychological capacity—pretend play on the one hand, egocentric speech on the other—as dysfunctional and doomed to disappear in the course of development. Closer analysis reveals that both capacities are actually positive and progressive in the sense that they are carried forward and play a role in the cognitive functioning of the adult.

My own account of the development of the imagination owes a great deal to Piaget's analysis of pretend play, as described in *Play, Dreams and Imitation* (Piaget, 1962). Piaget's description of the emerging sophistication and complexity of the pretend play of his own three children has turned out to be remarkably accurate and informative. Nevertheless, I ultimately share Vygotsky's more positive assessment of the status of pretend play and its continuity with the imaginative life of adults. I see three broad reasons for adopting that more positive stance (Harris, 2000).

In the first place, pretend play, especially the type of shared pretend play that we see among toddlers and young children, is distinctive of the human species and a good candidate for universality across very different cultures. Even in traditional village communities, where the burden of agricultural work or beliefs about what is appropriate for adult–child interaction may limit the support that adults provide, pretend play among young children still thrives (Göncü, Patt, & Kouba, 2002). For example, in her ethnography of Mayan children's activities in a Yucatan village, Gaskins (2000) reported a steady increase in the amount of time devoted to pretend play in early childhood. Pretend play emerges at about 18 months and by 6 to 8 years of age it takes up about half the time that children have for play activities, despite the fact that adults do little to support or stimulate such play. From an evolutionary perspective, it is difficult to maintain that an activity that manifests itself in such a regular, sustained, and relatively autonomous fashion in the course of childhood is maladaptive. It seems much more likely that such a capacity was positively selected in the course of human evolution. Certainly, it is plausible to suppose that any emerging capacity of the human species for contemplating alternatives to perceived reality was not just a form of escapism or wish fulfillment but enabled humans to act with greater judgment and foresight.

A second reason for taking a more positive stance toward pretend play and the imagination comes from the study of developmental psychopathology. Contrary to what we might expect from Piaget's account, it is not the presence or excess of pretend play but its absence or paucity that is associated with pathology. Thus, children suffering from autism are, by definition, restricted in their pretend play and also in their social relationships with other people. Although the exact connection between these two aspects of the syndrome of autism remains controversial, it certainly provides no grounds for the speculation that pretend play is a cognitive limitation that should be outgrown in the course of development.

A final reason for regarding pretense as a functional and progressive capacity emerges when we look closely at children's later deployment of the imagination. As I try to show, the available evidence indicates that the ability to imagine a state of affairs that one is not currently observing—one of the hallmarks of pretense—plays an important role in several key cognitive processes. In the next sections, I discuss three examples of such cognitive processes: reasoning from unfamiliar premises, judgments about obligation, and learning from testimony.

REASONING FROM UNFAMILIAR PREMISES

As part of a bold effort to show that even a basic cognitive process like logical reasoning is shaped by a person's cultural and educational experiences, Luria—in collaboration with Vygotsky—designed a large-scale research expedition to Uzbekistan (Luria, 1934, 1971). As part of that expedition, two groups of adults were given a set of reasoning problems. Luria found that peasants who had had no education balked at reasoning from an initial, general premise that lay outside their everyday experience. For example, if he said to them "In the Far North, where there is snow, all the bears are white. Novaya Zemlya is in the Far North. What color are the bears there?" Luria often received a protest along the following lines: "You've seen them, you know. I haven't seen them, so how could I say?" By contrast, those peasants who had received a minimal amount of schooling and literacy training—as part of Stalin's larger program of collectivist agriculture—adopted a different stance. Faced with the same problem, they could be coaxed into focusing on the wording of the problem and thereby drawing the appropriate conclusion. Luria concluded that the Soviet Revolution, and more specifically the exposure to education and literacy that many peasants were receiving in its wake, was bringing about a radical intellectual transformation. It was enabling peasants to contemplate and reason from propositions that were outside their ordinary realm of experience. The communist authorities suppressed Luria's dramatic findings for many years because they cast the traditional peasantry in a negative light. Luria abandoned cross-cultural research and eventually turned to the neuropsychological research that we usually associate with his name.

Nevertheless, Cole learned of the results obtained in Uzbekistan and initiated replication studies in West Africa (Cole, Gay, Glick, & Sharp, 1971). In due course, his colleague Scribner (1977) accepted and elaborated on Luria's basic conclusion. Reviewing studies of reasoning by adults and children in Uzbekistan, Liberia, and Mexico, she concluded that a relatively short exposure to schooling brings about a shift from an empirical to a theoretical orientation. Unschooled participants rely on their own empirical experience to supplement, distort, or reject the premises supplied by the experimenter. After a couple of years of schooling, however, participants are willing to focus on and reason from the supplied premises even when those premises do not fit into their everyday experience. Signs of each orientation can be discerned among Luria's protocols from Uzbekistan. Recall the protest of the traditional peasant quoted earlier when asked about the bears of Novaya Zemlya: "You've seen them, you know. I haven't seen them, so how could I say?" By contrast, more educated participants prefaced their correct conclusion with the phrase: "To go by your words…" or "If you say that…." Scribner reflected on the discourse genres that children and adults meet in school. They are exposed to a variety of problems with a formal structure that is similar to that of a syllogism. For example, they are invited to accept the premise that potatoes cost so much a pound, and to reflect on the total cost of 30 pounds. Their answer should be calculated and supplied independent of whether the price strikes them as plausible or whether they themselves would ever contemplate buying such a large quantity of potatoes. More generally, the school setting invites pupils to contemplate unfamiliar premises and to think through their implications. In this way, argued Scribner, schooling nurtures the so-called theoretical orientation.

At first glance, syllogistic reasoning might appear to have no affinity with children's imagination. However, our research has persuaded us otherwise. In a variety of studies, my colleagues and I have found that 2-year-olds engaged in pretend play with a partner are able to entertain a premise that is objectively false, to suppose that it is true, and to work out its implications (Kavanaugh & Harris, 1994). For example, an adult picks up a bottle of ketchup with the top firmly in place, inverts the bottle, and

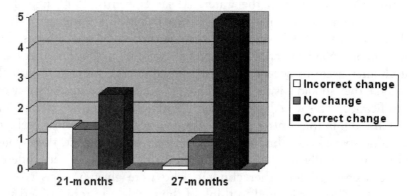

FIG. 9.1.   Mean number of choices (maximum = 6) devoted to each type of picture as a function of age (based on Kavanaugh & Harris, 1994).

makes pretend squeezing gestures above a toy pig. In watching the adult, children are effectively invited to suppose that ketchup is being squeezed out of the bottle. To assess whether they can work out the implications of that supposition, we showed them three pig pictures: one in which the pig was pink and pristine—the no change picture; one in which the pig had a white patch on its back—the incorrect change picture; and one in which the pretend consequence of the squeezing was appropriately illustrated—the pig was splashed with ketchup—the correct change picture. Children were asked to say what happened to the pig as a result of the supposed squeezing. Across a set of six such trials, 27-month-olds proved to be quite accurate—they mostly chose the picture depicting the correct change—but there was only a trend toward that correct choice among 21-month-olds (see Fig. 9.1). Note that if children had based their choice of picture on the observable, empirical situation, they would have chosen the no change picture. After all, the pretend squeezing had not actually altered the state of the toy pig.

These findings imply that young children can reason from premises that fly in the face of their empirical knowledge provided those premises are presented as temporary suppositions. They invite the speculation that young children might be able to engage in logical reasoning, and overcome the empirical bias, if they were given premises in a make-believe or pretend context. To explore this possibility, we gave 4- and 5-year-old children simple reasoning problems in which the first premise did not fit in with their everyday empirical experience; for example, "All fishes live in trees. Tot is a fish. Does Tot live in the water?" (Dias & Harris, 1990, Exp. 1). If children were to answer in terms of their empirical knowledge of fishes, they should say "yes"—and refer to what they know about fishes. This would correspond to Scribner's empirical orientation. On the other hand, if children were to accept the initial premise, and combine it with the second, they should answer "no" and refer back to the premises by way of a justification. This would correspond to Scribner's theoretical orientation.

Children in the control condition were given such reasoning problems with no special cues. Just as Scribner (1977) would expect, these young children typically displayed an empirical orientation. A very different pattern emerged for other children who were given various types of prompts. Whether invited to think of the problem in terms of a distant planet, or to make a mental image of the premises, or told the premises with a dramatic, storylike intonation, children were much more likely to adopt the theoretical stance, and to reason to a correct conclusion. Similar results were obtained more recently by Richards and Sanderson (1999). Indeed, they found that even 2- and 3-year-olds benefited from make-believe prompts.

The children in these studies, especially the very young children tested by Richards and Sanderson (1999), have clearly not had any exposure to formal schooling. How can we explain the fact that these uneducated children do so well, particularly in light of the apparently well-established claim that education is critical for reasoning from premises that lie outside of one's empirical experience? My conclusion is that the capacity for reasoning from such premises is available well before children go to school and has its roots in children's pretend play. Normally, a child hearing a premise that does not fit in with his or her empirical experience is inclined to resist that premise—unless prompted to do otherwise. Making the premise part of an imaginary or pretend world is one important way to overcome that resistance. Given such prompts, children display their ability to reason consequentially to new conclusions. Thus, what school appears to nurture is not the basic capacity to reason from such premises, but rather a greater readiness to take implausible premises seriously—in the absence of any explicit prompting—and to think about their implications. To borrow a phrase that is often used in connection with our stance toward fiction, school increases the child's willingness to suspend his or her disbelief. Nevertheless, our research indicates that the origin of this capacity antedates formal schooling and is closely connected to children's imaginative play.

JUDGING UNFULFILLED OBLIGATIONS

Children are often given rules that involve a conditional prescription, for example, if you do some painting, then you must wear an apron. A great deal of research with adults has suggested that they are quite alert to potential violations of such conditional prescriptions (Cosmides & Tooby, 1992) despite their difficulties in handling other types of descriptive conditionals; for example, if there is an odd number on one side of the card, there is a vowel on the other (Wason, 1966). We tried to find out if young children are also sensitive to such conditional prescriptions (Harris & Núñez, 1996).

To explore this issue, children were told about a child given permission to perform an action if a condition was met (e.g., to do some painting if an apron was worn) and they were then presented with four pictures showing the child performing the action or not, and either meeting or not meeting the condition. Figure 9.2 shows the type of picture that we used. It depicts one of the four combinations, namely the child performing the target action (painting) but not meeting the specified condition (i.e., not wearing an apron). We asked children to look at the four pictures and to choose the one where the child was being naughty and not doing what he (or she) was told. Three- and 4-year-olds proved to be remarkably accurate. The large majority chose the picture shown in Fig. 9.2, and ignored the other three.

The rule about wearing an apron when painting is likely to be familiar to young children, especially if they attend a preschool. Arguably, the high level of accuracy that we found in children's choice of the naughty protagonist was due to their familiarity with that rule and others like it that we included (e.g., If you ride a bicycle, then you must wear a helmet). Still, it is worth noting that children do not always get presented with such familiar—and prudent—conditional rules. Adults sometimes manufacture relatively arbitrary injunctions in pursuit of their own ends. Thus, a child might be told "If you watch TV, then you must put your pajamas on" or "If you finish your soup you can listen to a story." To find out if children understand the implications of such novel rules, we presented them with rules that they would never have encountered before. For example, we told them about a protagonist who was told this: "If you do some painting, you must wear a helmet" or "If you ride your bicycle you must wear an apron." Three- and 4-year-olds were again quite accurate when asked to indicate the picture in which the protagonist was being naughty. Thus, they picked out the child painting without a helmet or the child cycling without an apron.

FIG. 9.2. One of four choice pictures used by Harris and Núñez (1996). It depicts a "naughty" child performing the target action (painting) without meeting the prescribed condition (wearing an apron).

Children's choice data show that they are quite adroit at understanding both familiar and novel conditional rules. Again, as in the case of syllogistic reasoning, we can ask whether such understanding is in any way connected to children's imaginative capacity. The role of children's imagination emerged when we looked at the way that children justified their choices. We identified four different types of justification. As might be expected, some children offered an irrelevant justification; others simply

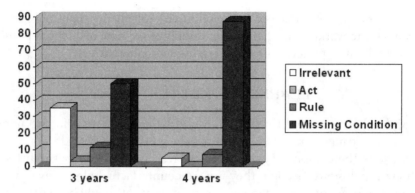

FIG. 9.3. Percentage of justifications falling into each of four categories as a function of age (based on Harris & Núñez, 1996).

echoed part of the rule (e.g., "He has to wear an apron"); others mentioned the critical action (e.g., "Doing some painting"); and still others pointed to the missing condition—they spelled out how the story protagonist had not satisfied the prescribed condition (e.g., "He hasn't got his apron on"). Figure 9.3 shows the frequency with which 3- and 4-year-old children produced each of these four types of justification.

Inspection of Fig. 9.3 reveals that the most frequent type of justification in each age group was a reference to the missing condition. A closer look at these justifications shows that children typically couch their statement in negative terms—they draw attention to what the protagonist was not doing or to something that is missing or absent. Apparently, in formulating such justifications, children compare what the protagonist is doing with some alternative course of action in which he or she could engage. More specifically, they compare what the protagonist is actually doing with what he or she should do. Thus, these simple justifications highlight the way that children—even in the preschool years—appraise what they observe in the light of some counterfactual but prescribed alternative. That alternative can be a very familiar rule (e.g., wearing an apron when you paint), but it can also be a completely new rule (e.g., wearing a helmet when you paint). By implication, preschool children readily assimilate such rules and then hold them up in their imagination as a mental prototype or standard against which people's actions are assessed. Thus, young children do not simply characterize reality in terms of the features it does possess; they also characterize it in terms of the features that it lacks when compared to some mental standard. In short, just beneath the surface of young children's judgments about obligation, we see the workings of their imagination; we see how reality is appraised in the light of prescribed—but often unmet—alternatives.

LEARNING FROM TESTIMONY

So far, I have argued that children use their imagination in two unexpected settings. First, they can entertain possibilities that do not correspond to their empirical experience and reason from those possibilities to new conclusions. Second, they invoke counterfactual alternatives when they make deontic judgments—they point to what should have happened but did not. I turn finally to another unexpected role for the imagination: in making sense of adult testimony, especially with respects to events, processes, or entities that are difficult for children to observe firsthand.

Before discussing any empirical findings, it is useful to consider the classic, Piagetian approach to early cognitive development. The child is assumed to gather knowledge and to revise his or her ideas primarily on the basis of firsthand observation. This emphasis on the key role of first-hand experience and exploration was taken up enthusiastically by some of the pioneers in early childhood education. Protocols from the Maltings experimental school run in Cambridge, England, by Susan and Nathan Isaacs show that children were prompted to seek answers on their own. When children put a question to an adult, the adult would often respond by asking how they could find out, and encouraging them to experiment for themselves (Isaacs, 1930). Echoes of the same positive assessment of independent discovery learning can be found in the writings of Montessori (1949/1967): "The greatest sign of success for a teacher," she wrote, "is to be able to say, 'The children are now working as if I did not exist'" (p. 283).

Yet there are many aspects of the world that children cannot observe firsthand or do experiments on. They cannot observe vast tracts of human history, they cannot observe distant objects or events, and they cannot easily observe microscopic processes. My hypothesis is that children learn a great deal about these unobservables by applying their imagination to the testimony that is provided by other people. Thus, as they listen to adults describing a historic battle, a remote galaxy, or the workings of a virus, children construct in their imagination a representation of what they are told.

In certain ways, however, this characterization of the link between imagination and testimony does not go far enough. A conservative interpretation of that link is that testimony simply expands the range of empirical phenomena that children can contemplate. Thus, testimony serves as a kind of microscope or telescope that gathers up and transmits information about mundane but hard-to-observe entities and events. Having listened to such testimony, children do not have the benefit of a firsthand encounter with such events but they can at least contemplate them in their imagination. On this view, testimony makes up for the fact that children—like adults—have limited powers of observation. A more radical interpretation is that testimony does not simply extend or amplify the range of observable phenomena that children can contemplate in their imagination. Rather testimony changes the very nature of the phenomena that children can contemplate. Indeed, to the extent that testimony serves as a type of guarantee, it encourages children to believe in the existence of beings and powers that no one can ordinarily perceive, even under the most favorable circumstances. By this interpretation, children end up with a different ontology, thanks to the joint contribution of their own imagination and other people's testimony.

Conceptualizing Metaphysical Phenomena

A first step toward establishing this more radical interpretation is to show that children readily conceptualize unobservable, metaphysical phenomena. For example, although children are told about distant lands or historical events that have been witnessed by observers in a relatively straightforward fashion, they are also told about religious phenomena that are beyond the reach of ordinary observation. How successful are young children in making sense of such metaphysical claims? Until recently, it was generally assumed that children's religious concepts are narrowly anthropomorphic. In particular, it has been assumed that children's conception of God is anthropomorphic. If that view were correct, it would suggest that although adults might offer children "radical" testimony about extraordinary beings or events, children will not fully assimilate what they are told. They will think of God as an ordinary human being with powers that are consistent with what they have observed to be true for human beings.

Recent evidence indicates, however, that this standard view of children's religious concepts gives them insufficient credit. Convincing evidence that young children are quite good at conceptualizing God's special powers has been reported by Barrett, Richert, and Driesenga (2001). Children were shown that some crackers had been taken out of a cracker box and put into a bag. They were then asked where various people, including their mother and God, would first look for the crackers: Would they mistakenly look in the cracker box or immediately know that they were in the bag? As might be expected from the large body of research on children's understanding of false or mistaken beliefs, there was a clear-cut improvement with age in the number of children who realized that their mother would mistakenly look in the cracker box. Children's replies with respect to God were quite different, however. By 5 and 6 years of age, children recognized that, unlike an ordinary human being such as their mother, God would not be mistaken about where to look for the crackers: He would immediately look for them in the bag. Thus, contrary to the standard view of young children as anthropomorphic, these findings indicate that children realize that God is not constrained by the need for perceptual access in the way that ordinary human beings are constrained. By implication, young children assimilate and understand what I have called radical testimony—claims about extraordinary beings that cannot be empirically checked in any standard fashion.

Still, one might insist that such attributions of knowledge to God are not so remarkable. Perhaps children are simply being egocentric—they attribute to God knowledge that they themselves possess. They know where the crackers are and they assume that God also knows. This line of interpretation is undermined by the recent findings of Giménez-Dasí, Gnerrero, and Harris (2005). Like Barrett et al. (2001), they interviewed children about God's knowledge as compared to that of a human being and obtained similar results. By the age of 5 years, children differentiated between the two beings. In addition, children were interviewed about God's lifecycle as compared to that of a human being. A similar pattern of results emerged in that 5-year-olds acknowledged biological constraints on the human life cycle but denied that those constraints applied to God. Thus, they recognized that God does not get older and will not die. In the context of the life cycle, it is not obvious that an egocentric strategy would help children to arrive at an appropriate conceptualization of God. These results therefore serve to reinforce the claim that young children can think about and conceptualize processes that neither they—nor anyone else—have ever observed.

However, it could be objected that these findings scarcely call for any reassessment of children's ontological beliefs. After all, the results described so far pertain only to children's understanding and not to their beliefs. Arguably, children listen to adult claims about God, understand their implications, but do not fully believe in those claims. For example, they might treat the religious discourse of adults as a kind of fairy story in which an extraordinary being does what is ordinarily impossible but only in the context of a special world akin to the fictional realm of "once upon a time." Certainly, it is feasible that the children interviewed by Barrett et al. (2001) and by Giménez-Dasí, Gunerrero, and Harris (2005) gave what they took to be correct answers about God's powers but had not committed themselves to a belief in God's existence. After all, even adult agnostics or atheists might be able to articulate the received, or theologically correct, view of God's special powers, whether or not they personally subscribe to God's existence.

Recent observations by Woolley (2000) are informative on this point. She noted that there are interesting parallels between making a wish on the one hand and saying a prayer on the other. In each case, there is a mental act—usually involving some form of utterance—and in each case, the act is aimed at bringing about a desired outcome by extraordinary means. Despite this similarity, the two practices are situated differently from a cultural perspective. Making a wish is typically regarded as a superstitious practice, something that we might encourage children to do on ritual occasions but not normally regarded as efficacious. By contrast, among believers at any rate, prayer is not regarded as a superstitious practice that the faithful should abandon. On the contrary, it is regarded as an effective and straightforward mode of communication with God.

Woolley and her colleagues invited children to assess the effectiveness of making a wish and saying a prayer (Woolley, 2000; Woolley, Phelps, Davis & Mandell, 1999). When asked about making a wish, an age change emerged. Among 3- and 4-year-olds, believers were in the majority, whereas among 5- and 6-year-olds, skeptics were in the majority. The developmental pattern was quite different for prayer: Among 3- to 5-year-olds, believers were in the majority—as for making a wish. Among 6- to 8-year-olds, however, the size of this majority waxed rather than waned. Thus, whereas children became increasingly dubious about the efficacy of making a wish as they got older, they became increasingly sure about the efficacy of prayer. These findings imply that when young children discuss God's special powers, they are not offering an agnostic but theologically correct view—they are conveying their own sincere beliefs. More generally, when taken in conjunction with one another, these findings on children's ideas about God's omniscience, God's immortality, and the efficacy of prayer suggest that children do not turn a deaf ear to radical testimony. It looks as if they listen to it, understand it, and indeed believe it. I now turn to a more explicit discussion of the implications of this claim for children's ontological judgments.

Ontological Judgments

To set the stage for the final set of findings that I want to describe, we can think of children as adopting either of two stances toward ontological matters. On the one hand, they might adopt the stance of a cautious empiricist. They might acknowledge and believe in the existence of all those entities and processes that they can observe firsthand but remain agnostic or skeptical toward everything else. Thus, they might readily believe in the existence of animals, rocks, and trees but remain doubtful about creatures that they never see for themselves, such as giants, mermaids, or monsters. Alternatively, children might adopt a more liberal and trusting stance. Alongside their belief in observable objects, they might also lend credence to entities that other people talk about but that they have not observed for themselves.

Given the routine assumption in research on cognitive development that children learn chiefly by virtue of their own active exploration, it is tempting to assume that cautious empiricism is their favored stance. Yet a moment's reflection should reveal that such caution on their part would actually amount to arch skepticism. It would imply that young children remain agnostic not just about God but also about the existence of historical personages that they have never met, countries they have never visited, and exotic animals that they have not had a chance to see for themselves. It would further imply that children doubt the existence of various tiny or invisible entities that they cannot see for themselves—entities such as viruses or genes. It is possible, of course, that children are indeed imbued with such extreme skepticism, but that does not easily square with their credulity in other respects. Most young children in North America believe in the Tooth Fairy, yet we may safely assume that few have ever seen her. In addition, the evidence reviewed in the previous section suggests that young children also believe in the existence of God. Again, it seems safe to say that few, if any, children base their belief in God on firsthand observation. They have learned of God's existence via adult testimony and they have no reason to doubt the assertions that are made. The implication of these reflections is that children are probably better described as trusting rather than skeptical in their ontological stance. More specifically, they listen to adult testimony and they accept the ontological assumptions of that testimony.

To explore these issues in more detail, we asked 4- to 5-year-olds and 7- to 8-year-olds about three types of entity: real and easily observable entities such as giraffes and rabbits, scientific but difficult-to-observe entities such as germs and oxygen; and nonexistent entities such as flying pigs and barking cats. Children were asked three questions of each entity—whether or not they believed in its existence, how sure they were of their judgment, and whether they knew what such entities looked like (Harris & Pons, 2003; Harris, Pasquini, Duke, Asscher, & Pons, 2006).

The findings were fully consistent with the expectations set out earlier. Children proved to be liberal or trusting in their ontological commitments rather than skeptical. First, as might be expected, children in both age groups claimed that entities such as giraffes and rabbits exist, they were confident of that judgment, and they also claimed to know what such entities looked like. Second, children in both age groups claimed that entities such as flying pigs or barking cats do not exist, they were also confident of that judgment, and they admitted to not knowing what such entities looked like. The most provocative findings emerged for hard-to-observe entities such as germs and oxygen. Both age groups claimed that they exist and they expressed confidence in that judgment. At the same time—and consistent with the idea that children's ontological judgments are not rooted in firsthand observation of such entities—they frequently admitted that they did not know what such entities looked like. Notice that there is nothing particularly unusual or naive about such an acknowledgment. Most adults would admit that cancerous cells exist yet, they would also admit that they are not able to distinguish between a cancerous cell and a healthy one. Our interpretation of these findings is relatively straightforward. Children often hear adults talk about germs or oxygen. In doing so, adults are likely to take the existence of such entities for granted. For example, a parent might warn a child not to touch something because it has germs or explain that germs can cause illness. We assume that children listen to these exhortations and explanations and take over the ontological presuppositions that they carry. Without reflecting on the matter, children simply go along with the adult assumption that germs exist.

Overall, these findings confirm that children are not cautious empiricists. They are guided by adult testimony in their ontological commitments. Thus, they deny the existence of some impossible entities (e.g., flying pigs), but they accept the existence of others (e.g., germs and oxygen). A major implication of these findings is that children's imagination enlarges the scope of ordinary reality. In the previous sections, I argued that children's imagination allows them to entertain alternatives to reality. Thus, when they reason, they can entertain a premise they know to be false and work out its implications. When they make deontic judgments, they can compare what has actually happened to some obligatory alternative and judge accordingly. In each of these cases, children are using their imagination to explore possibilities that have not been realized. In the case of children's ontological commitments, however, children use their imagination in a different way: Rather than allowing them to contemplate alternatives to reality, it leads them to expand their conception of reality itself. For the young child—as for the adult—reality comes to embrace all sorts of hidden and unobservable entities.

An important question for the future concerns the extent to which children differentiate among those unobservable entities. If the argument that I have made so far is correct, children readily accept the existence of God on the one hand and scientific entities such as germs on the other. In each case, their belief is based on the testimony that is provided by other people because children do not ordinarily have the opportunity to observe either phenomenon firsthand. Does this mean, then, that in the eyes of young children their ontological status is on the same footing? More specifically, is children's belief in God as unreflective and confident as their belief in germs? A review of the arguments that I have presented so far points to two different possible answers. Consider a child growing up in a home where belief in God is taken for granted, and everyday discourse frequently invokes God's causal role—whether with respect to creation or the answering of prayers. Such a child might reasonably draw the conclusion that people in his or her family take it for granted that God exists in roughly the same way that they take it for granted that germs exist. If this argument is correct, such a child would have no inkling that—for many people at least—germs are simply part of the normal ontological furniture of the world, whereas God enjoys a special status. Consider, by way of contrast, a child growing up in a diverse community that includes a variety of religious standpoints. Such a child might notice that people vary in the extent to which they invoke God: Some people might do so routinely, others might do so rarely, and still others might explicitly comment on variation in belief. Such diverse testimony might prompt children to attribute a different, and more equivocal, ontological status to God as compared to less controversial entities. On this argument, quite young children might show some embryonic ability to differentiate between two groups of unobservable entities—those that everyone takes for granted and those whose ontological standing varies from group to group. As we gain more insight into children's ability to monitor incoming testimony, we will be able to assess which portrait of the young child is more accurate.

CONCLUSIONS

In the introduction, I noted that Piaget portrayed early cognitive development as the gradual suppression of prerational, autistic thinking in favor of objectivity and logic. On this view, cognitive progress involves three interrelated characteristics. First, the child constructs increasingly objective hypotheses or theories. Second, these intellectual revisions and transformations are generally precipitated by the child's own active exploration and observation. Third, when the child is confronted with adult verbal instruction, there are the twin dangers that the child will resist what he or she is told—especially when it conflicts with autonomously constructed ideas—or that the child will gain, at best, a superficial verbal understanding of what is being taught. This portrait of cognitive development has had an enduring appeal; echoes of it can certainly be found in contemporary analyses of cognitive development (Gardner, 1991; Gopnik, Meltzoff, & Kuhl, 1999). Yet it is difficult to identify any sustained role for the imagination in Piaget's account. Insofar as he discussed the imagination, it was generally regarded as an unsatis-factory departure from reality—a feature of autistic as opposed to objec-tive thinking.

My conception of cognitive development is different from Piaget's. I share with Vygotsky the belief that the imagination plays a sustained rather than transient role in cognitive development. I am not convinced that children ineluctably progress toward a more objective conception of the world and I do not believe that children's imagination is suppressed in the wake of such progress. First, as I have tried to show, children manifest an early willingness to entertain premises that do not coincide with their empirical experience, and to reason from those premises to new conclu-sions. They bring that imaginative capacity to school with them, and it continues to underpin the expansion of children's intellectual horizons that good schooling can nurture. Second, children's appraisal of reality is con-stantly informed by normative and moral considerations. Faced with the actual world, children often refer to possibilities that would have been preferable. Again, therefore, we see children's imagination at work: They spontaneously refer to possibilities that have not been realized but could and should have been. The final role that I have sketched for the imagina-tion is in many ways the most potent. There are many domains in which children's active observation and exploration can yield virtually no useful data. For example, in the domains of history, cosmology, and religion, the key data are not available for firsthand observation. Accordingly, young children can scarcely act as scientific explorers. Rather, they are obliged to play the role of budding jurors—or disciples—who wonder what testimony to trust. They are obliged to listen to and sift through the variegated claims made by other people. Children's ability to make sense of these claims and to detect where consensus lies is no guarantee that they gradually move toward a more objective or rational picture of the world. The history of ideas offers many examples of collective folly and there is no reason to assume that the course of cognitive development escapes all of these siren calls. To my mind, then, it is plausible to suppose that children will increasingly subscribe to theories and precepts that have little basis in objective reality even if, in some domains, we judge them to show signs of progressive enlightenment. The human imagination, for better or for worse, makes each of these avenues possible.

REFERENCES

Barrett, J. L., Richert, R. A., & Driesenga, A. (2001). God's beliefs versus mother's: The development of non-human agent concepts. *Child Development, 72*, 50–65.

Cole, M., Gay, J., Glick, J. A., & Sharp, D. W. (1971). *The cultural context of learning and thinking.* New York: Basic Books.

Cosmides, L., & Tooby, J. (1992). Cognitive adaptations for social exchange. In J. H. Barkow, L. Cosmides, & J. Tooby (Eds.), *The adapted mind: Evolutionary psychology and the generation of culture* (pp. 163–228). Oxford, UK: Oxford University Press.

Dias, M., & Harris, P. L. (1990). The influence of the imagination on reasoning by young children. *British Journal of Developmental Psychology, 8*, 305–318.

Gardner, H. (1991). *The unschooled mind.* New York: Basic Books.

Gaskins, S. (2000). Children's daily activities in a Mayan village: A culturally grounded description. *Journal of Cross-Cultural Research, 34*, 375–389.

Giménez-Dasí, M., Gnerrero, S., & Harris, P. L. (2005). Intimations of immortality and omniscience in early childhood. *European Journal of Developmental Psychology, 2*, 285–297.

Göncü, A., Patt, M. B., & Kouba, E. (2002). Understanding young children's pretend play in context. In P. Smith & C. Hart (Eds.), *Blackwell handbook of childhood social development* (pp. 418–437). Oxford, UK: Blackwell.

Gopnik, A., Meltzoff, A., & Kuhl, P. (1999). *How babies think.* London: Weidenfeld & Nicolson.

Harris, P. L. (1997). Piaget in Paris: From "autism" to logic. *Human Development, 40*, 109–123.

Harris, P. L. (2000). *The work of the imagination.* Oxford, UK: Blackwell.

Harris, P. L., & Núñez, M. (1996). Children's understanding of permission rules. *Child Development, 67*, 1572–1591.

Harris, P. L., Pasquini, E. S., Duke, S., Asscher, J. J., & Pons, F. (2006). Germs and angels: The role of testimony in young children's ontology. *Developmental Science, 9*, 76–96.

Harris, P. L., & Pons, F. (2003, April). Germs, angels and giraffes: Children's understanding of ontology. Poster presented at the biennial meeting of the Society for Research in Child Development, Tampa, FL.

Isaacs, S. (1930). Intellectual growth in young children. London: Routledge.

Kavanaugh, R. D., & Harris, P. L. (1994). Imagining the outcome of pretend transformations: Assessing the competence of normal children and children with autism. Developmental Psychology, 30, 847–854.

Kerr, J. (1994). A most dangerous method: The story of Jung, Freud and Sabina Spielrein. London: Sinclair-Stevenson.

Luria, A. R. (1934). The second psychological expedition to central Asia. Journal of Genetic Psychology, 41, 255–259.

Luria, A. R. (1971). Towards the problem of the historical nature of psychological processes. International Journal of Psychology, 6, 259–272.

Montessori, M. (1967). The absorbent mind. New York: Holt, Rinehart & Winston. (Original work published 1949)

Piaget, J. (1962). Play, dreams and imitation. London: Routledge and Kegan Paul.

Richards, C. A., & Sanderson, J. A. (1999). The role of imagination in facilitating deductive reasoning in 2-, 3-, and 4-year-olds. Cognition, 72, B1–B9.

Scribner, S. (1977). Modes of thinking and ways of speaking: Culture and logic reconsidered. In P. N. Johnson-Laird & P. C. Wason (Eds.), Thinking: Readings in cognitive science (pp. 483–500). New York: Cambridge University Press.

Spielrein, S. (1923). Quelques analogies entre la pensée de l'enfant, celle de l'aphasique et la pensée subconsciente. (Some similarities between the thinking of children, the thinking of aphasics, and subconscious thinking) Archives de Psychologie, 18, 306–322.

Vygotsky, L. (1986). Thought and language. Cambridge, MA: MIT Press. (Original work published 1934)

Wason, P. C. (1966). Reasoning. In B. M. Foss (Ed.), New horizons in psychology 1 (pp. 135–151). Harmondsworth, UK: Penguin.

Woolley, J. D. (2000). The development of beliefs about direct mental–physical causality in imagination, magic, and religion. In K. S. Rosengren, C. N. Johnson, & P. L. Harris (Eds.), Imagining the impossible: Magical, scientific, and religious thinking in children (pp. 99–129). New York: Cambridge University Press.

Woolley, J. D., Phelps, K. E., Davis, D. L., & Mandell, D. J. (1999). Where theories of mind meet magic: The development of children's beliefs about wishing. Child Development, 70, 571–587.

10

Of Hobbes and Harvey: The Imaginary Companions Created by Children and Adults

Marjorie Taylor
Anne M. Mannering
University of Oregon

In his classic book *Play, Dreams and Imitation in Childhood*, Piaget (1962) carefully documented a series of imaginary companions created by his daughter Jacqueline. At 3;11, she invented an "aseau," a strange birdlike creature that could also be a dog, an insect, or any other animal that struck Jacqueline's fancy. The aseau was followed by an invisible dwarf and then a girl named Marecage, who played all the time and did not have to take naps. Piaget was interested in the many functions served by these companions and provided examples of how they comforted Jacqueline when she was afraid, helped her cope with being teased, and provided a vehicle for expressing opinions, emotion, and ideas related to reality.

Piaget's discussion presents a normative view that contrasts with the theories of his contemporaries, who tended to link imaginary companions with various types of disturbances and difficulties (e.g., Ames & Learned, 1946; Bender & Vogel, 1941; Benson & Pryor, 1973; Myers, 1976, 1979). On the other hand, Piaget (1962) cautioned his readers not to overinterpret interactions with imaginary companions as evidence of creativity or a developing imagination: "In reality, the child has no imagination, and what we ascribe to him as such is no more than a lack of coherence" (p. 131). For Piaget, imaginary companions were an intriguing mix of imitation and distorting assimilation that belonged to the preoperational period of development. He believed that the development of imagination consisted of a decrease in such constructions "in favor of representational tools more adapted to the real world" (p. 131).

Despite his negative interpretation of imaginary companions as evidence of immature thought, Piaget described the phenomenon of children's imaginary companions as the most interesting of all deliberate symbolic constructions. We agree with the latter part of this assessment. After more than a decade of studying the creation of imaginary companions and related types of pretend play, we continue to be amazed by the complexity, idiosyncrasy, and detail in children's reports. Also, like Piaget and more recent researchers (Bouldin & Pratt, 1999; Gleason, Sebanc, & Hartup, 2000; Manosevitz, Fling, & Prentice, 1977; Manosevitz, Prentice, & Wilson, 1973; Pearson et al., 2001; Singer & Singer, 1990), we consider the creation of imaginary companions to be normative, even common, during early childhood. However, in contrast to Piaget, we do not believe that interacting with an imaginary other is a curious phenomenon unique to early childhood. Instead, we have more of a life-span perspective on this type of activity and are convinced that there is much to be learned about the capabilities of the human mind and the development of imagination from the investigation of imaginary companions.

In what follows, we review recent research on the developmental course of imaginary companions, the functions they serve, the characteristics of children who create them, and parental reactions to them (e.g., Taylor, 1999; Taylor & Carlson, 1997; Taylor, Cartwright, & Carlson, 1993). We also discuss some of the methodological challenges presented by this area of research. Finally, we suggest a link between the creation of imaginary companions by children and the creation of imaginary characters by adult fiction writers.

DEFINITIONAL AND METHODOLOGICAL ISSUES

In general, there is considerable variability in the types of pretend activities that children enjoy. More specifically, imaginary companions come in all shapes, sizes, ages, genders, and species. They differ in vividness, personality development, longevity, and activities. Sometimes they are completely invisible and sometimes children use props to represent them, including a variety of idiosyncratic objects (a leaf, a stick, a finger, etc.), as well as toys such as dolls and stuffed animals. One of our research participants used a couch caster (i.e., the little hemisphere of metal that goes on the bottom of a couch leg to keep the carpet from tearing). He wore it on his thumb, and his thumb and the caster cap became "Johann." Some children consistently use a prop, others consistently do not use a prop, and others are inconsistent (i.e., sometimes they use a prop and sometimes the character is completely invisible). For example, Piaget's daughter sometimes used a shovel to represent her friend Marecage, who at other times was invisible. In addition, some children act out or impersonate the character themselves rather than treat it as a separate individual (e.g., a child who created a character named Super Lightning Bolt Aidan and pretended to be this character for many months). Finally, some children switch back and forth between impersonating the character and treating the character as a separate individual. This was true for Piaget's daughter Jacqueline. When she first invented the aseau, she ran around flapping her arms and was the aseau. Only later did the aseau become a separate entity who was her companion.

According to Harris (2000), all these pretend activities are similar in that they involve role play; the child imagines the thoughts, actions, and emotions of a person or creature. Within role play, Harris made distinctions based on the vehicle for the imagined character: (a) an object as vehicle, (b) nothing as vehicle (i.e., an invisible imaginary companion), or (c) the self as vehicle (i.e., impersonation). In our research, we have investigated all three types of role play, but here we focus primarily on the first two types in which a character (based on an object or invisible) can serve as a companion. Depending on the age of the children, about a third to half of imaginary companions are based on objects and the rest are invisible (e.g., Gleason et al., 2000; Taylor, 1999). Some authors have excluded objects as imaginary companions (Svendsen, 1934); however, we believe that children's imagined relationships with objects sometimes become so vivid and interactive that it is reasonable to consider them a type of imaginary companion. Parental report can help identify the toys that are more than casual playthings or transitional objects, but are instead toys with which children have a special relationship similar to the one depicted in the comic strip *Calvin and Hobbes*.

In our research we have found that the psychological characteristics that distinguish children with imaginary companions from other children are true for the children with toy imaginary companions as well as children with invisible imaginary companions (Taylor & Carlson, 1997). This is not to say, however, that toy-based and invisible imaginary companions are equivalent in all respects. Gleason et al. (2000) found that children tend to have relationships that resemble friendships with invisible imaginary companions, whereas with toy imaginary companions there is often a caretaking relationship. Although this is a general trend with many exceptions, it is an interesting finding and suggests that the type of imaginary companion that a child creates may provide insight into the social and emotional functions of the companion.

A variety of approaches have been used to examine the characteristics of children's imaginary companions. One frequently used method is to ask adults if they had an imaginary companion in childhood and if so to describe it. According to these retrospective reports, about 10% to 25% of adults report having had an imaginary companion (e.g., Hurlock & Burnstein, 1932). One limitation of retrospective reports is that many adults do not remember very much about their imaginary companions, and often what they report are secondhand accounts from their parents. In fact, when investigating imaginary companions in childhood, parents can be a valuable source of information, with 50% or more of parents reporting that their children have imaginary companions (Gleason et al., 2000). However, some parents are unaware that their child has created such a companion or have inaccurate impressions about the companion's characteristics. For example, one parent in our research described her child's imaginary companion Nobby as a little invisible boy, whereas the child reported that Nobby was a 160-year-old businessman (Taylor, 1999). In another study (Mannering & Taylor, 2003), a parent described her daughter's imaginary companion Olympia as a naughty invisible girl who was responsible for damages in child's room, whereas the child described Olympia as an invisible giraffe who turned different colors when she danced.

Given the limitations of parent reports, it is optimal to interview the children themselves. Children are the authorities on their imaginary companions, and many young children are quite capable of describing them (Friedberg & Taylor, 1997; Nagera, 1969; Singer & Singer, 1990; Taylor, Cartwright, & Carlson, 1993). However, child interviews present other methodological difficulties. For example, children may have a special way of referring to their imaginary companions ("fake friend," "ghost sister") and misunderstand questions about having a "pretend friend" (Taylor & Carlson, 1997). Further, sometimes children mistakenly describe real friends when asked about pretend friends. Interviewing parents as well as the children provides clarification in such cases. In light of these considerations, our preferred method has been to use a combination of child and parent interviews, and when possible we have interviewed both the children and the parents on two separate occasions to assess the reliability of the descriptions (Taylor & Carlson, 1997; Taylor et al., 1993).

CHARACTERISTICS OF IMAGINARY COMPANIONS

In the course of our research, we have collected 592 descriptions of imaginary companions: 327 descriptions from children, 76 descriptions from parents, and 189 retrospective reports from adults. These descriptions are from published studies (Taylor et al., 1993; Taylor & Carlson, 1997; Taylor, Carlson et al., 2004) and unpublished data collected in collaboration with Ariann Bolton, Stephanie Carlson, Thomas Dishion, Robert Kavanaugh, Vickie Luu, Jennifer Miner, and Alison Shawber. The children in our studies ranged in age from 3 to 12 years (73% were 5 years old or younger, 16% were 6–8 years old, and 11% were 12 years old). The parents all described the imaginary companions of children under 5 years of age, and although many of the adults did not report exactly how old they were when they played with their imaginary companions, most of the adult retrospective reports seemed to be of companions from early childhood. For the purpose of providing a broad picture of childhood imaginary companions we have collapsed across different sources of information.

Of the 592 descriptions, 236 (40%) were of special toys or objects that seemed to function as imaginary companions. These companions were not based solely on teddy bears and dolls, but represented a range of different species (rabbits, frogs, dogs, monkeys, Muppets, a kangaroo, a dinosaur, a hedgehog, a cow, a tiger, a horse, a dolphin, a Smurf, a Tasmanian Devil, a cat, a donkey, a squirrel, and a moose), as well as more idiosyncratic non-toy objects (Taylor & Carlson, 2002).

The remaining 356 descriptions (60%) were invisible companions. About 34% of invisible imaginary companions were regular everyday sorts of invisible girls and boys, consistent with the function of imaginary companions as playmates. However, many imaginary companions (16%) were not regular children in that they had special or magical characteristics—they could fly, change shape, exert special powers—or they had unusual physical characteristics like blue skin or tiny size. For example, Elfi Welfi was described by her 4-year-old creator as being especially tiny with tie-dye hair and skin and a bossy personality. This particular case illustrates another intriguing aspect of children's imaginary companions: They do not always comply with the child's wishes. Sometimes they disagree with the child, surprise the child with the things they say or do, and even boss the child around (e.g., Bouldin & Pratt, 1999; Nagera, 1969; Taylor, 1999). In fact, a few imaginary companions (1% in our sample) are predominantly mean or frightening to the child (e.g., "Invisible big blue furry thing that had red eyes, no clothes and was six feet tall. He was really scary.").

In addition to human imaginary companions, our sample included a large number of invisible animals (15%). The invisible animals typically have the ability to talk or otherwise communicate with the child, and about half are further embellished with magical powers or special characteristics. For example, one child described Dipper, an invisible flying dolphin who lived on a star, never slept, and could fly very fast (Taylor, 1999). In addition to invisible people and animals, children reported other categories of imaginary companions, albeit less frequently. Our sample included superheroes, ghosts, angels, and spirits (8%). Yet another 7% of the invisible imaginary companions were unique (e.g., a Cyclops who was a world traveler).

From the sample of descriptions presented, the diversity of children's imaginary companions is clear; they vary in size from a speck to 10 feet tall, they can be newborn infants or they can be ancient (e.g., 1,000 years old), they are every possible species, and they may even be from another planet. Further, the imaginary companions sometimes have families and lives of their own. For example, we recently learned about a little invisible boy named Bunsen. Bunsen often spent time with the child who created him, traveled in the family car with her, and had long conversations with her on the phone. However, Bunsen also had a family of his own, including parents (Peechop and Petreep), a sister (Bowie) who was born about the same time that the little girl's sister was born, and a dog (Pum-Pum) who died when a dog in the little girl's family died.

CHARACTERISTICS OF CHILDREN WHO CREATE IMAGINARY COMPANIONS

In our research we have found that about 28% of 3- and 4-year-olds have imaginary companions. What are the characteristics of the children who engage in this type of role play? First of all, at least in preschool, they are more likely to be girls than boys (Carlson & Taylor, 2005). Our research replicates many other studies that report a sex difference in the incidence of imaginary companions (e.g., Hurlock & Burnstein, 1932; Manosevitz et al., 1977; Mauro, 1991; Pearson et al., 2001; Svendsen, 1934). We have found, however, that this difference pertains to the form of the role play rather than the overall frequency of role play. Although preschool girls are more likely than boys to have imaginary companions, boys are more likely than girls to impersonate imaginary characters. These findings highlight the importance of including impersonation when investigating role play in preschool children, given that boys and girls appear to express fantasy orientation differently during the preschool period (e.g., Bach, 1971; Carlson & Taylor, 2005; Harter & Chao, 1992; Rosenfeld, Huesmann, Eron, & Torney-Purta, 1982; Svendsen, 1934). Another caveat about the sex difference in the creation of imaginary companions is that it seems to disappear as children get older. In recent longitudinal data, we found that by school age, boys and girls are equally likely to create imaginary companions (Taylor, Carlson, Maring, Gerow, & Charley, 2004).

A number of recent studies have investigated personality and other types of possible differences between children with and without imaginary companions. The emerging view is that, in most respects, the similarities between the two groups are more striking than the differences. However, fantasy activities during the preschool period are related to a number of positive social characteristics. For example, high-fantasy children are rated by teachers as showing higher levels of energy, concentration, self-reliance, and frustration tolerance (Tower, 1985). They also initiate and engage in more social play and are less likely to play alone (Singer & Singer, 1990). More specifically, other studies have found that young children who create imaginary companions show higher levels of positive affect and are more socially competent (e.g., Partington & Grant, 1984; for a review see Singer & Singer, 1990; Tower, 1985; although see Harter & Chao, 1992 for contradictory findings), and some research suggests that creating an imaginary companion in childhood is related to later creativity (e.g., Schaefer, 1969). Mauro (1991) found that although children with imaginary companions did not differ from their peers on most temperament measures, they were rated by their parents as being less shy and more able to focus and sustain attention than children without imaginary companions. Overall, research findings suggest that young children who do and do not create imaginary companions show considerable similarity in personality (e.g., Bouldin & Pratt, 1999, 2002; Manosevitz et al., 1977; Manosevitz et al., 1973; Taylor, 1999; Taylor et al., 2004); however, when differences are found, they tend to favor children with imaginary companions (Mauro, 1991; Taylor, 1999).

We have been particularly interested in the relation between having an imaginary companion and theory of mind development. By age 5, most children have developed an understanding of the role of the mind in guiding behavior, and this understanding is positively correlated with measures of social competence (e.g., Astington, 1993; Lewis & Mitchell, 1994; Wellman & Gelman, 1998). A number of researchers have suggested that children's involvement in pretense and fantasy contributes to theory of mind development, noting that role play in particular is a context in which children encounter and manipulate multiple perspectives (e.g., Astington & Jenkins, 1995; Harris, 2000; Leslie, 1987; Taylor & Carlson, 1997). Indeed, elaborate pretense often involves a good deal of negotiation between what the child is pretending and the real world. For children with imaginary companions, this negotiation involves integrating the companion into everyday activities, such as having an extra place set at the table and keeping others informed about the companion's behavior and mental states.

Taylor and Carlson (1997) found that compared to children who engaged in less role play, 4-year-old children who had imaginary companions or impersonated characters were significantly better at distinguishing appearance from reality, attributing a false belief to both themselves and a puppet, and recognizing the different perspective of another. Further, there was a .28 correlation between fantasy and theory of mind that was independent of verbal intelligence, age in months, and sex. Similarly, Carlson, Gum, Davis, and Molloy (2003) found that having an imaginary companion was positively related to understanding that a person can hold a false belief. In addition, Carlson et al. found that 24-month-olds who later created an imaginary companion showed a broad interest in fantasy, demonstrated greater understanding of visual perspective taking, and used more mental state words compared to children who did not create imaginary companions.

Thus, the findings from our own research and the research of others stand in sharp contrast to the view that children's involvement in fantasy, and the creation of imaginary companions in particular, reflects social and cognitive deficits. Whereas Piaget described imaginary companions as nothing more than distorting assimilation of reality to the child's own ego, we find that children's imaginary companions are positively associated with their performance on cognitive tasks that require accommodation of thought to reality. Rather than promoting an exclusive focus on the child's own subjective experience, role play involving imaginary companions is related to a greater ability to adopt the perspective of another person and to consider how mental representations are connected to but distinct from reality. Thus, our findings are consistent with Harris's (2000) claim that children's pretend play demonstrates their knowledge of reality, rather than confusion about it.

We clearly have a positive view of imaginary companions, but we do not mean to claim that troubled children do not create them. Pretend play is a resource that young children use to cope with a wide range of difficulties and adverse life circumstances (e.g., Bach, 1971; Bender & Vogel, 1941; Friedberg & Taylor, 1997; Myers, 1979; Nagera, 1969; Terr, 1990). For example, work by Putnam (e.g., 1996, 1997, 2000), Silberg (1998), and others (e.g., Sanders, 1992) indicates that sexually abused children who develop dissociative disorders are very likely to have imaginary companions. In addition to providing companionship, the imaginary companions created by these children also serve a number of coping functions not typically reported by nonabused children. Specifically, children and adolescents diagnosed with dissociative identity disorder report that their imaginary companions keep secrets, hold memories, endure the pain of abuse, and act as protectors (Putnam, 1997; Sanders, 1992). Similarly, Clark (chap. 12, this volume) presents some striking examples of how sick children use fantasy to cope with the challenges presented by their illnesses. For a variety of difficult situations or life problems, having an imaginary companion can be a positive and adaptive response. However, it is important to keep in mind that although children with problems often have imaginary companions, having an imaginary companion does not mean that the child has problems. In fact, children with imaginary companions tend to be particularly sociable individuals who enjoy the company of others and are somewhat advanced in social understanding.

PARENTAL ATTITUDES ABOUT IMAGINARY COMPANIONS

It is not just developmental psychologists who are curious about imaginary companions and wonder what they mean. Parents also express a range of positive and negative beliefs about the significance of imaginary companions. On the one hand, some parents are extremely positive about their children's imaginary companions, viewing them as markers of high intelligence and creativity (e.g., Manosevitz et al., 1973; Svendsen, 1934; Taylor & Carlson, 2000). In fact, some parents worry if their child does not have an imaginary companion. At the other extreme, parents sometimes hold negative views of imaginary companions, fearing that creating and interacting with an imaginary character reflects an inability to tell the difference between fantasy and reality or is evidence of emotional disturbance and risk for developing mental illness (Taylor & Carlson, 2000).

The wide range of parental reactions to imaginary companions raises a number of interesting questions: What are the bases for parental beliefs? For example, are they a function of culture and religion? Do they stem from experiences specific to the imaginary companions created by their own children? To what extent do parental beliefs influence children's fantasy behaviors? Do children whose parents discourage interactions with imaginary companions give them up more quickly or become more secretive about them? Perhaps these children would be less likely to have an imaginary companion in the first place.

As a first step in addressing these issues, we have investigated how parental attitudes about imaginary companions (personified objects and invisible) and impersonated characters vary as a function of the cultural, socioeconomic, and religious context in which the role play occurs (Carlson, Taylor, & Levin, 1998; Taylor & Carlson, 2000). For example, in one study, we compared the attitudes of 40 parents from a midsize U.S. city and 28 parents from Mexico City (Taylor, Miner, Legorreta, Luu, & Perez, 2004). The parents were told stories in which children engaged in a variety of behaviors involving different types of pretend play and then were asked to describe what the children were doing and their reactions to the children's behavior. The Mexican parents did not differ from the U.S. parents with respect to pretend play involving object substitution (e.g., the child pretends a block is a train), but they were significantly less approving of role play involving imaginary companions and expressed a variety of concerns about them (e.g., "I was afraid it was something supernatural. Their reassurance that they could see it frightened me.") Differences also emerged in the extent to which parents equated pretending with lying; whereas 25% of the Mexican parents associated pretending with lying, none of the U.S. parents did so.

In a related study, we compared the reactions of parents of low socioeconomic status whose children were in a Head Start preschool with the reactions of parents whose children were not enrolled in Head Start (Taylor, Miner et al., 2004). Both groups of parents were approving of pretend play involving object substitution. However, the Head Start parents were significantly less positive about role play involving imaginary companions than the other parents. We wonder if this difference could be related to differences in the content of the children's play. Children often explore negative themes in their play such as death, violence, disease, or negative aspects of ongoing events in their lives (e.g., Dunn & Hughes, 2001; Friedberg & Taylor, 1997). Although some degree of violence in the context of pretend play may be normative for children, it makes parents uneasy (Sutton-Smith, 1997). In this study, we did not collect systematic data about the content of the children's play, but some of the Head Start children had imaginary enemies rather than friends. For example, one child from this group described Sebastian, a nasty, violent invisible entity who was a threat to a second tiny imaginary companion the child protected by holding in the palm of her hand. In future research it would be interesting to more carefully investigate the relation between the content of children's fantasies involving imaginary companions and the circumstances the children are currently experiencing.

More generally, there have been a few recent studies that have focused on the correlates of particular themes in pretend play. Dunn and Hughes (2001) found that the enactment of themes involving the deliberate infliction of harm is related to a number of negative outcomes. Compared to their peers, the 4-year-old children who frequently engaged in violent fantasy showed poor executive control, frequent antisocial behavior, poor communication and coordination of play, and more conflict with a friend. At age 6, the tendency to engage in violent fantasy play was also related to a lack of empathy in moral judgments. These findings suggest that an emphasis on particular themes in fantasy play may be of greater concern than a high level of fantasy involvement.

FANTASY IN MIDDLE CHILDHOOD
AND ADOLESCENCE

Piaget (1962) described young children's pretense as an immature form of thinking that is replaced by more reality-oriented thought as children enter the concrete operational stage of development (e.g., Friedberg, 1995; Friedberg & Taylor, 1997; Newson & Newson, 1976). Some researchers, however, have argued that children's fantasy play does not disappear in middle childhood and adolescence but goes underground in response to implicit cultural expectations and explicit discouragement (Cohen & MacKeith, 1991; Pearson et al., 2001; Silvey & MacKeith, 1988; Singer & Singer, 1990). In particular, recent evidence challenges the view that imaginary companions are limited to early childhood (e.g., Bouldin & Pratt, 1999; Hoff, 2005; Pearson et al., 2001; Taylor, Carlson et al., 2004). For example, Taylor, Carlson et al. (2004) found that even at age 7 years, 31% of the children were currently playing with imaginary companions (compared with 28% of the children at age 4). Many of the 7-year-old children described imaginary companions that their parents did not know existed, perhaps because the imaginary companions of older children are played with more covertly (Newson & Newson, 1976). Another recent large-scale investigation of invisible imaginary companions found that

28% of 5- to 9-year-olds reported having a current imaginary companion (Pearson et al., 2001). Further, at least 9% of the 12-year-olds in this sample also reported having a current imaginary companion. Pearson et al. (2001) noted that this may be an underestimation, as some of the older children who denied having an imaginary companion reluctantly admitted after the interview that they actually did have one.

Other research indicates that adolescents also sometimes have imaginary companions. Seiffge-Krenke (1993, 1997) found that it is common for creative and socially competent adolescents to write to imaginary companions in their diaries. Moreover, continued interaction with imaginary companions is not the only form of active fantasy involvement found in older children and adolescents. For example, in a retrospective study of adults who created private, elaborate, and enduring imaginary worlds in childhood, Silvey and MacKeith (1988; Cohen & MacKeith, 1991) found that "paracosms" were most commonly created between the ages of 8 and 9. As with the imaginary companions of younger children, imaginary worlds provided an antidote to boredom and were not associated with adjustment difficulties (Cohen & MacKeith, 1991).

In summary, although relatively little research has examined fantasy and role play in middle childhood and adolescence, the available evidence does not support Piaget's assertion that imaginary companions and other forms of pretend play are displaced by games with rules after the preoperational period. In addition, research on imaginary companions beyond early childhood has implications for Piaget's claim that children's pretend play declines as they become more adapted to the social world and are increasingly able to satisfy the needs served by this form of play with real relationships. In contrast, the research we have presented has shown that imaginary companions are not replaced by real friends; rather, these imaginary relationships seem to go hand in hand with social competence.

IMAGINARY OTHERS IN ADULTHOOD

In light of the evidence that imaginary companions are not limited to early childhood but are created as late as adolescence, we have become interested in adult activities involving imaginary others. Most adults enjoy some sort of activity involving fantasy consumption (e.g., reading novels), but do they ever have imaginary companions? Adults with imaginary companions have sometimes been portrayed in movies such as *Harvey*, a story about a gentle adult man and his friendship with a giant invisible talking rabbit (Chase, 1944), but little is known about the extent to which this type of relationship occurs in real life. However, according to Caughey (1984), the social worlds of most people include a large number of individuals they know only through television, books, movies, and other forms of media, as well as the people they interact with face-to-face in their everyday lives. These relationships often go beyond interest and admiration and actually involve imagined conversations, meetings, and extended interactions. Such relationships are similar to the ones that children sometimes have with imaginary versions of real people (e.g., an imaginary companion based on a cousin who lives in another state).

In looking for an adult analog of childhood imaginary companions, we have turned to the activities of fiction writers. For fiction writers, creating an imaginary character or an invented world is all in a day's work. We have found that the reflections of fiction writers about the creation of their characters contain insights and observations that are fascinating and instructive. Of particular interest is how commonly writers report the experience of characters becoming almost real (Watkins, 1990). For example, writers report that their characters sometimes take control of the writing process; characters tell the story to the author who then writes it down. In addition, writers sometimes develop personal relationships with their characters in which the characters are experienced as real, separate, independent beings with minds of their own. We describe this experience as the *illusion of independent agency* (Taylor, Hodges, & Kohanyi, 2003). The essence of this illusion is the sense that the characters are independent agents not directly under the author's control—a fictional character is experienced by its creator as having its own thoughts, feelings, and actions.

At first glance, the illusion of independent agency is reminiscent of flow (Csikszentmihalyi, 1990). *Flow* is the pleasurable experience of becoming so absorbed in an activity that the sense of the passage of time is suspended, one loses track of the self and immediate surroundings, and the activity becomes effortless and unselfconscious. Authors do report the experience of flow while writing (Perry, 1999), but the illusion of independent agency differs from flow in that there can be considerable discord. The characters often argue with the author about the direction the novel is taking and their actions in it. "The characters arrive when evoked, but full of the spirit of mutiny. For they have these numerous parallels with real people, they try to live their own lives and are consequently often engaged in treason against the main scheme of the book" (Forster, 1927/1985, pp. 66–67).

The sense of uncontrollability and discord in the relationships between authors and their characters is something that we have also encountered in children's descriptions of their imaginary companions. In a study with 90 preschoolers, 36 had imaginary companions (40%) and answered questions about control. Only 1 child described her imaginary companion as completely compliant and cooperative. The other 35 children had a range of complaints: the imaginary companions did not always show up when summoned, would not go away when the children wanted them to, would not share, or refused to play what the child wanted to play.

To investigate the illusion of independent agency more systemically, we interviewed 50 adults who had been writing fiction for at least 5 years (Taylor et al., 2003). About a third of the writers had published their work, and some were professional writers, including one award-winning novelist (35 men, 15 women; age 20–73 years; M age = 37). The procedure involved the writers filling out a variety of questionnaires (we measured dissociation, empathy, and history of imaginary companions) and being interviewed about the characters in their novels. We asked about the characters' evolution, the author's perceived control over what the characters do and say, whether the characters did or said surprising things, and the extent to which the writers felt that the characters were the ones writing the story.

The most striking result was that almost all the writers (46 of the 50 writers, 92%) reported experiencing the illusion of independent agency. This finding was unanticipated. In fact, we expected to find that some writers experienced the illusion of independent agency and that others did not. Based on this expectation, we had planned to examine the extent to which the experience of the illusion of independent agency was related to a variety of factors, such as having an imaginary companion as a child, dissociation, and empathy. The low level of variability in the writers' experience of the illusion of independent agency precluded these analyses; however, we did find that our 50 writers were a special population. For example, 40% of these writers remembered having imaginary companions as children—a high proportion for a retrospective study. In addition, the writers scored higher on dispositional perspective taking than would be expected in the general population as assessed by the perspective taking subscale of the Interpersonal Reactivity Index (Davis, 1983).

One hypothesis about the illusion of independent agency is that it is related to expertise. The idea is that someone who pretends extensively, whether child or adult, could be considered an expert pretender. With increased practice, the performance of a skill eventually requires little or no conscious processing. Perhaps for some writers, the creative process becomes automatized so that it is no longer consciously experienced, creating the illusion that the imagined character is the one who is speaking and acting. The character's words and actions begin to be perceived, listened to, and recorded rather than consciously created. Consistent with this hypothesis, we found that expertise (having been published) was related to more detailed reports of the illusion. In future research with expert pretenders (both children and adults), we hope to discover how expertise is experienced in the domain of fantasy, and in particular how it is possible to experience an imaginary other as an independent agent. We also hope to address whether the experiences of adult authors are related to what children experience day after day when thinking about and interacting with imaginary companions. In our view, the research on the illusion of independent agency in fiction writers provides further evidence against Piaget's claim that the creation of imaginary characters is rare after childhood. Rather, fiction writers present at least one example of adults inventing and interacting with imaginary others.

CONCLUSION

Recent research indicates that the creation of imaginary companions is a healthy and common activity in early childhood and beyond. This body of research contradicts Piaget's (1962) assertion that the invention of imaginary others declines with the emergence of concrete operational thought and disappears by adulthood. As our review has shown, although the specific forms these imaginary others take in childhood and adulthood show developmental differences, research suggests continuity in this type of imaginative activity across the life span. Further, findings from our own research as well as the research of others suggest that the relationships children develop with their imaginary companions may have positive implications for their ability to successfully navigate the social world. The correlational nature of the available data precludes any claims regarding the direction of the relationship between imaginary companions and children's cognitive and social development; however, it is an intriguing relationship that warrants further investigation. Clearly, there is much to be learned about the phenomenology of sustained fantasies about imaginary others and the role of these relationships in our lives.

REFERENCES

Ames, L. B., & Learned, J. (1946). Imaginary companions and related phenomena. *Journal of Genetic Psychology, 69*, 147–167.

Astington, J. W. (1993). *The child's discovery of the mind.* Cambridge, MA: Harvard University Press.

Astington, J. W., & Jenkins, J. M. (1995). Theory of mind development and social understanding. *Cognition & Emotion, 9*, 151–165.

Bach, S. (1971). Notes on some imaginary companions. *The Psychoanalytic Study of the Child, 26*, 159–172.

Bender, L., & Vogel, B. F. (1941). Imaginary companions of children. *American Journal of Orthopsychiatry, 11*, 56–65.

Benson, R. M., & Pryor, D. B. (1973). When friends fall out: Developmental interference and the function of some imaginary companions. *Journal of the American Psychoanalytic Association, 21*, 457–468.

Bouldin, P., & Pratt, C. (1999). Characteristics of preschool children and school-aged children with imaginary companions. *Journal of Genetic Psychology, 160*, 397–410.

Bouldin, P., & Pratt, C. (2002). A systematic investigation of the specific fears, anxiety level, and temperament of children with imaginary companions. *Australian Journal of Psychology, 54*, 79–85.

Carlson, S. M., Gum, J., Davis, A., & Molloy, A. (2003). *Predictors of imaginary companions in early childhood.* Poster presented at the annual meeting of the Jean Piaget Society, Chicago. June.

Carlson, S. M., & Taylor, M. (2005). Imaginary companions and impersonated characters: Sex differences in children's fantasy play. *Merrill-Palmer Quarterly, 51*, 93–118.

Carlson, S. M., Taylor, M., & Levin, G. R. (1998). The influence of culture on pretend play: The case of Mennonite children. *Merrill-Palmer Quarterly, 44*, 538–565.

Caughey, J. L. (1984). *Imaginary social worlds: A cultural approach.* Lincoln: University of Nebraska Press.

Chase, M. (1944). *Harvey.* New York: Dramatists Play Service.

Cohen, D., & MacKeith, S. A. (1991). *The development of imagination: The private worlds of childhood.* New York: Routledge.

Csikszentmihalyi, M. (1990). *Flow: The psychology of optimal experience.* New York: HarperCollins.

Davis, M. H. (1983). Measuring individual differences in empathy: Evidence for a multidimensional approach. *Journal of Personality and Social Psychology, 44*, 113–126.

Dunn, J., & Hughes, C. (2001). "I got some swords and you're dead!": Violent fantasy, antisocial behavior, friendship, and moral sensibility in young children. *Child Development, 72*, 491–505.

Forster, E. M. (1985). *Aspects of the novel.* New York: Harcourt Brace. (Original work published 1927)

Friedberg, R. D. (1995). Allegorical lives: Children and their imaginary companions. *Child Study Journal, 25*, 1–21.

Friedberg, R. D., & Taylor, L. A. (1997). Imaginary friends and amazing stories: Clinical implications of children's metaphorical communications. In

L. Vandecreek, S. Knapp, & T. L. Jackson (Eds.), *Innovations in clinical practice: A source book* (pp. 97–109). Sarasota, FL: Professional Resource Press/Professional Resource Exchange, Inc.

Gleason, T. R., Sebanc, A. M., & Hartup, W. W. (2000). Imaginary companions of preschool children. *Developmental Psychology, 36,* 419–428.

Harris, P. L. (2000). *The work of the imagination.* Oxford, UK: Blackwell.

Harter, S., & Chao, C. (1992). The role of competence in children's creation of imaginary friends. *Merrill-Palmer Quarterly, 38,* 350–363.

Hoff, E. (2005). Imaginary companions, creativity, and self-image in middle childhood. *Creativity Research Journal, 17,* 167–180.

Hurlock, E. B., & Burnstein, M. (1932). The imaginary playmate: A questionnaire study. *Journal of Genetic Psychology, 41,* 380–391.

Leslie, A. M. (1987). Pretense and representation: The origins of "theory of mind." *Psychological Review, 94,* 412–426.

Lewis, C., & Mitchell, P. (1994). *Children's early understanding of mind: Origins and development.* Hillsdale, NJ: Lawrence Erlbaum Associates, Inc.

Mannering, A. M., & Taylor, M. (2003). *Young children's role-play: Social cues and fantasy orientation.* Poster presented at the annual meeting of the Jean Piaget Society, Chicago. June.

Manosevitz, M., Fling, S., & Prentice, N. M. (1977). Imaginary companions in young children: Relationships with intelligence, creativity and waiting ability. *Journal of Child Psychology and Psychiatry, 18,* 73–78.

Manosevitz, M., Prentice, N. M., & Wilson, F. (1973). Individual and family correlates of imaginary companions in preschool children. *Developmental Psychology, 8,* 72–79.

Mauro, J. (1991). *The friend that only I can see: A longitudinal investigation of children's imaginary companions.* Unpublished doctoral dissertation, University of Oregon, Eugene.

Myers, W. A. (1976). Imaginary companions, fantasy twins, mirror dreams and depersonalization. *Psychoanalytic Quarterly, 45,* 503–524.

Myers, W. A. (1979). Imaginary companions in childhood and adult creativity. *Psychoanalytic Quarterly, 48,* 292–307.

Nagera, H. (1969). The imaginary companion: Its significance for ego development and conflict solution. *The Psychoanalytic Study of the Child, 24,* 165–196.

Newson, J., & Newson, E. (1976). *Seven years old in an urban environment.* London: Allen & Unwin.

Partington, J. T., & Grant, C. G. (1984). Imaginary playmates and other useful fantasies. In P. K. Smith (Ed.), *Play in animals and humans* (pp. 217–240). New York: Basil Blackwell.

Pearson, D., Rouse, H., Doswell, S., Ainsworth, C., Dawson, O., Simms, K., et al. (2001). Prevalence of imaginary companions in a normal child population. *Child Care, Health and Development, 27,* 13–22.

Perry, S. K. (1999). *Writing in flow: Keys to enhanced creativity.* Cincinnati, OH: Writer's Digest.

Piaget, J. (1962). *Play, dreams and imitation.* New York: Norton.

Putnam, F. W. (1996). Child development and dissociation. *Child and Adolescent Psychiatric Clinics of North America, 5,* 285–301.

Putnam, F. W. (1997). *Dissociation in children and adolescents: A developmental perspective*. New York: Guilford.

Putnam, F. W. (2000). Dissociative disorders. In A. J. Sameroff, M. Lewis, & S. M. Miller (Eds.), *Handbook of developmental psychopathology* (2nd ed., pp. 739–754). New York: Kluwer Academic/Plenum.

Rosenfeld, E., Huesmann, L. W., Eron, L. D., & Torney-Purta, J. V. (1982). Measuring patterns of fantasy behavior in children. *Journal of Personality and Social Psychology, 42*, 347–366.

Sanders, B. (1992). The imaginary companion experience in multiple personality disorder. *Dissociation, 5*, 159–162.

Schaefer, C. E. (1969). Imaginary companions and creative adolescents. *Developmental Psychology, 1*, 747–749.

Seiffge-Krenke, I. (1993). Close friendship and imaginary companions in adolescence. In B. Laursen (Ed.), *New directions for Child Development: Close Friendships in Adolescence* (pp. 73–87). San Francisco: Jossey-Bass.

Seiffge-Krenke, I. (1997). Imaginary companions in adolescence: Sign of a deficient or positive development? *Journal of Adolescence, 20*, 137–154.

Silberg, J. L. (1998). *The dissociative child: Diagnosis, treatment, and management* (2nd ed.). Lutherville, MA: Sidran Press.

Silvey, R., & MacKeith, S. (1988). The paracosm: A special form of fantasy. In D. Morrison (Ed.), *Organizing early experience: Imagination and cognition in childhood* (pp. 173–197). Amityville, NY: Baywood.

Singer, D. G., & Singer, J. L. (1990). *The house of make-believe: Children's play and the developing imagination*. Cambridge, MA: Harvard University Press.

Sutton-Smith, B. (1997). *The ambiguity of play*. Cambridge, MA: Harvard University Press.

Svendsen, M. (1934). Children's imaginary companions. *Archives of Neurology and Psychiatry, 2*, 985–999.

Taylor, M. (1999). *Imaginary companions and the children who create them*. New York: Oxford University Press.

Taylor, M., & Carlson, S. M. (1997). The relation between individual differences in fantasy and theory mind. *Child Development, 68*, 436–455.

Taylor, M., & Carlson, S. M. (2000). The influence of religious beliefs on parental attitudes about children's fantasy behavior. In K. S. Rosengren, C. N. Johnson, & P. L. Harris (Eds.), *Imagining the impossible: Magical, scientific, and religious thinking in children* (pp. 247–268). New York: Cambridge University Press.

Taylor, M. & Carlson, S. M. (2002). Imaginary companions and elaborate fantasy in childhood: Discontinuities with nonhuman animals. In R. W. Mitchell (Ed.), *Pretending and imagination in animals and children* (pp. 167–180). New York: Cambridge University Press.

Taylor, M., Carlson, S. M., Maring, B. L., Gerow, L., & Charley, C. (2004). The characteristics and correlates of high fantasy in school-aged children: Imaginary companions, impersonation and social understanding. *Developmental Psychology, 40*, 1173–1187.

Taylor, M., Cartwright, B. S., & Carlson, S. M. (1993). A developmental investigation of children's imaginary companions. *Developmental Psychology, 29*, 276–285.

Taylor, M., Hodges, S., & Kohanyi, A. (2003). The illusion of independent agency: Do adult fiction writers experience their characters as having minds of their own? *Imagination, Cognition and Personality, 22*, 359–378.

Taylor, M., Miner, J., Legorreta, D., Luu, V., & Perez, E. (2004). *Cross cultural differences in parental reactions to elaborate fantasy in young children*. Unpublished data.

Terr, L. (1990). *Too scared to cry: Psychic trauma in childhood*. New York: Harper & Row.

Tower, R. B. (1985). Preschoolers' imaginativeness: Subtypes, correlates, and maladaptive extremes. *Imagination, Cognition and Personality, 4*, 349–364.

Watkins, M. (1990). *The development of imaginal dialogues: Invisible guests*. Boston: Sigo Press.

Wellman, H. M., & Gelman, S. A. (1998). Knowledge acquisition in foundational domains. In W. Damon (Series Ed.) & D. Kuhn & R. S. Siegler (Vol. Eds.), *Handbook of child psychology: Vol. 2. Cognition, perception and language* (5th ed.; pp. 523–530, 538–546). New York: Wiley.

11

The Interplay of Play and Narrative in Children's Development: Theoretical Reflections and Concrete Examples

Ageliki Nicolopoulou
Department of Psychology
Lehigh University

This chapter explores the relationship between symbolic play and narrative in the process of development. There has been a great deal of developmental research on each of these subjects, and in fact both have attracted increasing interest in the past several decades—not just for their own sake, but also in terms of their connections to broader issues of socialization and development, including cognition, imagination, social competence, and education (e.g., Bamberg, 1997; Bruner, 1992; Fireman, McVay, & Flanagan, 2003; Nicolopoulou, 1993, 1997a; Roskos & Christie, 2000; Saracho & Spodek, 1998). For example, a growing body of research has argued convincingly that the mastery of narrative skills by children in their preschool years serves as one crucial foundation for emergent literacy and long-term school success (e.g., McCabe & Bliss, 2003; Tabors, Snow, & Dickinson, 2001). Other lines of research have linked children's play to their learning and development in the domains of cognition, language, morality, social understanding, and social competence (for one overview, see Saracho & Spodek, 1998). However, there have been relatively few attempts to address children's play and narrative in an integrated way, and to examine the relationship between them concretely and systematically.

The prevailing mutual isolation between developmental research on play and narrative is both unfortunate and surprising, because theoretical considerations and existing empirical research point toward important affinities and interdependence between them. A major form of children's play, pretend play, centers precisely on the enactment of narrative scenarios. One body of research, reviewed later, has found that children's participation in sociodramatic play improves their narrative skills. Research dealing explicitly with the effects of children's narrative abilities and development on their play has been more rare, but a good deal of work has strong implications for this relationship. For example, Wells and others have argued that the experience of narratives—both listening to stories and telling them—helps to bring home to children "the symbolic potential of language: its power to create possible and imaginary worlds through words" (Wells, 1986, p. 156; cf. Bruner, 1986; Wolf & Heath, 1992). Children's developing ability to produce and understand stories also enables and encourages them to appropriate the rich array of genres and other symbolic resources available in their culture, and to use these flexibly and creatively for their own purposes (Cohen & MacKeith, 1991; Miller, Hengst, Alexander, & Sperry, 2000; Miller, Hoogstra, Mintz, Fung, & Williams, 1993; Rowe, 1998, 2000; Wolf & Heath, 1992). Constructing possible and imaginary worlds through the creative appropriation and reworking of cultural elements involves precisely the kinds of cognitive and imaginative capacities expressed in and promoted by children's pretend play. For these and other reasons, more systematic examination of the dynamic interplay between play and narrative in development can help enrich both areas of research and, in the process, contribute significantly to our larger understanding of the development of cognition and imagination.

Pursuing this examination effectively requires theoretical and empirical approaches that can do justice both to the similarities and interdependence between children's play and narrative and also to their differences. Building on previous research in this area and on my own ongoing studies of preschool children in naturalistic contexts, I argue that the active interplay and cross-fertilization between children's pretend play and narrative can significantly advance their development in a range of domains, but this active interplay is neither given nor automatic. Rather, young children's pretend play and their storytelling seem to start out as mostly separate and parallel activities, and the potential for fruitful coordination and cross-fertilization between them is a developmental achievement that children first need to master. I thus propose a model that sees children's pretend play and storytelling as distinct but complementary modes of their narrative activity, which offer children complementary challenges and benefits, and suggest some ways that they begin to come together in the course of development.

RESEARCH PERSPECTIVES: NARRATIVE IN PRETEND PLAY AND STORYTELLING

Some researchers have usefully explored the connections between pretend play and narrative in children's experience and development (e.g., Engel, 1995; Fein, Ardila-Rey, & Groth, 2000; Goldman, 1998; Sutton-Smith, 1984a, 1984b). One key point of intersection between them is that a central element of pretend play is the enactment of narrative scenarios, and recognition of this fact has informed work on children's "play narratives" (e.g., Pellegrini & Galda, 1990; Wolf, Rygh, & Altshuler, 1984). In fact, for a number of purposes it is useful to see children's pretend play and storytelling as complementary modes of their narrative activity, on a continuum ranging from the discursive exposition of narratives in storytelling to their enactment in pretend play (Nicolopoulou, 1997a, 2002).

This insight has perhaps been formulated most vividly by Paley (1990), who has consistently argued that "play...[is] story in action, just as storytelling is play put into narrative form" (p. 4) and that children's "fantasy play and storytelling are never far apart" (p. 8). Paley has further asserted "that this view of play makes play, along with its alter ego, storytelling and acting, the universal learning medium" (p. 10). Following the lead of Paley and others in this respect, I have argued that we should approach children's play and narrative as closely intertwined, and often overlapping, forms of socially situated symbolic action—and that Vygotsky's sociocultural analysis of children's play, for example, offers valuable theoretical resources for grasping the interplay between the two from this perspective (Nicolopoulou, 1997a; Vygotsky, 1933/1967). Both play and storytelling should be viewed as complementary expressions of children's symbolic imagination that draw from and reflect back on the interrelated domains of emotional, intellectual, and social life.

The Research Focus: From Pretend Play to Storytelling

These ideas offer useful starting points for further developmental research, but so far they have only begun to be followed up. Most research that has systematically explored the relationship between children's play and narrative has focused on one aspect of this relationship—the ways that pretend play (i.e., enacted narratives) can help promote the skills necessary for the production and comprehension of stories (i.e., discursive narratives). Various studies have found that children's participation in dramatic storybook reenactments (e.g., Galda, 1984; Martinez, Cheyney, & Teale, 1991; Pellegrini & Galda, 1982, 1993) or spontaneous socio-dramatic play with peers (e.g., Smilansky, 1968) improved children's abilities to remember, reproduce, and comprehend stories—not only the enacted stories themselves (Pellegrini & Galda, 1982), but also other stories that were neither enacted by nor familiar to the children (Silvern, Taylor, Williamson, Surbeck, & Kelley, 1986). Furthermore, this research found that the children's narrative skills were promoted not only by their participation in the play enactment itself, but also by the "metaplay" communication and interaction surrounding it, which included conversation and negotiation in setting up the play and conflict resolution within the play episode (Pellegrini & Galda, 1993; Williamson & Silvern, 1990, 1991, 1992).

An emphasis on the developmental priority of play also predominated in Kavanaugh and Engel's (1998) perceptive overview of this and other research on pretend play and narrative as distinct but interconnected expressions of children's symbolic thought. They argued that pretend play, both solitary and social, emerges first and helps lay crucial foundations for discursive narrative skills. For example, in joint pretend play between 2-year-old children and adult caregivers, the adult often brings out and elaborates the "implicit narrative structure" (p. 92) of the child's pretend gestures, thus providing "a thematic structure that gives meaning and coherence" to the child's initially fragmentary actions (p. 88). As one illustration, they offered a play interaction between a mother and her 2-year-old daughter using two small action figures, Lantern Man and Spider Man.

> As the child begins to move the figures about, her mother supplies a thematic narration, saying, "Oh look, Lantern Man is chasing Spider Man. Oh no, he is pushing him down. Spider Man says, …Help, Lantern Man is grabbing me.' Look, Spider Man is getting away." (p. 88)

"[I]t is likely," they suggested, "that episodes such as these underlie the acquisition of the child's own storytelling abilities. Long before children can construct their own narratives," such playful interactions "fore-shadow the stories they will tell in the preschool years and beyond" (p. 88). For slightly older children, collaborative pretend play with peers, especially role play, "encourages children to imagine the world from someone else's point of view" (p. 85) and to explore their own inner thoughts and feelings and those of others. It thus promotes children's abilities to represent and coordinate multiple points of view—skills that are important for story production and comprehension and for the broader development of social cognition (pp. 84–88, 92–93).

These analyses are generally convincing and illuminating, but a one-sided focus on the priority of play would seem to capture only part of the ongoing interplay between children's pretend play and storytelling. As Kavanaugh and Engel (1998) themselves acknowledged, "fledgling" forms of narrative discourse emerge very early and are promoted by various types of adult–child talk in addition to pretend play interactions (pp. 89–91). Other research has found that even 2-year-olds use discursive narratives, both factual (e.g., Nelson, 1989) and fictional (e.g., Miller et al., 2000; Miller et al., 1993), to work over and make sense of their experience, and that they have already begun to develop rudimentary narrative strategies for these purposes. Furthermore, one could plausibly infer from Kavanaugh and Engel's (1998) approach that young children's enacted play narratives should be more advanced and sophisticated than their comparable discursive narratives. One study of 4- and 5-year-old middle-class children by Benson (1993) explicitly tested a hypothesis along these lines, independently of Kavanaugh and Engel but in accord with their basic model, and did not find support for it. In two play tasks, the children were presented with character figurines and other props and asked to play with them; in two storytelling tasks, the children were presented with drawings of the same characters and asked to make up a story about them. Contrary to Benson's expectation, the plots of the discursive narratives that the children composed in the storytelling tasks were more complex and sophisticated than those of their play narratives.

Toward a More Dialectical Approach

Thus, I propose that the contributions of the research just reviewed can usefully be incorporated into a less one-sided, more reciprocal, and more complex approach to the developmental relationship between pretend play and narrative. As I go on to explain more fully, there are both theoretical and empirical grounds for treating young children's pretend play and storytelling as initially parallel and complementary modes of their narrative activity, with at least partially distinct origins and developmental trajectories, that children are only gradually able to integrate effectively. As this integration is achieved, it allows for an increasingly complex and mutually enriching interplay and cross-fertilization between pretend play and storytelling. The key tasks are therefore to delineate the processes by which this occurs and the developmental dynamics that underlie them.

YOUNG CHILDREN'S PRETEND PLAY AND STORYTELLING: INITIAL THEMATIC DISJUNCTION AND GROWING CROSS-FERTILIZATION

My own research on 3- to 5-year-old children in a range of preschool classes (e.g., Nicolopoulou, 1996, 1997b, 2002; Nicolopoulou, Scales, & Weintraub, 1994) provides evidence that supports this proposed model. In these classes, a storytelling and story-acting practice pioneered by the teacher/researcher Vivian Paley (e.g., 1986, 1988, 1990) was a regular component of the preschool curriculum. During the period allotted each day to "choice time," any child who wishes can dictate a story to a designated teacher, who writes it down with minimal intervention. This storytelling is a voluntary activity, and each story dictation is typically child-initiated. Later that day, during "group time," each of the stories composed that day is read aloud to the entire class by the teacher, while the child author and other children, whom he or she chooses, act out the story. This is an apparently simple technique with complex and powerful effects, as all children in the class typically participate in three interrelated roles: composing and dictating stories, taking part in the group enactment of stories (their own and those of other children), and listening to (and watching the performance of) the stories of the other children in the class. There is strong evidence that these conditions lead children to produce narratives that are richer, more ambitious, and more illuminating than when they compose them in isolation from their everyday social contexts and in response to agendas shaped directly by adults (Nicolopoulou, 1996, 2002).

Eleven of the classes studied were in preschools serving children from predominantly middle-class backgrounds, and seven were in Head Start programs serving poor and otherwise disadvantaged children. For all these classes, I obtained the entire corpus of spontaneous stories composed by the children during the school year. For most of the classes from middle-class preschools, my assistants and I also visited the classrooms regularly (at least twice a month) and wrote detailed field notes about the conduct of the storytelling and story-acting practice and about other classroom activities, including the children's unstructured free play. So far, only two of the Head Start classes have been studied for an entire year in this manner (a large-scale multiyear study of preschoolers in a metropolitan Head Start system is currently in preparation), but I visited all of them several times and wrote detailed field notes for each visit.

In constructing their stories, the children drew themes, characters, images, plots, and other elements from each other's stories; they also incorporated elements into their narratives from a wide range of other sources, including fairy tales, children's books, TV (and popular culture more generally), and their own experience. However, they did not simply imitate other children's stories, nor just passively absorb messages from adults and the larger culture. My analysis has shown that, even at this early age, they were able to appropriate these elements *selectively*, and to *use* and rework them for their own purposes—cognitive, symbolic, and social-relational.

A Puzzling Disjunction

Given this pattern of narrative appropriation and cross-fertilization, which includes an ongoing interchange and reworking of themes between different children's stories, one would also expect to find extensive thematic interchange between the children's storytelling and pretend play. In fact, preschoolers often do use common themes in their stories and play scenarios. However, to my surprise, I have consistently found that among the younger preschoolers, and those with weaker narrative and play skills, the overlap of themes and other symbolic elements between their discursive narratives and the narrative scenarios they enact in pretend play is at first minimal or absent. At that stage, as I have suggested, the children's pretend play and storytelling appear to operate as parallel activities with surprisingly little thematic interchange or mutual influence. The integration between them, as expressed by the use of common themes in both activities, takes some time to become established. Research findings from middle-class preschools and from Head Start classes can help to illuminate different aspects of this overall pattern.

Middle-Class Preschools

In Paley's accounts of her preschool classes, one encounters numerous examples of children using (and reworking) similar themes in their play and storytelling. In my own studies of middle- and upper middle-class preschoolers, I have also observed frequent continuity of themes between children's play and their stories. However, there is at first a sharp disjunction between the themes that children use in these two activities, and the thematic continuity between them has to be developed over time.

To provide one illustration of this pervasive pattern, I use a middle-class preschool classroom studied during the 1999–2000 school year. This mixed-age class included 17 children (9 girls and 8 boys). My examples come from two time periods (in December and May) in which the children's classroom play was observed and audiotaped for 2 consecutive days. In both observational periods, the children who told stories also engaged in pretend play episodes. However, in December, as in previous months, the extent to which they used common themes in their pretend play and storytelling was minimal, whereas by May it had increased substantially.

During the first day of the December observation period, we did not see much sustained pretend play, but the next day 5 children, later joined by 2 more, participated in a joint play episode lasting over an hour that centered on "fire truck" and "firefighter" themes. This play episode seems to have been at least partly inspired by props that the teacher brought into the classroom (i.e., she placed tires next to a large block structure on which children could sit), and during the play she actively but gently scaffolded it (e.g., adding hoses once the firefighter theme was established). Different children took on the firefighter paradigm and actively elaborated it in their own way, responding only intermittently to the teacher's suggestions. The children engaged in the play episode developed and recycled a cluster of loosely connected themes: putting out a fire, helping a dead person, washing the fire truck, driving the fire truck around, and putting gas in the fire truck.

Later in the day, two of the dominant children in this play episode dictated stories to the teacher, but their stories showed barely a trace of the central play themes. There was no mention of fires, fire trucks, or firefighters. One story did mention "a hose"—"Ben blowed on the hole of the hose" (Jason,[1] 5; 0)—which may have been a reference to the hoses

---

[1]Pseudonyms have been assigned to children whose stories and play activities are discussed.

used to put gas in the make-believe fire truck. In the other story, told by Rhys (5; 1), there was mention of a "dead person"—a role that this child had played briefly during the play episode. In both stories, these were no more than brief (and ambiguous) references to isolated elements from the play episode, with no effort to incorporate and elaborate the central themes of the pretend play narrative. This lack of sustained thematic interchange was a pattern we observed consistently in this class throughout the fall semester.

By May, in contrast, themes from the children's pretend play appeared frequently in their stories and vice versa, and there was often a fluid continuity between the narrative scenarios in the two activities. For example, two boys, Tillian and Jason, played together with the themes of Power Rangers and fighting. Later that day, they coauthored a story using the same themes:

A story about fighting.

One day there was two men. Then there was a Power Ranger. Then one man punched the other man. And then that man fell down a mountain. And then he climbed back again. And punched the guy back. Then the Power Ranger chased those fighting guys out of the world forever. And then came the end. (Tillian, 5; 2 & Jason, 5; 6, 5/25/00)

That same day, Holly, one of the youngest children in the class, was playing with figurines of various farm animals, arranging and rearranging them in different configurations. At one point she announced to a teacher and a nearby child that she had created a "horse school." This other child joined her briefly in playing with the figurines. Later that day, Holly told the following story:

A toy story.

Once upon a time there was a big horse. And then there was a little sheep. And there was a goose and a chicken. They both had babies, two babies and three babies. And then there was a little horse and a little goat. And there was a black cat. They played candy land. The end. (Holly, 3; 9, 5/25/00)

These examples capture the larger pattern indicated by the analysis of pretend play and storytelling of children in the middle-class preschools studied. At first, the use of common themes in these two modes of narrative activity was minimal, and tended to include only isolated elements. (The main exceptions were children in their second year of preschool who began the school year already having participated in this storytelling and story-acting practice the previous year.) By the spring, however, thematic continuity and cross-fertilization between their pretend play and storytelling was considerably more frequent and comprehensive.

Head Start Classrooms

This initial disjunction between the thematic content of children's stories and their pretend play scenarios has been even more striking in the Head Start classes I have studied. Here is one example from a Head Start program in a large city, a few weeks after I had introduced the storytelling and story-acting practice in this class. I was playing with a group of children at a waist-high sand table with figurines representing animals, cars, and superheroes. What follows is an excerpt from my field notes (2/28/03):

> At one moment I was playing with some kids at the sand table. I noticed that the children were rather imaginative in their play, taking on the role of a character/superhero flying around, hitting others, etc. I pretended I did not know what to do with my character and some of the kids were directing me. A regular volunteer in this classroom, an older woman from the community, urged me to take down a story from one of these children, Dasai, because she mentioned he was very imaginative. I had noticed his imaginative engagement in the sand table play (that is, having his action-hero character perform various stereotypic actions). After he lost interest in the sand table and was looking around for another activity, I asked him whether he wanted to tell me (i.e., dictate) a story. He was eager to do that, and I thought that he would tell me a story that followed (or had some elements of) his sand table play. However, his story just recounted some simple ordinary events, and resembled a number of stories I was getting from the children in this and other Head Start classrooms.

> **Dasai:** Me and my brother played outside. We went to the store.
> **AN:** (Because he stopped, I asked): What kind of store?
> **Dasai:** Gumstore. That's it.

This pattern was brought out especially well in a more intensive study of a Head Start class of 17 children in a semirural area in the northeastern United States conducted during the 1997–1998 school year (Nicolopoulou, 2002). These children came from backgrounds of poverty combined, in most cases, with family difficulty or instability. The teacher introduced the storytelling and story-acting practice into the classroom that year with my assistance. In addition to monitoring its operation, for a 2-day period each month an assistant and I conducted systematic observations of other classroom activities, including the children's free play.

The children in this class began the school year with significantly weaker narrative skills than corresponding middle-class children or even children in some other Head Start classes I have studied. For example, they showed less familiarity with the basic conventions for telling a free-standing, self-contextualized story—such as marking beginnings and endings, explicitly relating events in temporal sequence, and constructing a complete narrative scenario—and less mastery of the relevant language skills. Their narrative skills improved significantly during the year, but even in the spring these were still less advanced than those of equivalent-aged children in middle-class preschools I have studied. Early in the school year the children's pretend play was also rather limited and fragmentary—generally restricted to a small range of stereotyped roles, with minimal scenarios and very little play-related communication. Both the quantity and quality of their pretend play increased during the school year but, again, it remained relatively weak in most cases.

Thus, although the children immediately displayed great enthusiasm for telling stories, at first they had some difficulty doing this effectively. In their early attempts at storytelling, they simply listed a string of characters (and sometimes mentioned other potentially relevant elements), usually without providing actions, descriptions, or plots. After several weeks of this protonarrative groping, one child, April, produced a story that met the minimal standards for a free-standing fictional story:

> Wedding girl and wedding boy, and then there was a baby. And then there was the person that brought out the flowers. And then there was some animal that wrecked the house, the church house that people were getting married in. And a person was listening to a wedding tape. And that's all. (April, 5; 1)

This story was not very complex, but it did include a relatively coherent and explicit scenario, a set of interrelated characters, and a sketchy but readily discernible plot. It also introduced and combined a set of organizing themes that were to prove powerfully appealing to other children in the class: first, a wedding, featuring the two linked characters of wedding girl and wedding boy; and second, animal aggression.

The dynamics of the storytelling and story-acting practice then set in motion a process of narrative borrowing and mutual cross-fertilization. A few weeks later another child, Anton, who had acted as the wedding boy in April's story, composed a story using these themes and adding his own elaborations. In Anton's story, the wedding couple got married and then went on to have children (an event that, incidentally, happens very rarely in boys' stories). Shortly afterward, April told a slightly reworked version of her story. Over time this story paradigm was gradually taken up and reused, with variations and elaborations, by other children in the class, until it became pervasive in the children's storytelling. By the spring, all the children in the class told at least some stories that included this bundle of themes, and more than half of them used it in most of their stories. This narrative paradigm became a cultural tool that was shared and elaborated by the classroom peer group as a whole (for more details, see Nicolopoulou, 2002).

Given the extent to which this cluster of themes captured the children's attention and imagination, and the enthusiasm with which different children appropriated it for their own storytelling, one might have expected these themes to appear in their pretend play as well. However, this was not the case for most of the year. In fact, not until May did we observe a play episode in which three girls, who had used these themes profusely in their stories, enacted a wedding girl–wedding boy scenario. The classroom teacher confirmed that this was the first time she had noticed the children using these themes in their play, although the same girls subsequently used them in a few more play episodes. Nor did the characteristic themes in the children's play appear in their stories. In short, there was a striking contrast between the rapid and pervasive thematic cross-fertilization in the children's storytelling and the relative lack of thematic cross-fertilization between their storytelling and their pretend play narratives.

COMPLEMENTARY EMPHASES IN EARLY PLAY AND STORYTELLING: CHARACTER REPRESENTATION VERSUS PLOT

These and other findings support the proposition that young children's pretend play and storytelling start out as relatively distinct and parallel symbolic activities, and that the ability to engage in flexible coordination and cross-fertilization between them is a developmental achievement that requires some time and effort to accomplish. The explanation for this developmental pattern still needs to be worked out, but it is possible to offer some informed hypotheses to help orient research on these questions.

As noted earlier, a key point of contact between pretend play and the production and comprehension of stories is that both involve constructing and understanding narrative scenarios. However, fully developed narrative combines a number of different elements. It seems plausible that, at least in their early phases, these elements—and the skills associated with them—develop in partly independent ways, tend to be linked unevenly to different activities, and need to be integrated to achieve full narrative competence. I argue that young children's pretend play and storytelling require and promote somewhat different but complementary clusters of narrative-related skills, build on different strengths, and pose different challenges for the children. This complementary relationship between the two activities is an important reason why their coordination and cross-fertilization can be beneficial, but it helps explain why bringing them together requires significant effort and development.

DIMENSIONS OF NARRATIVE AND NARRATIVE COMPETENCE

What are the elements into which a well-formed narrative can be analytically decomposed to pursue this hypothesis? As a conceptual starting point, I propose that we draw on a useful suggestion by Bruner (1986), who argued that successful narrative must simultaneously construct and effectively integrate two landscapes: "a landscape of action" that links sequences of actions and events in physical settings, and a "landscape of consciousness" that portrays "what those involved in the action know, think, and feel" (p. 14). These two landscapes are analytically distinct, but it is their integration that gives successful narrative its full power and coherence. To reframe this distinction somewhat, fully developed narrative must coordinate actions and events in a coherent *plot*, which must simultaneously be integrated with a rich and effective representation of *characters*, including the portrayal and coordination of their subjective points of view.

This model dovetails with Harris's (2000) analysis of "the work of the imagination" in cognitive and language development. Harris argued that there are "important continuities" (p. 51) between the cognitive capacities that underpin the production and comprehension of narrative scenarios in pretend play and in stories. "The key concept for linking the two functions is what has become known as the *situation model*" (p. 192), a concept initially developed by cognitive psychologists to capture the ways that adults process oral or written narratives (Zwaan, 1999; Zwaan & Radvansky, 1998). To create or understand a narrative scenario, children and adults must construct a mental model of the narrative situation being portrayed—one that is independent of their actual spatio-temporal context but is internally coherent—and then transform it appropriately as the narrative unfolds. For our purposes here, what is striking is the extent to which the key features of the situation model identified in this analysis correspond to the elements of narrative just emphasized. Constructing and transforming a situation model requires both (a) the ability to link actions and events into a coherent plot, including the recognition and imputation of causal connections within the imagined narrative situation, and (b) the ability and disposition to enter into the point of view of characters within the narrative. This account once again poses the questions of how young children develop these complementary abilities—and the ability to integrate them effectively.

Complementary Narrative Emphases in Early Pretend Play and Storytelling

From the beginning, of course, young children struggle with both plot construction and character representation in both pretend play and storytelling, and these two aspects of narrative can never be entirely independent. However, I would argue that, in the earliest phases of development, the two activities tend to emphasize and promote different dimensions of narrative and narrative skills. In comparative terms, early pretend play emphasizes increasing depth and richness in character representation, whereas early storytelling emphasizes increasing complexity, coherence, and sophistication in plot construction.

For example, there is considerable evidence (summed up by Kavanaugh & Engel, 1998) that pretend play, especially sociodramatic role play, highlights and fosters children's abilities to understand and coordinate multiple mental perspectives. Children's identification with characters whose roles they enact heightens their interest and emotional engagement in the activity. At the same time, this role playing has an important cognitive dimension. It pushes the child to see the world from the point of view of the character being represented—which involves constructing a relatively consistent perspective for this character—and also to coordinate this imagined perspective with those of other protagonists in the play scenario. Thus, it promotes the ability and inclination to understand people's actions in terms of motives, beliefs, desires, and other internal mental states in addition to externally observable phenomena—in short, to construct a "landscape of consciousness." For example, Wolf et al. (1984) found that, in pretend play with figurines, even 3-year-olds began to explicitly attribute to characters emotions, cognitions, obligations, and moral judgments; this is at least several years earlier than the great bulk of narrative research has found such mentalistic descriptions in children's stories (e.g., Berman & Slobin, 1994; for an overview, see Nicolopoulou & Richner, in press). There is also ample research suggesting that children who participate more frequently in role play and other forms of joint pretend play demonstrate greater understanding of internal mental processes, including the role of false beliefs (e.g., Astington & Jenkins, 1995; Schwebel, Rosen, & Singer, 1999; Taylor & Carlson, 1997; Youngblade & Dunn, 1995). My own observations suggest that young children's play narratives often begin to portray vivid, substantial, and reciprocally coordinated characters before they develop complex, sophisticated, or even minimally coherent plots.

By comparison, in their storytelling, young children initially show a greater preoccupation with constructing, elaborating, and extending coherent plots. As indicated earlier, some children may start out with a protostory phase in which they simply list characters to act out, but as soon as they grasp that the character's actions have to be described explicitly, they begin to construct sequences of actions and events that become increasingly extended, complex, and imaginative. My observations accord with Benson's (1993) finding that the plots of preschoolers' stories are usually more complex and sophisticated than those of their pretend play narratives. For some time, however, this increasing sophistication in plot construction is usually not matched in the development of character representation. Young children are certainly capable of including a range of characters in their stories, and some of them (particularly girls) begin quite early to link characters in family or quasi-family relationships. However, at first these characters tend to remain generic types, described with little detail or psychological depth. They are portrayed largely in terms of their actions, especially by boys, or in terms of their social ties, especially by girls (Richner & Nicolopoulou, 2001). Only later do the children's stories begin to portray individuated characters with more detailed characteristics, perspectives on the world, and internal mental states (Nicolopoulou & Richner, in press).

Integrating the Elements of a Complete Narrative Scenario

In both their pretend play and their storytelling, young children gradually master the ability to construct a full narrative scenario, and, correspondingly, a coherent cognitive situation model. That is, they achieve the capacity to routinely produce and understand narrative scenarios that effectively combine coherent and complex plots with rich and substantial character representations, including portrayal of a "landscape of consciousness." I would suggest that achieving this level of development in at least one of their two central narrative activities, pretend play or storytelling, is a key factor that accelerates active and fruitful narrative cross-fertilization between the two activities. We still need to determine how much the attainment of a full narrative scenario takes the form of a gradual and self-reinforcing process or a more sharply defined developmental break-through, but in either case it constitutes an important developmental threshold that serves as a basis and impetus for further development. One reason is that the ability to produce and understand a full narrative scenario, if only in minimal form, integrates the two crucial elements of narrative emphasized by early pretend play and storytelling, respectively, and helps enable children to build cognitive bridges between them.

DEVELOPMENTAL TRAJECTORIES IN STORYTELLING AND PRETEND PLAY: DIFFERING ROUTES IN CONSTRUCTING NARRATIVE SCENARIOS

To flesh out the model just proposed and assess it systematically, we still need to map out the processes by which the narrative scenarios in young children's pretend play and narrative converge to an extent that enables active interplay and fruitful cross-fertilization between them. Drawing on relevant findings from different lines of research, I highlight some of the developmental patterns that appear to be especially significant.

The discussion that follows is necessarily exploratory, especially with respect to pretend play. It is also important to note that the developmental trajectories outlined here should not be expected to unfold in uniform or automatic ways. The developmental pathways followed by individual children are complex, uneven, and diverse, in narrative as in other domains, and they can be significantly shaped and promoted by differing social contexts and interactions (for some elaboration, see Nicolopoulou, 1996, 2002). However, some broad developmental tendencies can be discerned on the basis of existing research, and they accord with the pattern of narrative complementary and convergence I have suggested.

Storytelling: From Plot to Perspective

Addressing these issues is complicated by the fact that most developmental research on children's story production and comprehension during the past several decades has tended to focus heavily on linguistic or plot structure, with considerably less attention to character representation (for more extended discussion, see Nicolopoulou, 1997a; Nicolopoulou & Richner, in press). As I indicated earlier, it is necessary to develop approaches that can effectively capture both of these aspects of narrative and the relationships between them. It is also important to recognize that the processes by which narratives are constructed and used are simultaneously processes of cultural appropriation. In constructing their narratives, children, like adults, necessarily draw on a range of cognitive and symbolic resources from the culture around them, including themes, images, characters, and genres. As Feldman, Bruner, Kalmar, and Renderer (1993) and others have argued, narrative genres provide constitutive mental models for ordering and interpreting the world and our own experience, in ways that are both constraining and enabling, and therefore provide us with crucial tools for thought and action as well as communication. However, children must develop their abilities to master and appropriate these genres and other narrative resources to use them flexibly and creatively.

From this perspective, one revealing feature of young children's earliest storytelling efforts is the difficulty they experience in mastering the narrative resources they try to use. As indicated earlier, some children may start out with protonarratives, merely listing characters, although they soon move beyond that. On the other hand, 3-year-olds from middle-class families have usually been read a great many stories by adults before they arrive in preschool, and they often begin by using some of their favorite stories as models for their own storytelling. However, their first attempts to reproduce these stories tend to be fragmentary and not very coherent.

> It's about a thunderstorm and Bambi and fire.

> There is a thunderstorm and some fire. Bambi's trying to call her mama and they are fawns. They goed home and saw some good little friends. The end. (Daphne, 3;3, 9/14/93)

Other children, in both middle-class preschools and Head Start programs, become able to retell fragments of stories they have heard in considerable detail, sometimes displaying an impressive memory for disconnected story elements. However, on close examination, it is clear that they are repeating stories rather than constructing them—or, to put it another way, that they are imitating narrative models rather than genuinely appropriating them as resources for their own storytelling.

Over the course of the school year, children's stories almost invariably show significant improvements in quality and complexity. One strategy that some children use is to focus on a few basic story paradigms or plot-lines—or even a single paradigm—for an extended period, returning to them over and over and reworking them with incremental variations. In these cases, adults often feel that the child's stories are becoming monotonous, and teachers occasionally complain that these children are "stuck in telling the same stories." However, if one follows the pattern of these stories over time it is clear that the children are methodically working through narrative possibilities of the material and gradually producing more complex and effective stories (for further discussion, see Nicolopoulou, 1996). At first, these advances are manifested primarily in improved plot structure. Later, this begins to be combined with increased depth and richness of character representation.

Some illustrations can be taken from the stories of Joshua (4; 8), who began by telling stories organized around three elements: Ninja Turtles (characters often favored by boys), fighting, and eating. Here is his first story of the school year:

> Ninja Turtles. They fight. Then they eat pizza. And then they fight again. Then pizza again. And then they ate cake and ice cream. And then they fight again. And that's the end. (Joshua, 4; 8, 9/08/93)

Somewhat unusually, but usefully for illustrative purposes, Joshua stayed exclusively with this single story format for more than a semester. His stories gradually became longer and more complicated, primarily by adding more characters (drawn largely from the Ninja Turtles cartoons) and more actions:

> Ninja Turtles eat pizza. And then they fight the foot soldiers. And Bebop and Rocksteady and Shredder came and the Ninjas fighted them. And then they go on the Turtle van. And then they fighted with the foot soldiers 11 times. And then Donatello throw Bebop to the river. And then Donatello throws boulders on top of Bebop's head. And then boulders come tumbling down on Bebop another time. And then Ninja Turtles eat chocolate cake, ice cream, and hot chocolate and candy bars. And then the Ninjas swim in the pond. The end. (Joshua, 5; 2, 3/24/94)

Toward the spring semester, although Joshua's stories were still organized around the alternating themes of fighting and eating, he now used characters drawn from a wider range of sources, and his plots included a wider variety of actions, with more continuity and causal connections in action sequences. Furthermore, the characters began to be described in more detailed, specific, and differentiated ways, although still without much depth:

> The good knights fight the bad knights. And then the bad knights climbed up the castle wall. And the good knights shot them off with bows and arrows. And then the good knights came and put three more of the bad knights in the prison. And then they gave the bad knights some water and food. And then the bad guys escaped from prison. And the good knights fight them again with bows and arrows and swords. Then the good knights went swimming and then they ate chocolate cake and ice cream. Then the good knights go to bed. And in the morning they rode their horses into battle and then the good knights shot the bad knights with bows and arrows. The end. (Joshua, 5; 3, 4/4/94)

Unlike Joshua's stories, which tended to become increasingly sprawling, the following story by another boy, Mickey, offers an example of a more tightly organized narrative depicting a conflict and its resolution. The characters (a man, a woman, and two dinosaurs) are well coordinated with each other within the plot, but none of them is portrayed in detail or with any inner mental life.

> Once upon a time there was a man and one girl. They found some dinosaurs in the stick house and they were Tyrannosaurus Rex and Packiasefalasaurus. They rode on them and the man was bad and the woman was good. The woman was on Packiasefalasaurus and the man rode Tyrannosaurus Rex. And they fighted while they were on the dinosaurs. Packi bited Tyrannosaurus with his head. And Tyrannosaurus bit him with his teeth. And Packi won the fight. (Mickey, 4; 7, 12/1/88)

Other stories by preschoolers achieve a more sophisticated integration of plot complexity with depth of character representation. These stories by Nora, who was in the same preschool class as Mickey, offer a good illustration. We can compare a relatively early story, composed in October, with two stories from the next semester.

> Once upon a time there was a bunny and a duck and they played in the park on the swing. And then they went back to their house and there was a monster. And then they were into their room there was another monster. The end. (Nora, 4; 9, 10/18/88)

This was Nora's fourth story of the school year. At the end of January (after composing another 10 stories in the meantime), she told the following two stories in sequence:

Once upon a time there was a mom and a dad and a sister. They lived in a house in the forest. And one morning the sun came up and they weren't awake yet. But then a fox came looking for food. But then the sister woke up, and she heard the fox. And then the fox came knocking in her door. Then the sister peeked out the door. And then she slammed it closed. And then she ran to tell her mommy and dad. They opened the door and the fox ran away. (Nora, 5; 0, 1/26/89)

Once upon a time in a forest there was a tiger and a bunny. They played hide and seek. And then they found a person and they thought it was a stranger. They ran and then got up a tree, and then the person ran away. They were all scared. And then came a whole family. Then they took the bunny back to their house. And they had dinner there. And then all went to bed. And then in the morning, they woke up. And then they looked out the window. And then they saw snow falling down. (Nora, 5; 0, 1/29/89)

This contrast brings out some key developmental advances. The first story is brief, and each character performs a limited number of actions that are described in generic terms (e.g., they played, they went back home). The later stories have considerably more specificity and complexity: A background is established, and then an interrelated sequence of actions is initiated and elaborated (with the second story combining a general and a specific temporal marking device, "once upon a time" and "one morning"). Overall, the plot structure is more complex and sophisticated. In the second and third stories, for example, a series of dramatic *problems* are posed (the fox goes looking for food, then the sister hears the fox at the door, etc.), which are then *resolved*. In the third story, which has a looser form than the second, elements from two episodes are nevertheless coordinated into a continuous story. In addition, the characters are more fully developed, with a number of specific actions attributed to each, and the relations between the characters are more clearly and carefully worked out. Furthermore, we see the attribution of motives and the depiction of "internal" points of view, with incidents in the story being related from the perspective of one or more of the characters (e.g., the girl hears, then sees, the fox; the tiger and bunny think the person is a stranger and are scared). (For a somewhat more extended analysis see Nicolopoulou, 1996, where Nora's stories are also discussed.)

In each of these later stories, in short, complexity and coherence of plot structure is effectively integrated with depth of character representation within a fully formed narrative scenario. However, this completed narrative scenario with its successful "dual landscape" is a developmental achievement, not a starting point.

Pretend Play: From Intersubjectivity to Plot

With respect to young children's pretend play, I cannot draw directly on my own research, and only a limited number of studies have systematically addressed the issues raised in this chapter. However, findings from several lines of developmental research, when considered in combination, also lend support to the model I have proposed. That is, in their earliest phases young children's play narratives seem to focus primarily on increasing depth and richness of character representation, and only later begin to generate more complex and coherent plots.

As noted earlier, a good deal of research has shown that pretend play, especially collaborative play, engages and promotes children's abilities to represent and coordinate multiple points of view and to understand the role of internal mental processes—skills that are critical for constructing a "landscape of consciousness" in narrative. This is true not only for children's participation in play enactment itself, which involves portraying and identifying with characters, but also for the "metaplay" communication and interaction used in setting up, negotiating, and managing play collaboration. In fact, a number of researchers have argued, explicitly or in effect, that these metaplay processes should be treated as an integral component of play (e.g., Farver, 1992; Goldman, 1998; Göncü, 1993a, 1993b; Sachs, Goldman, & Chaille, 1984; Sawyer, 1997; Trawick-Smith, 1998). For example, Göncü (1993a, 1993b) suggested convincingly that a key dimension in the development of pretend play during the preschool years is the achievement of increasingly effective intersubjectivity—that is, children's abilities to establish and build on understandings and to organize and maintain play collaboration. This line of analysis has also been pursued and elaborated, using somewhat different terminology, by Sawyer (1997) and others.

As Sawyer (1997) himself recognized, these analyses of intersubjectivity in metaplay interaction still need to be coordinated more fully with developmental analyses that focus on the structure and symbolic content of the enacted play narratives themselves. However, existing play research already offers further evidence for the developmental priority of character representation in young children's pretend play narratives. For example, according to the extensive body of developmental research on social pretend play synthesized by Howes, Unger, and Matheson (1992), young children begin by acting out vague and generic roles in relatively disconnected ways, with a tendency to repeat a few stereotypic actions. In later phases, the characters are increasingly fleshed out, individuated, and portrayed with psychological depth. In addition, roles are more tightly linked with each other and role enactments are increasingly coordinated, in complementary or even directly reciprocal fashion. This greater richness and depth in character representation develops in tandem with children's increasing skills in achieving successful intersubjectivity and extended play collaboration. However, for some time the plots of their play narratives remain rudimentary, with little complexity or coherence (in this connection, the findings reported by Howes et al., 1992, are strongly reinforced by the perceptive analysis of Sachs et al., 1984). It is not until later during the preschool years, usually after age 5, that children begin to construct and enact well-articulated plots in their pretend play, thus moving toward the effective integration of plot and character representation in their play narratives.

CONCLUSIONS AND OPEN QUESTIONS

This chapter has proposed an approach to understanding the developmental relationship between pretend play and storytelling that treats them as initially parallel and complementary modes of children's narrative activity, with at least partly distinct origins and developmental pathways, that young children are gradually able to integrate effectively. Children's play and narrative should not be artificially separated or studied in mutual isolation, but should be viewed as closely intertwined, and often overlapping, forms of socially situated symbolic action. The active interplay and cross-fertilization between pretend play and storytelling can significantly promote children's learning and development in a range of domains. However, children's ability to engage flexibly and fruitfully in this active interplay is neither automatic nor simply given. Instead, it is a developmental achievement that, in turn, serves as a foundation and impetus for further development.

Some empirical support for this model is provided by my findings of initial thematic disjunction and increasing thematic cross-fertilization between the narrative scenarios in children's storytelling and their pretend play. However, this developmental pattern still needs to be delineated and explained more fully. I propose that part of the explanation lies in the tendency for children's pretend play and storytelling, at least in their earliest phases, to emphasize and promote different but complementary dimensions of narrative and narrative skills. The earliest phases in pretend play emphasize and encourage increasing depth and richness in character representation, whereas the earliest phases in storytelling emphasize increasing complexity, coherence, and sophistication in plot construction and comprehension. Building on these complementary strengths and challenges, in both of these activities young children gradually master the ability to integrate these elements so as to produce and understand complete narrative scenarios— ones that effectively combine coherent and complex plots with rich and substantial character representations, including the portrayal of what Bruner (1986) termed a landscape of consciousness that conveys characters' inner mental states, motives, and perspectives on the world. Achieving this capacity to produce and understand a complete narrative scenario is a key factor enabling active and flexible cross-fertilization between the two activities.

Of course, this does not imply that at any point there is a sharp and rigid separation between these two modes of young children's narrative activity. And as I noted earlier, the developmental pathways followed by young children are complex, uneven, and diverse, so the patterns outlined in this chapter will never be entirely uniform in practice. For example, it seems clear that even very young children can sometimes experience vivid identification and deep imaginative involvement with characters in stories they hear and tell (e.g., the 2-year-old described in Miller et al., 1993; see also Miller et al., 2000). However, as I have argued in this chapter, there are both theoretical and empirical grounds for believing that the model presented here captures some fundamental developmental patterns.

This analysis, in short, has been offered as an orienting framework and working hypothesis for further research. To the extent that it can be fol- lowed up, confirmed, and refined, the developmental model of narrative complementarity and convergence suggested here can potentially have significant implications for both research and practice. In theoretical terms, for example, I would argue that whereas the concept of a cognitive "situation model" as used by Harris (2000) and others is extremely valu- able and illuminating for narrative research, children's ability to con- struct and employ a coherent situation model is itself a developmental achievement, so that the effective integration of its different elements cannot simply be taken as given. It also seems clear that the develop- mental dynamics of children's pretend play and storytelling, and children's abilities to benefit from the active interplay between them, can be powerfully facilitated, shaped, and encouraged by different social con- texts and practices, including adult–child interactions and peer-group activities (important starting points for research along these lines include rich ethnographic studies such as Paley, 1986, 1988, 1990; Rowe, 1998, 2000; Wolf & Heath, 1992). More systematic and theoretically informed investigation of the complex interplay between play and narrative can help us better understand and more effectively encourage the potential value of children's symbolic activities for promoting the development of cognition and imagination.

REFERENCES

Astington, J. W., & Jenkins, J. M. (1995). Theory of mind development and social understanding. *Social Cognition and Emotion, 9*, 151–165.

Bamberg, M. (Ed.). (1997). *Narrative development: Six approaches.* Mahwah, NJ: Lawrence Erlbaum Associates, Inc.

Benson, M. S. (1993). The structure of four- and five-year-olds' narratives in pretend play and storytelling. *First Language, 13*, 203–223.

Berman, R., & Slobin, D. I. (Eds.). (1994). *Relating events in narrative: A crosslinguistic developmental study.* Hillsdale, NJ: Lawrence Erlbaum Associates.

Bruner, J. (1986). *Actual minds, possible worlds.* Cambridge, MA: Harvard University Press.

Bruner, J. (1992). The narrative construction of reality. In H. Beilin & P. Pufall (Eds.), *Piaget's theory: Prospects and possibilities* (pp. 229–248). Hillsdale, NJ: Lawrence Erlbaum Associates.

Cohen, D., & MacKeith, S. A. (1991). *The development of imagination: The private worlds of childhood.* New York: Routledge.

Engel, S. (1995). *The stories children tell: Making sense of the narratives of childhood.* New York: Freeman.

Farver, J. M. (1992). Communicating shared meaning in social pretend play. *Early Childhood Research Quarterly, 7*, 501–516.

Fein, G. G., Ardila-Rey, A. E., & Groth, L. A. (2000). The narrative connection: Stories and literacy. In K. A. Roskos & J. F. Christie (Eds.), *Play and literacy in early childhood* (pp. 27–43). Mahwah, NJ: Lawrence Erlbaum Associates.

Feldman, C., Bruner, J., Kalmar, D., & Renderer, B. (1993). Plot, plight, and dramatism: Interpretation at three ages. *Human Development, 36*, 327–342.

Fireman, G. D., McVay, T. E., & Flanagan, O. J. (2003). *Narrative and consciousness.* New York: Oxford University Press.

Galda, L. (1984). Narrative competence: Play, storytelling, and story comprehension. In A. D. Pellegrini & T. D. Yawkey (Eds.), *The development of oral and written language in social context* (pp. 105–117). Norwood, NJ: Ablex.

Goldman, L. R. (1998). *Child's play: Myth, mimesis, and make-believe.* New York: Berg.

Göncü, A. (1993a). Development of intersubjectivity in social pretend play. *Human Development, 36*, 185–198.

Göncü, A. (1993b). Development of intersubjectivity in the dyadic play of preschoolers. *Early Childhood Research Quarterly, 8*, 99–116.

Harris, P. (2000). *The work of the imagination*. Malden, MA: Blackwell.

Howes, C., Unger, O., & Matheson, C. C. (1992). *The collaborative construction of pretend: Social pretend play functions*. Albany: State University of New York Press.

Kavanaugh, R. D., & Engel, S. (1998). The development of pretense and narrative in early childhood. In O. N. Saracho & B. Spodek (Eds.), *Multiple perspectives on play in early childhood education* (pp. 80–99). Albany: State University of New York Press.

Martinez, M., Cheyney, M., & Teale, W. H. (1991). Classroom literature activities and kindergartners' dramatic story reenactments. In J. F. Christie (Ed.), *Play and early literacy development* (pp. 119–140). Albany: State University of New York Press.

McCabe, A., & Bliss, L. S. (2003). *Patterns of narrative discourse: A multicultural, life-span approach*. Boston: Allyn & Bacon.

Miller, P. J., Hengst, J., Alexander, K., & Sperry, L. (2000). Versions of personal storytelling/Versions of experience: Genres as tools for creating alternate realities. In K. S. Rosengren, C. N. Johnson, & P. L. Harris (Eds.), *Imagining the impossible: Magical, scientific, and religious thinking in children* (pp. 212–246). New York: Cambridge University Press.

Miller, P. J., Hoogstra, L., Mintz, J., Fung, H., Williams, K. (1993). Troubles in the garden and how they get resolved: A young child's transformation of his favorite story. In C. A. Nelson (Ed.), *Memory and affect in development: The Minnesota Symposia on Child Psychology* (Vol. 26, pp. 87–114). Hillsdale, NJ: Lawrence Erlbaum Associates.

Nelson, K. (Ed.). (1989). *Narratives from the crib*. Cambridge, MA: Harvard University Press.

Nicolopoulou, A. (1993). Play, cognitive development, and the social world: Piaget, Vygotsky, and beyond. *Human Development, 36*, 1–23.

Nicolopoulou, A. (1996). Narrative development in social context. In D. I. Slobin, J. Gerhardt, J. Guo, & A. Kyratzis (Eds.), *Social interaction, social context, and language: Essays in honor of Susan Ervin-Tripp* (pp. 369–390). Mahwah, NJ: Lawrence Erlbaum Associates.

Nicolopoulou, A. (1997a). Children and narratives: Toward an interpretive and sociocultural approach. In M. Bamberg (Ed.), *Narrative development: Six approaches* (pp. 179–215). Mahwah, NJ: Lawrence Erlbaum Associates, Inc.

Nicolopoulou, A. (1997b). Worldmaking and identity formation in children's narrative play-acting. In B. D. Cox & C. Lightfoot (Eds.), *Sociogenetic perspectives on internalization* (pp. 157–187). Mahwah, NJ: Lawrence Erlbaum Associates, Inc.

Nicolopoulou, A. (2002). Peer-group culture and narrative development. In S. Blum-Kulka & C. E. Snow (Eds.), *Talking to adults: The contribution of multiparty discourse to language acquisition* (pp. 117–152). Mahwah, NJ: Lawrence Erlbaum Associates, Inc.

Nicolopoulou, A., & Richner, E. S. (in press). From actors to agents to persons: The development of character representation in young children's narratives. *Child Development*.

Nicolopoulou, A., Scales, B., & Weintraub, J. (1994). Gender differences and symbolic imagination in the stories of four-year-olds. In A. H. Dyson & C. Genishi (Eds.), *The need for story: Cultural diversity in classroom and community* (pp. 102–123). Urbana, IL: NCTE.

Paley, V. G. (1986). *Mollie is three: Growing up in school.* Chicago: University of Chicago Press.

Paley, V. G. (1988). *Bad guys don't have birthdays: Fantasy play at four.* Chicago: University of Chicago Press.

Paley, V. G. (1990). *The boy who would be a helicopter: The uses of storytelling in the classroom.* Cambridge, MA: Harvard University Press.

Pellegrini, A. D., & Galda, L. (1982). The effects of thematic-fantasy play training on the development of children's story comprehension. *American Educational Research Journal, 19,* 443–452.

Pellegrini, A. D., & Galda, L. (1990). The joint construction of stories by preschool children and an experimenter. In B. K. Britton & A. D. Pellegrini (Eds.), *Narrative thought and narrative language* (pp. 113–130). Hillsdale, NJ: Lawrence Erlbaum Associates, Inc.

Pellegrini, A. D., & Galda, L. (1993). Ten years after: A reexamination of symbolic play and literacy research. *Reading Research Quarterly, 28,* 163–175.

Richner, E. S., & Nicolopoulou, A. (2001). The narrative construction of differing conceptions of the person in the development of young children's social understanding. *Early Education and Development, 12,* 393–432.

Roskos, K. A., & Christie, J. F. (2000). (Eds.). *Play and literacy in early childhood.* Mahwah, NJ: Lawrence Erlbaum Associates, Inc.

Rowe, D. W. (1998). The literate potentials of book-related dramatic play. *Reading Research Quarterly, 33,* 10–35.

Rowe, D. W. (2000). Bringing books to life: The role of book-related dramatic play in young children's literacy learning. In K. A. Roskos & J. F. Christie (Eds.), *Play and literacy in early childhood: Research from multiple perspectives* (pp. 3–25). Mahwah, NJ: Lawrence Erlbaum Associates, Inc.

Sachs, J., Goldman, J., & Chaille, C. (1984). Planning in pretend play: Using language to coordinate narrative development. In A. D. Pellegrini & T. D. Yawkey (Eds.), *The development of oral and written language in social context* (pp. 119–128). Norwood, NJ: Ablex.

Saracho, O. N., & Spodek, B. (Eds.). (1998). *Multiple perspectives on play in early childhood education.* Albany: State University of New York Press.

Sawyer, R. K. (1997). *Pretend play as improvisation: Conversation in the preschool classroom.* Mahwah, NJ: Lawrence Erlbaum Associates, Inc.

Schwebel, D. C., Rosen, C. S., & Singer, J. L. (1999). Preschoolers' pretend play and theory of mind: The role of jointly constructed pretense. *British Journal of Developmental Psychology, 17,* 333–348.

Silvern, S. B., Taylor, A., Williamson, P. A., Surbeck, E., & Kelley, P. (1986). Young children's story recall as a product of play, story familiarity, and adult intervention. *Merrill-Palmer Quarterly, 32,* 73–86.

Smilansky, S. (1968). *The effects of sociodramatic play on disadvantaged preschool children.* New York: Wiley.

Sutton-Smith, B. (1984a). The origins of fiction and the fictions of origin. In E. M. Bruner (Ed.), *Text, play, and story: The construction and reconstruction of self and society* (pp. 117–132). Washington, DC: American Ethnological Society.

Sutton-Smith, B. (1984b). Text and context in imaginative play. In F. Kessel & A. Göncü (Eds.), *Analyzing children's play dialogues: New directions for child development* (pp. 53–70). San Francisco: Jossey-Bass.

Tabors, P. O., Snow, C. E., & Dickinson, D. K. (2001). Homes and schools together: Supporting language and literacy development. In D. K. Dickinson & P. O. Tabors (Eds.), *Beginning literacy with language: Young children learning at home and school* (pp. 313–334). Baltimore: Brookes.

Taylor, M., & Carlson, S. M. (1997). The relation between individual differences in fantasy and theory of mind. *Child Development, 68*, 436–455.

Trawick-Smith, J. (1998). A qualitative analysis of metaplay in the preschool years. *Early Childhood Research Quarterly, 13*, 433–452.

Vygotsky, L. S. (1967). Play and its role in the mental development of the child. *Soviet Psychology, 12*, 6–18. (Translation of a stenographic record of a lecture given in Russian in 1933)

Wells, G. (1986). *The meaning makers: Children learning language and using language to learn.* Portsmouth, NH: Heinemann.

Williamson, P. A., & Silvern, S. B. (1990). The effects of play training on the story comprehension of upper primary children. *Journal of Research in Childhood Education, 4*, 130–136.

Williamson, P. A., & Silvern, S. B. (1991). Thematic-fantasy play and story comprehension. In J. F. Christie (Ed.), *Play and early literacy development* (pp. 69–90). Albany: State University of New York Press.

Williamson, P. A., & Silvern, S. B. (1992). "You can't be grandma; You're a boy": Events within the thematic fantasy play context that contribute to story comprehension. *Early Childhood Research Quarterly, 7*, 75–93.

Wolf, S. A., & Heath, S. B. (1992). *The braid of literature: Children's worlds of reading.* Cambridge, MA: Harvard University Press.

Wolf, D. P., Rygh, J., & Altshuler, J. (1984). Agency and experience: Actions and states in play narratives. In I. Bretherton (Ed.), *Symbolic play: The development of social understanding* (pp. 195–217). Orlando, FL: Academic.

Youngblade, L. M., & Dunn, J. (1995). Individual differences in young children's pretend play with mother and siblings: Links to relationships and understanding other people's feelings and beliefs. *Child Development, 66*, 1472–1492.

Zwaan, R. A. (1999). Situation models: The mental leap into the imagined worlds. *Current Directions in Psychological Science, 8*, 15–18.

Zwaan, R. A., & Radvansky, G. A. (1998). Situation models in language comprehension and memory. *Psychological Bulletin, 123*, 162–185.

12

Therapeutic Advantages of Play

Cindy Dell Clark

Pennsylvania State University

Children commandeer play when facing troubles, even without the guidance of formal play therapy. Preschoolers who survived the 1995 Oklahoma City bombing played "hospital" using play figures with missing limbs. Children who experienced Hurricane Hugo in 1989 were observed to play with broccoli at dinner, pretending that the broccoli sprouts were trees, then dousing the broccoli with gravy to represent rushing flood waters (Sleek, 1998). Children in a hospital outpatient waiting room, stocked with toys, awaited their own surgery by throwing themselves into playing doctor: listening to the doll's heartbeat, taking the doll's temperature, putting on a curative bandage, and all the while reassuring the doll—or sometimes a human playmate—in the most gentle tones: "This will be alright. This won't hurt at all" (L. Thomasen, personal communication, November 26, 2003). Youngsters in need of gentle reassurances, or in want of control amidst chaotic threat, enact on playthings forms of self-consolation. Children's creative and unguided uses of play are salient reminders that play holds important power for coping.

However, little is currently documented about the scope of child-initiated therapeutic play within children's lives, nor about the incidence of such coping across varied groups of children facing stressors. Neither is very much known about the efficacy or therapeutic impact of child-initiated therapeutic play. By comparison, investigations of the efficacy of formal

275

play therapy interventions, although not exhaustive (Russ, 2004), are relatively more available. Empirical studies of play therapy (in which a child plays aided by the accompaniment and interpretations of an adult therapist) have found that overall, play therapy is about as effective in treating children as psychotherapy is in treating adults (LeBlanc & Ritchie, 2001). Questions remain, however, for instance about whether or not divergent forms of supervised play therapy assist coping to a comparable extent. Children participating in formal play therapy play as a means to address troubles, in a manner reminiscent of child-initiated therapeutic play. Play therapy, I argue, can be a relevant model through which to better understand child-initiated therapeutic play, which exhibits both similarities to and distinctions from play therapy.

This chapter shows how play therapy and child-initiated therapeutic play appear to be not-distant cousins in terms of their semiotic RNA; that is, common dynamic structures of meaning appear to underpin each respective process. Both forms of play touch on five common dynamic issues: (a) the child undertaking an active role as self directing; (b) the role of others in supporting or scaffolding the child's play; (c) an implicit sort of ontological "framing" that encourages suspended disbelief and an engagement with an as-if version of reality, through play; (d) an orientation that is open to unresolved ambiguity, that allows for multivocal symbolism and flexible meanings; and (e) within the play, an experience of restructured meaning accompanied by an affect-laden release or relief. Child-initiated play, which I have elsewhere called *imaginal coping* (Clark, 2003), can be explicated as a process using these five dimensions, through comparison with known principles of play therapy.

The discussion in this chapter is not intended to review the field of formal play therapy, which has been adequately introduced elsewhere by clinical experts (e.g., Axline, 1947; Gil, 1994; O'Connor, 1991; Schaeffer, 1993; D. G. Singer, 1993, 1994; Webb, 1999). Rather, the intent is to chart the waters of child-initiated play by engaging knowledge about play therapy. My goal, in other words, is to explore how the workings of child-initiated therapeutic play correspond to, and differ from, the dynamics of play therapy, as a means of instruction about child-initiated imaginal coping.

A main resource in this analysis will be my own ethnographic study of chronically ill 5- to 8-year-olds, conducted in children's homes (and sometimes in area summer camps) in urban and suburban Chicago (Clark, 2003). The youngsters in my study—suffering from diabetes or severe asthma—brought to my attention the phenomenon of child-initiated therapeutic play, through the sheer prevalence of such play in their lives.

Imaginal coping was recorded again and again in photos, drawings, and interviews about children's illness experiences, and in written journals kept by parents about their child's daily living with illness. Through play children addressed and reframed predicaments of illness, using imagination to render troubles in new ways. A young girl in need of protection, hospitalized for diabetes at age 3, imagined that a large toy tiger in her hospital room was capable of preventing the doctors and nurses from mortally harming her during hurtful procedures. An asthmatic boy imagined that the characters pictured on his bed sheets, the Teenage Mutant Ninja Turtles, would save him at night from death by flying off the sheets to fetch the doctor if the boy was gravely ill. Children's imaginings, which were routine occurrences in the lives of many young illness sufferers, systematically enabled children to remake a safer, more defended world and self, through play. Children gained resiliency through playful transformation. The dynamics by which children accomplished such feats, reframing and reconceiving the troubles they faced, compels profound interest in therapeutic play, especially for scholars or practitioners concerned with issues of meaning, imagination, resilience, and coping. Flexibility of meaning, as it turns out, is instrumental to the therapeutic value of play, and to a child's capacity to be resilient. Better delineation of the dynamics of playful self-coping may ultimately yield insights into how children who come under stress can make sense of, and thereby deal with, their distress.

THE CHILD AS SELF-DIRECTOR OF PLAY

In therapeutic play—both clinically prescribed play therapy and the unprescribed therapeutic play of the child in a nonclinical environment—play provides a flexing dynamic that accommodates a shift in the child's personal system of significance. The child, having come to a troubling impasse in his or her system of signification, makes flexible use of cultural forms to configure and reconfigure dilemmas of meaning (J. L. Singer, 1994). The boy who commandeered the Teenage Mutant Ninja Turtles, pictured on his bed sheets, to take on the superheroic job of saving his life faced a dilemma directly threatening to selfhood: the possibility of death through suffocating asthma symptoms. His symptoms were worse at night, when his parents slept at the end of a long, dark hallway. His asthma was sufficiently severe that his mother (under direction of a physician) had prohibited the boy from sleeping with any stuffed (perhaps asthma-triggering) toys that might otherwise have been a source of trusting reassurance. Undaunted by the lack of a conventional velveteen rabbit or teddy bear as a transitional object, the boy directed his own imagination to make use of the illustrations on his bed sheets. This play-like imagining was instigated and directed by the child, without adults even being aware of the child's creative portrayal.

During interviews a familiar experience to me was for children to confide, in an atmosphere of privacy, about acts of imaginal coping that they had not yet revealed to others. A youngster with asthma, required to sit still for a prolonged period and inhale medication through a machine nebulizer, said he imagined that his toy airplane could fly away through the nebulizer's exuding mist, thus (in pretense) transporting him away from being tethered to the machine. An 8-year-old with diabetes took his Power Ranger action figure with him during a doctor's visit, imagining the Ranger to be diabetic, and to share the ordeal of being examined and pricked alongside the boy. The young owner of the Power Ranger thereby gained appreciated company-in-misery, unbeknownst to his mother or physician. Children's acts of playful coping were often covert, with children serving as their own agents of imaginal experience, unbeknownst to adults or peers. The sheer privacy of such play can be assumed to have social consequences, of course. In the case of the toy tiger mentioned earlier, the girl's imaginings about the tiger were not made public, with the result that the nurses were oblivious to the tiger's meaning for the child. They removed the tiger from her hospital room, because they thought it frightened her, resulting in the girl's profound loss and grief; she sobbed uncontrollably when remembering the event 3 years later.

As these cases illustrate, children exercise creative powers of imagining at their own volition, sometimes without intentional social sharing. Children's making of meaning through play is directed by their own choices, often highly creative ones. Taylor (1999) wrote about the fact that adults know little and are poor informants about children's imaginary companions, a phenomenon closely related to imaginal coping because it can involve coping with trauma or processing unsettling events. Taylor observed that children's initiatives often underlay the development of imaginary companions.

In professional play therapy, by comparison, the therapist directly observes the child at play, and is interactive with the child in discussing interpretive insights about play behaviors (Webb, 1999). Play therapists set a range for play by providing a preselected array of play materials. Yet despite the active involvement of the professional therapist—in providing a setting and materials, in witnessing the child's play, and in volunteering interpretations of play—a premise of play therapy stipulates that the adult therapist should not impose meaning on the child. Indeed, research shows that the imposition of an a priori interpretation is known to inhibit rather than to illuminate the therapeutic process (Birch, 1997). In prescribed play therapy, the therapist seeks a relationship of rapport and common ground, but ironically this groundwork is meant to enable the child to freely explore and set his or her own direction. As the influential and well-known practitioner of play therapy Axline (1947) once stated, the therapist is advised to consciously avoid dictation or direction of the child's actions but should "let the child lead the way"—whereupon the therapist should follow in turn. In that sense, formal play therapy and imaginal coping share a quality, both being in an important respect, child-driven, child-discovered, and child-directed activities. Play therapy may involve more adult assistance than does imaginal coping, but the crucial child-directed aspect of play—the child's privilege to fire his or her imagination at will—characterizes both contexts.

SUPPORT AND SCAFFOLDING OF THERAPEUTIC PLAY

As just discussed, play therapists adopt a conscious ideal of having children lead the way in therapy, although professionals do support youthful play by providing a conducive setting, materials, and interpretive involvement. Indeed, one might argue that the whole notion of formal play therapy aims to scaffold a child's coping through play, by predefining a bracketed time and space, tailor-made for such an endeavor. The process of formal play therapy sets an expectation that a child will head out in some direction bent on playing therapeutically, and will actively mold his or her own play. Still, this does not imply that the child is isolated or that the activity is asocial. The therapist generally leaves the direction and script of the evolving play to the child, yet actively interacts with the child to earn and maintain trust, encourage playful involvement, and monitor the play and its meaning (Schaefer, 1993; Webb, 1999). The famed British child therapist Donald Winnicott invented and disseminated a play therapy technique called the "squiggle game" (Claman, 1993; Frankel, 1997), specifically focused on interactive engagement in play therapy. Winnicott drew a squiggle on a sheet of paper and enticed the child to then draw his or her own line on the paper. Turn by turn, child and therapist interactively completed squiggle drawings, each improvising as they drew. Winnicott, although he commented on children's productions, did not dominate the interaction (Clancier & Kalmanovitch, 1984). The squiggle-drawing method has earned many proponents because it puts children at ease and ready to make spontaneous gestures and approaches. (Indeed, the game aims to have the hierarchy of child and adult drop away, creating a liminal space in which the child's role is not secondary to the adult therapist's role.) Play therapists, as the instance of the squiggle game implies, actively scaffold children's therapeutic play, in a manner that nevertheless does not obviate children's agency.

Based on my ethnographic work with chronically ill children, imaginal coping was not always a solitary pursuit for these children either, but frequently involved social interaction in one sense or another. For example, a recurring form of fantasized interaction was role-reversal play, in which children playfully took the ascendant pretend role of doctor or caregiver and played out that role with an imagined subordinate patient. The as-if patient could be an animal toy, a pet or a doll—but also was often a human playmate. Diabetic children, for instance, dispensed insulin injections with toy syringes to playmates. Inverting roles during pretend treatment provoked children to recognize and identify with an alternative point of view, that of the caregiver. (This role inversion will be discussed more later.) Another example occurred among school-age children with asthma who attended an overnight camp, and who together staged various forms of play, such as making music together with their "spacers," gadgets used in taking inhaled medicine that make a noise to signal improper inhalation. The spacer's sound signal was redirected by children as a means of interactive musical entertainment. In a skit performed at camp, children jointly produced a performance poking fun at a traumatic aspect of asthma, disabled breathing: In the skit, the wolf antagonist from the story "The Three Little Pigs" was depicted as breathing so poorly he could not summon the breath to blow down any pig's house. Sometimes, play at camp was instigated with the help of adult-provided materials. At a camp attended by children with diabetes, empty syringes filled by counselors with paint became instruments for art in a gleefully shared activity.

Chronically ill children played in interaction with others, also, when receiving medical treatment at home. Such play, which superficially seemed to be a way of distracting attention from the medical act, carried meaningful, socially shared content. In one such instance, a boy with diabetes pretended that the syringe used by his mother to inject insulin was (in pretense) not a syringe, but a zebra. As the mother began the injection, she narrated that the zebra was about to kiss the boy. However, because the injection hurt, the boy stomped on the empty syringe in retaliation for the hurtful "kiss." In this pretend play interaction, mother and son were able to transform meaning, jointly, through the mother's pretense of a "kiss" (a loving motivation) and the boy's open expression of annoyance at pain. Both the loving act of care and its unintended painful effects were expressed in the play.

During treatment, children joined companions in a variety of invented games. A diabetic girl made wagers with her uncle about what the numerical test reading from a blood test would be, associating a pleasurable game of chance with the irksome procedure. Two brothers, both with diabetes, drew blood and began their blood test while making a race out of the act. A girl encouraged her mother to playfully clap and count (in varying languages) as the girl inhaled her asthma medication to the prescribed count of 10.

During medical procedures and at other times, someone besides the child sometimes instigated play. A father suggested to his diabetic son that he sing out "Alleluia" (using Handel's well-known melody) after receiving his insulin shot. The boy followed the suggestion, and from then on enthusiastically sang "Alleluia" after other injections, even when his father was not present. At a camp for children with asthma, the camp director loaned a homesick camper a stuffed dog (complete with a leash that stood up without being held). The director told all the children that this toy animal had asthma and needed care. The homesick camper took the director's suggestion and became responsible for the toy dog's "care" for 4 days. This play (a role-reversing caregiving) seemed to relieve the girl's severe homesickness. In another situation, a hospital nurse gave a newly diagnosed diabetic boy a teddy bear, which the boy (at his own instigation) used for medical play, administering his entire diabetic regimen in pretense. The boy's mother made available injection gear, blood test meter, and lancets used in blood tests—all augmenting the boy's role-reversal play with the teddy bear.

Like a play therapist, family members and medical care providers can be catalysts to remind a child that play is acceptable, in the course of providing ideas, supplies, or companionship for children's therapeutic play. The reverse can also be true. Family members may interfere with coping by removing toys from a child's room (e.g., for intended allergic prevention). Medical professionals sometimes refuse to allow a child to bring a toy along to a procedure (as happened in one X-ray room, or in a number of hospital rooms). Physicians or nurses several times had a child's trusted plaything (e.g., the girl's large stuffed tiger) removed in stressful circumstances, even though the child was being consoled by the item now banned.

Although unprescribed therapeutic play—imaginal coping—is in an important sense child directed, then, it is not socially isolated. Just as in prescribed play therapy, an adult can set the stage by providing particular play materials and by tolerating or encouraging play. It is a simple act to make available toys that might encourage improvisation about a child's troublesome experiences, such as toys for medical play, or toys representing relevant qualities such as strength (tigers, bears), free mobility (planes, cars), vulnerability (stuffed dog-patient), and so forth. The adult's receptivity to play, as an activity, supports imaginal coping. By being a willing "patient" in role-reversing medical play, or welcoming games or play during actual medical procedures, parents and caretakers scaffold therapeutic play.

Nevertheless, therapeutic play cannot be in any sense dictated to the child, because therapeutic play reflects and plays off of issues of person-based meaning. Children have the power to actively resist play therapy, which is a common dilemma of play therapists (Bow, 1993). Adults and peers, like play therapists, can support, but not dictate, the direction a child takes when coping through play.

FRAMING AN "AS-IF" REALITY

Children's ability to remain "well adjusted" is not a mere matter of adjusting to the external world, for that would imply a steady diet of reality testing, without the "as-if" experience of fantasy, with its willing suspension of disbelief. Playing therapeutically involves a withdrawal from reality testing, a throwing aside of external constraints (Garbarino, Dubrow, Kostelny, & Pardo, 1992). Play invites remakings of experience, casting off ontological correctness. To suspend disbelief in this way requires a sense of trust on the part of the child. Some children, traumatized and too psychologically hurt to extend trust and suspend disbelief, may lack the flexibility to play in a manner that reorders meaning and thereby aids coping. This is the dilemma of the child with posttraumatic stress who compulsively repeats a scenario, but truly cannot play (Raynor, 2002). To be therapeutic, play presumes the ability to inhabit a parallel universe, in a figurative sense, and to playfully manipulate and maneuver its contents and events. Therapeutic play is flexible, unfixed, and transforming of meaning. This is true both in formal play therapy and in unprescribed imaginal coping.

Take, as illustration, an example from D. G. Singer's (1993) play therapy practice. Her client Perry, just past 5 years old and behaving aggressively in preschool, was the child of drug-dependent parents. Perry expressed concern that when his father drinks beer, he "gets real mad, grrr grr, grrr, like that!" When Singer attempted to probe Perry about this concern, he made an angry face but would not speak, and avoided the subject. When Perry set out to play in Singer's office, he put aside the literal world of beer and fathers. Using Play-Doh from Singer's playroom, Perry sat and made a "volcano" out of blue and yellow clay, making noises to signify loud eruptions, and adding rocks made of red clay, commenting "This explodes all over, just watch it go!" Perry repeated his volcano play at a subsequent session with Singer, volunteering that he liked the "explosions" in the play.

Perry's parents behaved violently, but rather than literally reflect on this, Perry's play represented explosiveness through an "as-if" universe made and controlled by him. So too, when children play in unprescribed, child-initiated imaginal coping, they are apt to cast issues in terms of an imagined scenario, rather than to literally mull over what troubles them.

Bruce, a 6-year-old with asthma, did not like hospital food when he was an overnight patient. He also worried that the hospital would be boring, because the Nintendo machine in the hospital room was out of order. He further worried about receiving shots and other hurtful procedures. His father brought, from home, videos of the Teenage Mutant Ninja Turtles. Bruce pretended, even when not watching the videos, about one of the Turtles. He pretended that the superturtle was under water, but did not get hurt under the water, because the creature could "blow bubbles" with his turtle respiration, and had protective bombs for any sharks in the water. The imagined Turtle character ate pizza rather than hospital food. As Perry imagined it, the nurse kept pouring water on the Ninja Turtle, an act of care needed by turtles out of water. Thus, Bruce did not ponder directly issues of disliked food, worrisome medical procedures, or hampered respiration. Instead, he pondered an as-if plane of reality—where remarkably, some of these same issues recurred in a context that could be directly manipulated by the imagining boy.

Conforming to literal reality is not required by play, although the alternate plane of reality created by play may carry stowed-away themes that reflect troublesome issues in a child's everyday world. Conforming to external reality is not the point of play. Still, in therapeutic play, kids face themes that, in normal existence, trouble them. Kids consider the issues (laden with fear, anger, vulnerability, loss, etc.) by reworking them, in pretense, within an as-if universe of each child's own making.

AMBIGUITY AND FLEXIBLE MEANING-MAKING

It is well known that play is a realm of significance that is open to unresolved ambiguity (Sutton-Smith, 1997). Play accommodates multiple meanings and mixed messages. The pretend enactment by which a mother and son turned a syringe filled with insulin into a "zebra" leaves space for equivocation: Is the zebra mean or loving? Play allows the zebra to be both, or either, and allows flexibility in choosing a satisfying interpretation. Play is dense with meaning, in this way, containing what Ricoeur (1976) called a surplus of meaning.

The equivocation and ambiguity of play allows a child to pivot, flexibly, across layers of signifying. This facilitates a dynamic remaking of what is significant to the child. It also ensures that meaning is discoverable by the individual person, rather than determined, fixed, or dictated. Play involves "trying on" transient self-representations or identifications (Birch, 1997), such as venturing to take the role of doctor before surgery, or the role of a breathless, ineffectual wolf at asthma camp. It involves exploring possible worlds, such as imagining a world in which superheroic protection is at hand to counter threat. Whether play is formally prescribed or not, it is an opportunity to flex the human capacity to remake meaning. Openness to such flexing is implicitly encouraged by play therapists, and exercised on a more informal basis by children in imaginal coping.

Play, then, is in some respects a free for all, a context in which nuances and frameworks are up for grabs. A child who brings an open-minded, flexible stance to playing draws from the act a kind of tensile strength, a flexibility to reassess, shift, and even invert issues. A good example of this transforming dynamic is role-reversal play, play in which an ill child, who is usually a receiver of care, in play takes on the part of a would-be caregiver, such as a doctor. This play represents a turnabout of roles, in which the power-deficient party impersonates the powerful. Numerous acts of turnabout medical play occurred among the chronically ill children I studied. Through topsy-turvy reversal, ill children administered countless doses of medicine, injections, tests, and so forth to dolls, pet turtles, dogs, cats, toy snakes, and human friends. By playing doctor (or veterinarian or nurse or mother)—reversing roles and claiming ascendancy over a play patient—the caregiver–receiver dialectic was released from the usual position. This meant that the usually sick child took control. In the inverted balance of power, no matter how fleeting, children were able to recognize and identify with an alternate point of view—caregiving—a role ultimately crucial in the self-care of children with chronic illness (Irwin & Curry, 1993). Role play, which is an approach used in play therapy, as well, facilitates empathy for other viewpoints and identification with other possibilities.

Anthropologist Turner (1969) described how particular cultural rituals, in which usual social positions and classifications are suspended, provide both communitas (collective sharing and connection) and liminality (involving "antistructure" in which to rethink relatedness). Role-reversal play, like ritual, suspends rank and introduces liminality, a kind of leveling of social roles. The ill child is temporarily unencumbered by subordination, and the play companion who feigns illness provides communitas (enacted company) through the mock sick role so familiar to the ill child. The turnabout act of playing doctor turns the tables so that the child examines and gains empathy for his or her own role as patient, and also gains a better appreciation of the ambivalent necessities of caretaking.

Particular linguistic forms, specifically metaphor and narrative, often seem to characterize children's unprescribed therapeutic play. This pattern of figurative language structures is paralleled in play therapy. Metaphor, a subject to which I turn shortly, has been explicitly recommended for use in formal play therapy with children, because it is inherent to childhood discourse (Mills & Crowley, 1986) and a promising mode of intervention (Frey, 1993; Linden, 2003). Likewise, storytelling is commonly an explicit, intended focus during play therapy, as in the mutual storytelling technique (Gardner, 1993) and other storytelling-based therapies (Kaduson & Schaefer, 1997). (Narrative or story is also a framework that has been implicated as fundamental in adult psychotherapy and coping; see Kleinman, 1988.) It is not surprising to observe that children at play are storytellers, using the improvisational power of story to shape and narrate an account they find satisfying. The narrative form spans both prescribed therapy and unprescribed imaginal coping. The children I interviewed became storytellers even when asked to draw. One boy drew the cartoon character Pink Panther, and told me stories of how the Pink Panther (who was presumed to have diabetes, too) behaved in the face of being ill. Children fantasized that their toys came to life, and wove stories about ensuing events. A boy with asthma, who kept a toy car at ready most of the time, was driven by flare-ups of illness to imagine tales of escape by car. Children also took pleasure in weaving stories about a time when their illness would be cured, when happy endings became imaginable.

Perhaps story, a pervasive structure in imaginal coping, is a structure that aids flexible, child-driven interpretation. Narrative operates as a holding structure for a range of meanings, such that the young storyteller can examine issues from multiple stances and imagine an outcome that best suits the child.

Metaphor, on the other hand, is a structure that is, in some sense, inherent to pretend play. Play sets up a plane of as-if experience, yet issues and dilemmas from literal reality are reflected in the play, made even more vivid, tractable, and concrete when used as trope, in play. Thus play connects one field of experience as rendered through another field of experience, the defining quality of metaphor. Metaphor abounds in therapeutic play: syringe as kissing zebra, blood test as wager, car or plane as escape from fear or encumbrance, Ninja Turtle as protector, volcano as inflamed feelings, and so on. More than constituting poetic flourish, metaphors morph ideas into embodiments or avatars, such that what was formless or inchoate is rendered into a graspable, concretized form (Fernandez, 1986). Such figurative transformation provides thick possibilities of interpretation, as the symbols can be manipulated and have a dense potentiality for meaning.

In play therapy, metaphor makes it possible to dynamically navigate issues that are charged and difficult to engage directly. Frey (1993) wrote about a young female client who had difficulty maintaining a transformation of personal behavior over the course of therapy. The girl did not express this concern directly to the therapist, yet sang and gestured to her therapist about the "itsy bitsy spider," a song telling of a spider who repeatedly fails to maintain upward progress in a rain-soaked waterspout. The metaphor of the itsy bitsy spider vividly placed the issue of backsliding behavior before Frey, in an as-if, nonliteral manner.

Metaphor entails a limberness of meaning making, because a person sets the metaphoric linkages and outcomes for himself or herself, and brings an attitude of limberness to the process. Metaphor contrasts with fixed, static, inert, or mechanical ways of understanding a problem. Explaining illness to oneself as a biomedical fact, for example, involves learning a given knowledge construct that is essentially preordained. Children with chronic illness, in settings such as camp or medical offices, are generally taught about the biomedical facts of their disease in didactic terms rather than figuratively or playfully. By contrast, children's metaphoric imaginings are nonliteral and unfixed, inviting transformative twists and turns in how the symbolic material is used by the child.

There is figurative dynamism and improvisation in metaphoric forms of thought. Among the ill children I studied who received frequent medical treatments, many approached these treatments with uninhibited, flexible modes of representation. The tube-connected face mask that a child had to wear during a nebulizer treatment for asthma was imagined (at various times, by various children) to be a fireman's smoke mask, an elephant's trunk, the oxygen mask of a *Top Gun* fighter pilot, and so on. The mist emanating from the nebulizer was taken to be cloud mist, or dragon "smoke," or the misty abode of a dinosaur. The machine at a children's hospital that took a sample of blood from patients with diabetes, was said (by hospital staff) to be named "Herbie," and this led children to imagine relationships with Herbie, sometimes very positive in tone. Among diabetic children, syringes became animals, such as zebras or polar bears. The child's illness experience contained a menagerie of meanings, a cavalcade of tropes by which treatment was morphed to suit that child's ways and means of representing.

If figurative forms such as narrative and metaphor are common to both play therapy and imaginal coping, perhaps this underscores how such forms foster improvisational reinterpretation, inherent to both domains. Whether play is prescribed or child-initiated, its therapeutic use entails revising, inverting, and even rendering roles topsy turvy. Play, with its very thick and agile possibilities of interpretation, is an asset in coping precisely because of its elasticity.

AFFECT-LADEN MEANING TRANSFORMATION

Given how intricately involved feelings are in therapy, play therapists theorize that affective processes are central to the workings of play therapy. Two examples of the way affective involvement is theorized are: (a) catharsis, defined as a process in which unexpressed, unconscious, or hidden emotions are released to relieve tension and anxiety (Ginsberg, 1993); and (b) abreaction, a process by which one's reaction to a stimulus brings to mind previous experience, leading to a reduction of painful or difficult feelings (Erikson, 1950; Oremland, 1993). Thus, play therapy is hypothesized to release feelings (through catharsis) or to reduce undesirable feelings (through abreaction).

Humor, an aspect of playful activity that I observed (outside therapy) during ethnographic research with chronically ill children, involves clear, physically manifested expressions of affect. Just at the point when a child "gets" the double meaning of the joke, there is an accompanying subjective sense (a pleasurable, even elated, feeling) and often a sense of affective release (Wolfenstein, 1954). Accompanying this feeling is a display of affect through laughter, smiling, and other physical signs.

Humor shares several of the qualities of play. Humor shifts or shuffles meaning, as is transparent in puns and other intended doublings of sense. Humor, like play, is layered with ambiguity. Amidst layered meanings, it is up to the child to "get" the joke, to actively complete the reaction. (A joke, as any comedian knows, is only successful after an audience member actively reframes essential meanings.) As in play, a joking child actively imputes meaning—and in making sense of the joke, maintains interpretive control. "Getting" the joke is not predetermined, but depends on a child's active engagement.

Humor, perhaps even more so than play, has been claimed to have value for coping, through empirical investigations linking humor to improved psychosocial adjustment, such as among childhood cancer patients (Dowling, Hockenberry, & Gregory, 2003). In play therapy, humor holds value for reducing initial resistance and tension (Bow, 1993), as well as facilitating the extended therapeutic process.

At summer camp, humor was rampant in the discourse of young chronically ill campers, who poked fun at their own vulnerabilities, made light of treatments, and turned irksome aspects of illness into fodder for joke—such as the skit about a breathless, ineffectual wolf and the three little pigs. Campers sang songs that lampooned the slings and arrows of diabetes treatment. A song mocking blood tests went something like this: "Don't take a prick at my finger, my finger. My fingers *hurts* [screamed loudly]." Insulin reaction, which encompasses a set of disconcerting hypoglycemic symptoms, was the mocked subject of another song: "What a reaction, what a reaction, doodlelee do. Some folks shake and some get clammy, doodly doo." A third song was sung to the tune of Foster's "Oh, Susanna": "Oh I went to diabetic camp,/With my needle and my syringe/ They made me prick my finger./'Til I thought I would cringe." Humor was also common in the lives of chronically ill children at home.

As a form of mood moderation, humor asks a child to see a new meaning, and if he or she does, this is apt to be accompanied by a pulse of affect, accompanied by laughter. The joke leads to reappraising meanings, including at times, laughing off a subject that once seemed daunting and serious (syringes, needles, symptoms of insulin reactions, breathlessness, etc.). At the asthma camp performance of "The Three Little Pigs," the loudest, most prolonged laughter by the audience occurred when the wolf was tested for poor breathing: The living wolf's measurement of breathing ("peak flow") yielded a number too low to sustain life. The watching crowd of asthmatics could not contain their uproarious laughter. Humor, like play, turns on one's willingness to put aside well-worn scripts of construing meaning, no matter how solemn or imposing, and to reconsider how meaning is constructed.

Neither humor nor play represents a reductive, pat system of signifying—underscoring the importance of appropriately viewing play, or humor, dynamically and intricately, when doing research. Unfortunately, the hydraulics of humor—by which joking contributes to adjustment to stress through revised interpretations—has been too little studied, in any framework. Humor is fleeting, but has visible signposts through its physiological display of affect. The affective dynamics of coping, observable to the attentive researcher through humor, invites further investigation.

Aside from humor, more subtle forms of play, about which researchers of coping know even less, also call out for further investigation. Very little is known about imaginative play as a mechanism of affective release or relief. The questions raised by my own ethnographic research are many: How is fear overcome by transitional objects, imaginary companions, or other fantasies? In encouraging children to accept a treatment regimen for illness, how does play contribute? Is a playful attitude toward treatment (brought about by reframing treatment as lighter hearted) helpful in encouraging, affectively, adherence to treatment over time? Does play have an impact on feelings associated with being powerless, needing control, feeling socially isolated, and a myriad of other issues that threaten selfhood in illness? The questions abound, and multiply when considering that imaginal coping may be a characteristic response to many traumas and crises, not simply for illness.

CONCLUSION

Therapeutic modes of remaking meaning (within play therapy and in child-initiated imaginal coping) have been too little studied by researchers, especially given the rich window these processes provide into how children navigate the world using their capacities to frame and reframe meaning. The knowledge that children cope with stressors through self-initiated therapeutic play presents a compelling reason for wider investigation of therapeutic play. Children's modalities of sense making are for them a resource leading to adaptability. Children are not pathogenic when they use imagination to reassess significance. On the contrary, a hallmark of the human species is adaptability, and children creatively and playfully exercise this human capacity through their own imaginal coping.

Resilience has been defined as the individual's capacity to function competently, and to adapt despite experiencing traumatic or chronic adversity. A critical element in determining the path toward an adaptive (vs. maladaptive) response involves how the individual actively exerts a self-organizing capacity (Cicchetti & Toth, 1998). Protection from maladaptive pathways does not come from a trait fixed within the individual, according to resilience theory, but from an active process involving dynamic feedback. Seen in these terms, playfulness is a component of resilience, in which cognitive control is exerted to modify affect (Cicchetti & Toth, 1998). Children reorganize cognitive structures through play, transforming the associative significance of scripts and constructs to a more adaptive arrangement. Through this process of play, medical treatment becomes easier to accept, and threats to survival are able to be more bravely met. Play is a source of tensile strength for children under stress, allowing them to bend without breaking when the going gets tough.

The study of play as therapeutic presents challenges. Play is ambiguous rather than definitive, fluid rather than fixed, vivid rather than formalist, and reticular rather than patently mappable. Animated by imagination, therapeutic play engages transformation by writ of openness and multivocality. Studying the dynamics of this sort of play will require flexible research approaches able to keep pace with a vagarious, poetic process. Yet despite these challenges of studying play, investigating play as coping holds theoretical advantages. The variability and ambiguity of play, as Sutton-Smith (1997) postulated, models the adaptive variability of human functioning. Play intensifies and exemplifies that human behavior embodies alternatives. The study of play as a coping behavior holds particular potential for tracing how an as-if enactment of a range of alternatives facilitates adaptation in adversity. This avenue of investigation might take us beyond the study of the cognitive dimensions of as-if experience, to its implications for adaptability and resilience.

Play varies with cultural milieu as well, adding another challenge when considering play in other cultural environments. If not through play, how else do children cope with adversity in less play-intensive cultures? Are there other modes of as-if enactment that instantiate adaptive alternatives, such as ritual or prayer? How are the dynamics of meaning making similar or different?

Improving our knowledge, in North American culture, of the intriguing dynamics of coping through play can provide insights into how children navigate a problematic world, sustaining resilient selves, with helpful support from others. In practice, adults (parents, caretakers, and play therapists included) can choose to scaffold or undermine playful coping. The value of play for coping lies in its limberness or elasticity of meaning making. Play cannot be dictated to the child. Rather, adults aiming to support therapeutic play would do best to foster poetic processes that invite the child to a self-directed, flexible process of expression. Stories can be helpful springboards to coping, but are best when carrying latent, ambiguous significance rather than flat, didactic, literal messages. The impulse to present children with stories that are literal expositions of personal problems (Feinberg, 2004) may, ironically, be less therapeutic than fantasy narratives that hold richer metaphoric meaning and call on the child's imagination. Adults can provide props for play as well, but the child is best empowered to make use of playthings as tools in freely exercised imaginings. Any attempt to tame or direct imagination, on the part of a teacher, parent, or helpmate, could be stifling of a process best left unhindered by well-intentioned realism. Didactic teaching may not point the way as readily as less engineered playfulness. This last point may be especially relevant in working with young children who have chronic illness, who seem to adapt well through metaphoric play rather than didactic, biomedical facts.

At stake in play is the children's capacity for resilience, as imaginal coping aids affective adjustment. Deprivation and hardship can give rise to rich, fictive experience. Fantasia, through its flexibility, concocts new meanings and provides helpful revelations that make hardships more bearable.

REFERENCES

Axline, V. (1947). *Play therapy*. New York: Ballantine.

Birch, M. (1997). In the land of counterpane: Travels in the realm of play. *The Psychoanalytic Study of the Child, 52*, 57–75.

Bow, J. (1993). Overcoming resistance. In C. E. Schaefer (Ed.), *The therapeutic powers of play* (pp. 17–40). Northvale, NJ: Aronson.

Cicchetti, D., & Toth, S. (1998). Perspectives on research and practice in developmental psychopathology (pp. 479–583). In W. Damon (Ed.), *Handbook of child psychology*. New York: Wiley.

Claman, L. (1993). The squiggle-drawing game. In C. E. Schaefer & D. M. Cangelosi (Eds.), *Play therapy techniques* (pp. 177–189). Northvale, NJ: Aronson.

Clancier, A., & Kalmanovitch, J. (1984). *Winnicott and paradox: From birth to creation*. London: Tavistock.

Clark, C. D. (2003). *In sickness and in play: Children coping with chronic illness*. New Brunswick, NJ: Rutgers University Press.

Dowling, J. S., Hockenberry, M., & Gregory, R. L. (2003). Sense of humor, childhood cancer stressors, and outcomes of psychosocial adjustment, immune function, and infection. *Journal of Pediatric Oncology Nursing, 20*(6), 271–292.

Erikson, E. (1950). *Childhood and society*. New York: Norton.

Feinberg, B. (2004). *Welcome to Lizard Motel: Children, stories, and the mystery of making things up*. Boston: Beacon Press.

Fernandez, J. W. (1986). *Persuasions and performances: The play of tropes in culture*. Bloomington: Indiana University Press.

Frankel, R. (1997). The clay squiggle technique. In H. Kaduson & C. Schaefer (Eds.), *101 favorite play therapy techniques* (pp. 87–92). Northvale, NJ: Aronson.

Frey, D. (1993). Learning by metaphor. In C. Schaefer (Ed.), *The therapeutic powers of play* (pp. 223–239). Northvale, NJ: Aronson.

Garbarino, J., Dubrow, N., Kostelny, K., & Pardo, C. (1992). *Children in danger: Coping with the consequences of community violence*. San Francisco: Jossey-Bass.

Gardner, R. A. (1993). *Storytelling in psychotherapy with children*. Northvale, NJ: Aronson.

Gil, E. (1994). *Play in family therapy*. New York: Guilford.

Ginsberg, B. G. (1993). Catharsis. In C. Schaefer (Ed.), *The therapeutic powers of play* (pp. 107–141). Northvale, NJ: Aronson.

Irwin, E. C., & Curry, N. E. (1993). Role play. In C. E. Schaeffer (Ed.), *The therapeutic powers of play* (pp. 167–188). Northvale, NJ: Aronson.

Kaduson, H., & Schaefer, C. E. (1997). *101 favorite play therapy techniques*. Northvale, NJ: Aronson.

Kleinman, A. (1988). *Rethinking psychiatry: From cultural category to personal experience*. New York: Free Press.

LeBlanc, M., & Ritchie, M. (2001). A meta-analysis of play therapy outcomes. *Counseling Psychology Quarterly, 14*, 149–163.

Linden, J. H. (2003). Playful metaphors. *American Journal of Clinical Hypnosis, 45*, 245–250.

Mills, J. C., & Crowley, R. J. (1986). *Therapeutic metaphors for children*. Philadelphia: Brunner/Mazel.

O'Connor, K. J. (1991). *The play therapy primer*. New York: Wiley.

Oremland, E. K. (1993). Abreaction. In C. E. Schaefer (Ed.), *The therapeutic powers of play* (pp. 143–165). Northvale, NJ: Aronson.

Raynor, C. (2002). The role of play in the recovery process. In W. N. Zubenko & J. A. Capozzoli (Eds.), *Children and disasters* (pp. 124–134). New York: Oxford University Press.

Ricoeur, P. (1976). *Interpretation theory: Discourse and the surplus of meaning*. Fort Worth: Texas Christian University Press.

Russ, S. (2004). *Play in child development and psychotherapy*. Mahwah, NJ: Lawrence Erlbaum Associates, Inc.

Schaefer, C. E. (1993). *The therapeutic powers of play*. Northvale, NJ: Aronson.

Singer, D. G. (1993). *Playing for their lives: Helping troubled children through play therapy*. New York: Free Press.

Singer, D. G. (1994). Play as healing. In J. H. Goldstein (Ed.), *Toys, play and child development* (pp. 147–165). New York: Cambridge University Press.

Singer, J. L. (1994). The scientific foundations of play therapy. In H. Hellendoorn, R. V. D. Kooij, & B. Sutton-Smith (Eds.), *Play and intervention* (pp. 27–38). Albany: State University of New York Press.

Sleek, S. (1998). After the storm, children play out their fears. *APA Monitor, 29*(6). Retrieved September 2001 from APA Website.

Sutton-Smith, B. (1997). *The ambiguity of play.* Cambridge, MA: Harvard University Press.

Taylor, M. (1999). *Imaginary companions and the children who create them.* New York: Oxford University Press.

Turner, V. (1969). *The ritual process: Structure and anti-structure.* Ithaca, NY: Cornell University Press.

Webb, N. B. (1999). *Play therapy with children in crisis.* New York: Guilford.

Wolfenstein, M. (1954). *Children's humor: A psychological analysis.* Bloomington: Indiana University Press.

Author Index

Note: Page numbers in *italic* refer to reference pages.

Subject Index

Note: Page references in **boldface** refer to tables. Those in *italic* refer to figures.